AF334643

Chaucer Yearbook

A Journal of Late Medieval Studies

Volume 5 (1998)

Chaucer Yearbook: A Journal of Late Medieval Studies is devoted to the critical examination of British literature written between 1350 and 1500. Please send submissions (two copies, double-spaced, maximum of 35 pages, Chicago-style, endnoted) to either

Jean E. Jost
Department of English
Bradley University
Peoria, IL 61625

or

Juris G. Lidaka
Department of English
West Virginia State College
Institute, WV 25112

Chaucer Yearbook

A Journal of Late Medieval Studies

Volume 5 (1998)

Edited by
MICHAEL N. SALDA *and* JEAN E. JOST

D. S. BREWER

First published 1999
D. S. Brewer, Cambridge

ISBN 0 85991 537 9

ISSN 1063–1836

D. S. Brewer is an imprint of Boydell & Brewer Ltd
PO Box 9, Woodbridge, Suffolk IP12 3DF, UK
and of Boydell & Brewer Inc.
PO Box 41026, Rochester, NY 14604–4126, USA

This publication is printed on acid-free paper

Printed in Great Britain by
Antony Rowe Ltd, Chippenham, Wiltshire

CONTENTS

ESSAYS

REVIEWS

The Rapes of Chaucer

WILLIAM A. QUINN, *University of Arkansas*

"It is quite possible, of course, that the matter was concerned with some real wrong .... " – G. K. Chesterton[1]

In 1380, Geoffrey Chaucer was released from all further legal actions regarding his alleged *raptus* of Cecilia Chaumpaigne. Extant documents report only the proceedings that led to the dismissal of all claims against Chaucer. A deed of release was enrolled in chancery court on May 1, 1380, which was acknowledged on May 4. On July 2, John Grove officially recognized a debt of £10 to Cecilia Chaumpaigne, which was canceled upon payment the following Michelmas, September 29.

The biographical implications of the four documents that F. J. Furnivall made public in 1873 remained highly debatable precisely because the denotations of their references to *raptus* proved so imprecise (until recently clarified by Christopher Cannon). Martin M. Crow and Clair C. Olson summarized the two most plausible theories "to explain the situation: (1) that it was a case of physical rape or seduction; (2) that it concerned the kidnapping or abduction of a young person, possibly in order to make an advantageous marriage."[2] Between Caxton and Furnivall, readers of *Chaucer* had remained blissfully ignorant of any such allegations. And throughout the first half of this century, most Chaucerians hoped to hold the poet above reproach by diminishing both the legal and moral implications of the *raptus* incident. But P. R. Watts and Theodore Plucknett,[3] arguing from more rigorous legal perspectives, insisted that a suspicion of *violentus concupitus*, the most damning interpretation of "Chaucer's Escapade," could not be summarily dismissed. Cecilia Chaumpaigne's original and lost

[1] G. K. Chesterton, *Chaucer* (1932; rev. ed., 1956; reprint: New York: Greenwood, 1969), 97.

[2] *Chaucer Life-Records*, ed. Martin M. Crow and Clair C. Olson (Oxford: Clarendon Press, 1966), 345.

[3] P. R. Watts, "The Strange Case of Geoffrey Chaucer and Cecilia Chaumpaigne," *Law Quarterly Review* 63 (1947): 491–515; and Theodore F. T. Plucknett, "Chaucer's Escapade," *Law Quarterly Review* 64 (1948): 33–36.

complaint probably entailed more than just Chaucer's third-party participation in an elopement.

Having discovered a heretofore overlooked document of release dated May 7, Christopher Cannon reviewed the entire case in terms of "its immediate legal context."[4] The most significant revision of the May 7 "memorandum," which was copied for the criminal rolls in King's Bench for 3 Richard II, is its omission of the specific phrase "de meo raptu" as recorded in the May 4 entry for the close rolls. In its specifically legal context, the charge of *raptus* would have "seemed just as inflammatory to Chaucer's contemporaries as it has seemed to its more modern readers." The most felonious allegation against Chaucer, thus, "had to be quietly, but emphatically, retracted."[5]

Regarding the inherently ambiguous implications of this "Cecilia Chaumpaigne Affair," Chaucer's biographers and critics have had persistently contrary predispositions. The former have pursued as precise a definition of *raptus* as possible,[6] while the latter have largely dismissed such biographical factoids as

[4] Christopher Cannon, "*Raptus* in the Chaumpaigne Release and a Newly Discovered Document Concerning the Life of Geoffrey Chaucer," *Speculum* 68 (1993): 76.

[5] Cannon, "*Raptus*," 93–94.

[6] Chaucer's biographers typically defend the poet's honor, even though they do not all presume his innocence. Marchette Chute pronounced it "useless to search in Chaucer's poetry for clues to his private life; ... it is almost impossible to find him speaking for himself" (*Geoffrey Chaucer of England* [New York: E. P. Dutton, 1946], 61), and she vehemently objected to any "premature conclusion" that Chaucer could have been guilty of actual rape (144). G. G. Coulton observed that if *raptus* signified felonious rape "a mere deed of renunciation on Cecilia's part could not have legally settled the matter." After noting the involvement of Chaucer's own father as victim in another *raptus* incident, Coulton also considered it "piquant to find our errant poet himself among the commissioners appointed to inquire into a case of *raptus*, just seven years after his own escapade" (*Chaucer and His England* [New York: Russell and Russell, 1957], 54–55). Edward Wagenknecht upheld A. C. Baugh's opinion that biographical judgment should be suspended so that readers can maintain a pose of critical indifference; Chaucer's poetry, however, provides a strong prejudice in favor of its poet (*The Personality of Chaucer* [Norman: Univ. of Oklahoma Press, 1968], 107–9). Derek Brewer explained "the uncomfortable fact" that Chaucer was charged with rape as symptomatic of the era's pervasive violence (*Chaucer in His Time* [New York: Longman, 1973], 74). Brewer subsequently ridiculed the "delightfully fizzy" name of Cecilia Chaumpaigne and doubted her good standing in court "if she was a lady." Noting that the case's very "publicity is notable," Brewer approved – though not without qualification – the interpretation that the charges represent a legal fiction brought against Chaucer for a financial technicality (*Chaucer and His World* [New York: Dodd, Mead, 1978], 149–50). John Gardner took "a darker – or perhaps more cheerful – view" when he speculated that busy Chaucer took sufficient time to seduce a "pretty wench" and "slipped into bed with a pretty and soft baker's daughter" (*The Life and Times of Geoffrey Chaucer* [New York: Knopf, 1977], 252–53). Donald Howard suspected that Cecilia Chaumpaigne's dominant motive was greed and doubts that she was the real victim in this affair (*Chaucer: His Life, His Works, His World* [New York: Dutton, 1987], 317–20).

Carolyn Dinshaw observed a tacit, but disturbing bias among many Chaucerians – "a strain of scholarly treatment of this incident that without much distress (indeed, with some contentment, even at time[s] with relish) accepts the idea that Chaucer raped; this is, I think, because it

critically impertinent.[7] Indeed, most readers of *Chaucer* now programmatically absent Chaucer himself from the interpretive play of the texts in hand. I would insist that neither premise – neither a factually fixative, nor a theoretically oblivious posture – is valid, if absolute, because neither addresses the tonal dynamics of Chaucer's histrionic strategies as first presenter of his own texts.

Any retrieval of the circumstantial resonances introduced by Chaucer's immediate presence must remain only suggestive. Indeed, the precise chronology of Chaucer's canon remains putative at best. Furthermore, the contention that Chaucer himself recited much of his poetry late into the 1380s has hardly been proven beyond the shadow of a doubt. Nevertheless, on some occasions in certain settings between 1380 and 1387, Chaucer had to hide his private concerns regarding the implications of *raptus* in some very public places. Whatever the legitimacy of the specific charges brought against him, Chaucer was forced to exonerate himself by drawing "on the most highly placed friends he could find for support in what was certainly an unsavory and perhaps also a potentially dangerous affair."[8] Orbiting around the central denotation of *raptus* in its legal sense are several, still more ambiguous contexts affecting its poetic resonances. Chaucer's contemporaries may not have known any more about his actual guilt or innocence than we do. They could, however, witness the kinesics by which he indicated his own latent feelings. As a performing persona (which was not always distinguishable from his role as defendant), Chaucer had to address *raptus* in terms of its received literary applications. More dramatically, however, Chaucer also had to anticipate how his immediate audiences, especially his personal acquaintances, would respond to any of his own references to rape.

Though there is no need now to try the poet *in absentia*, the proposition that after 1380 Geoffrey Chaucer read all references to rape *in propria persona* as both a putative performer and alleged rapist requires that such references be read again in terms of the poet's own highly individualized enactments. On the one hand, Chaucer's own voice would have quieted many interpretive controversies now attributable to his absence; "[b]ecause of the way Chaucer delivered his

is just such an incident that will establish the robust masculine reputation of a national poet – the 'father' of English poetry" ("Rivalry, Rape and Manhood: Gower and Chaucer," in *Chaucer and Gower: Difference, Mutuality, Exchange*, ed. R. F. Yeager [Victoria: Univ. of Victoria, 1991], 148n30). Derek Pearsall has most recently opined that some positive significance may emerge from all the dark speculation: "The incident, though enigmatic and the focus of many questions, provokes some possibly pertinent speculation on Chaucer's attitude to women" (*The Life of Geoffrey Chaucer: A Critical Biography* [Oxford: Blackwell, 1992], 138).

[7] John Matthews Manly attributed no critical significance to the Cecilia Chaumpaigne case. He did, however, note that "[t]he public for which Chaucer wrote would infallibly recognize immediately his allusion" to Pembroke because of his association with Sir William de Beauchamp, who appeared as a witness on Chaucer's behalf (*Some New Light on Chaucer* [New York: Holt, 1926], 90).

[8] Lee Patterson, *Chaucer and the Subject of History* (Madison: Univ. of Wisconsin Press, 1991), 35.

dramatic monologues, the response of the audience may have been more confident and unequivocal than it has been since."[9] On the other hand, any retrieval of Chaucer's own voice remains a highly disputable contention; "'dramatic enactment' must be considered a dangerously attractive *adaptation* of a Chaucerian text."[10] On the one hand, Chaucer himself cannot now be subpoenaed to read aloud. On the other hand, readers should not now summarily dismiss consideration of the interpretive overtones that Chaucer's own recitals once gave his references to rape.

In all of Chaucer's works composed prior to 1380, as well as in those texts that he wrote at any date for presentation *in absentia* – that is, for another reader's isolated or normatively "silent" reading – only one of fifty-eight or more explicit references to ravishment clearly denotes forced sex.[11] This predominantly figurative conception of *ravishment* in texts composed prior to 1380 and in those texts never intended for a real audience's communal *delit* suggests that Chaucer rather innocently – which is not to say inoffensively – maintained certain conventional tropes regarding rape. After 1380, however, Chaucer more often than not does refer to rape quite literally, and even his more oblique references to rape seem more graphic, more negative and much more personally relevant.

Although the extant texts of the *Romaunt of the Rose* and *Boece* may not be Chaucer's own translations, and neither seems to have been intended for courtly performance, both texts did provide Chaucer with conventional, though divergent, treatments of rape. Both texts also exemplify, however, a literary tradition that largely ignored the literal significance of ravishment. Among the *Roman de la Rose*'s numerous references to what might be translated as *rape*, the most amusing and, therefore, possibly most offensive is Amis's extremely cavalier advice (7525–7794). The fragmentary Middle English translation of the *Romaunt*, however, makes only two explicit and figurative references to "ravishment." In a passage as sincere as Guillaume de Lorris, Love declares that

[9] Beryl Rowland, "*Pronuntiatio* and its Effect on Chaucer's Audience," *Studies in the Age of Chaucer* 4 (1982): 51. George Kane, whose critique of "the autobiographical fallacy" has proven especially influential as a deterrent to speculative criticism, himself acknowledged the interpretive significance of considering Chaucer's role as the proto-reciter of his own texts, especially of his early dream visions (*The Autobiographical Fallacy in Chaucer and Langland Studies* [London: H. K. Lewis, 1965]).

[10] Alan Gaylord, "Reading Chaucer: What's Allowed in 'Aloud'?" *Chaucer Yearbook* 1 (1992): 87.

[11] All citations of Chaucer's works are from *The Riverside Chaucer*, ed. Larry D. Benson, 3d ed. (Boston: Houghton Mifflin, 1987). To survey Chaucer's explicit references to rape, I have consulted *A Concordance to the Complete Works of Geoffrey Chaucer and to the Romaunt of the Rose*, ed. John S. P. Tatlock and Arthur G. Kennedy (Washington: Carnegie Institute, 1927), and *A Complete Concordance to the Works of Geoffrey Chaucer*, ed. Akio Oizumi, 12 vols. (Hildesheim: Olms-Weidmann, 1991), *s.vv.* "ravisable," "ravish," "ravished," "ravishdest," "ravisheth," "ravishing," and "reven."

Amans is "ravysshed" (2462) by the sight of his beloved. Guillaume genuinely celebrates the affective power of feminine beauty. Jean de Meun, however, has Dame Reason correct the grammar of Love's imperatives by differentiating between an affection which deprives man of "al thi wit" (5198) and "love leful ... and good" (5195). In a passage replete with double entendre, Reason then debunks Love's (and Guillaume's) periphrasis, including his dislocation of the real denotations of rape.

The *Romaunt* preserves some indication of Chaucer's familiarity with both Guillaume's highly romanticized and Jean's fully satiric conceptions of *raptus*, even though the climactic taking of the Rose herself is never actually recorded in the translation. Indeed, explicit acknowledgments of rape *per se* throughout the Middle English text remain, at most, nominal. The *Boece*, however, addresses "ravishment" with extraordinary frequency and translates a far more tonally problematic set of conventions generated by the allegorization of *raptus*.

Speaking from an almost completely deliteralized lexicon of rape, Lady Philosophy, who has herself been physically abused by violent men – that is, by the misusers of dialectic – refers to rape only abstractly. S/he – that is, the authority of the text – rebukes any ravishment of the human imagination by idols. Expelling first all whorish Muses, Philosophy compares the allure of false rhetoric to a raping of the mind. She likewise renounces the ravishing but foolish reasoning of Stoics and Epicureans (1.pr.3.34, 70, 81). Lady Philosophy diagnoses such ravishment of the imagination as folly, a disease that denies reason free choice.

More often than not, however, the Middle English translator uses his text's *ravishment*-motif to suggest either dynamic activity or emotional intensity. Boethius pleads, for example, that the Maker of the Wheel and First Mover of the "ravysschynge sweighe" (1.m.5.4) save some part of mankind from "the ravysschynge flodes" of injustice (1.m.5.56). The orbit of Ursa Major is also described as "ravysschynge" (4.m.6.9), which here simply means "violent." In praise of God's Plenty, Lady Philosophy acknowledges that the world offers as many riches as the sea produces sand when "moeved with ravysshynge blastes" (2.m.2.4–5), but she then rebukes anyone who would idolize creation rather than adore the Creator: "Whi artow ravyssched with idel joies?" (2.pr.5.68–70). Less sensate passions ravish better imaginations. Many are seduced by fame. Yet, both heroes and poets do, in fact, wholly die; "o cruel day schal rayssche you" (2.m.7.28). Philosophy even condemns the philosopher's excessive fondness for the enrapturing *cantum* of her own words (3.pr.1.21). A more common and much baser temptation is greed; minds so ravished are especially repulsive because avarice bestializes the wit. Foxlike, the greedy then ravish the wealth of others "be wiles" (4.pr.3.111).

Such recurrent references to *raptus*, whether positive or negative according to context, hardly convey the literal import of rape *per se*. The motif, therefore, consists primarily of rather dead metaphors that resonate with little or no personal investment on the part of the text's presenter.[12] Only once, late in the translation, does a reference to ravishment clearly denote violent sex when Boethius complains that wicked men who "ravysschen medes of vertu" often escape justice while good folk are tortured (4.pr.5.23–24). But the poet-narrator under arrest vehemently dissociates himself from such "schrewes." And *ravishment* in *Boece* finally comes to signify one's ascent to Neoplatonic rapture (4.m.6.37, 5.pr.6.91).

As a private reader of either the *Roman de la Rose* or *De consolatione Philosophiae* – that is, free in his study from any familiar audience's immediate reactions – Chaucer seems to have been too often, too comfortable with the metaphor of *raptus* prior to 1380. Such persistent deliteralizing of rape may seem inherently indifferent to the trauma of real rape. The simplest explanation is that prior to 1380 the literal implications of *raptus* remained an abstractly bookish trope, personally irrelevant and, as such, unreal for Chaucer. The public record, however, reminds "us that there are not only *figurative* rapes – the writer's intent raped by the scribe's pen, the text as woman's body violated by interpretations of literary and exegetical tradition ... that there are not only *fictional* rapes ... but there are *real* rapes as well."[13] And, after 1380, the first audiences of Chaucer (especially the ladies of court whose reactions his texts occasionally anticipate explicitly) would have forced the public performer to remember much the same.

The *Parliament of Fowls* probably represents Chaucer's first public presentation of a text composed immediately after the Cecilia Chaumpaigne case. In it, Chaucer mentions "ravyshyng" only once and does so most coyly. He uses the adjective as a compliment to the harmony of the birds (198). There is no other diction that explicitly recollects rape even though the *Parliament* itself offers a ludic commemoration of the negotiations leading to a regal *raptus* – that is, the bride-taking of Anne of Bohemia.[14] The formel is granted a limited choice among suitors, but she is not permitted by Nature to remain permanently free. What seems Nature's concession that she "hireself shal han hir eleccioun" (621) is, in fact, a command (617). Even queens must yield to natural law. The formel receives only one year's respite before she too must choose "by kynde." And her kind consists of the birds of ravine who, when most outrageous, take tyrannically.[15] Despite a flock of opportunities and contextual motives, Chaucer

[12] Metrum 7 of Book 4, which celebrates manly virtue, makes an oblique reference to rape by alluding to the "wrekere Attrides," avengers of Helen's *raptus*. Boethius also calls Hercules a ravisher, but only of apples.

[13] Carolyn Dinshaw, *Chaucer's Sexual Poetics* (Madison: Univ. of Wisconsin Press, 1989), 11.

[14] Richard married Anne in January of 1382. Though a specific date for Chaucer's first recitation of the *Parliament* remains unknown, Nature's suggestion that the formel postpone her choice for one year makes February 14, 1381 – little more than six months after Chaucer had been fully exonerated from the charge of *raptus* – a plausible guess.

[15] See *The Riverside Chaucer*, 1000a, n334.

avoids any more explicit references to *raptus* throughout the *Parliament.* Ten years earlier, Chaucer had started the *Book of the Duchess* with a confession of amorous insomnia, and such comic narcissism is not entirely repressed in the *Parliament.* Again, Chaucer reads and then dreams. The excerpts cited from the *Somnium Scipionis* include a warning that "brekers of the lawe, soth to seyne / And likerous folk, after that they ben dede, / Shul whirle aboute th'erthe alwey in peyne" (78–80). But any more explicit references to *raptus* would have sounded too proximate, inherently more problematic, and as such tonally disruptive during Chaucer's first recitation of the *Parliament.*

None of Chaucer's lyrics make any explicit reference to "ravishment." Little can be said about this absence of a phenomenon, except that the motives for Chaucer's lyric silence may have been manifold. Some of Chaucer's short poems (e.g., "Gentilesse" or "Lak of Stedfastnesse") simply assume too magisterial a voice to suffer such self-referentiality; so, Chaucer's most laureate "I" avoids mentioning *raptus* even though rape conventionally served as a metonymy for tyranny. Antithetically, any domestic "ditees" that Chaucer composed after 1380 may have avoided mentioning rape precisely because the topic would have seemed entirely too relevant and embarrassing for the poet to discuss without some narrative mask. Even as late as 1396, the most explicit acknowledgment of *raptus* that Chaucer made in his lyric voice remains obscure at best (i.e., "lest thow do worse" than marriage ["Lenvoy de Chaucer à Bukton," 17]).

Chaucer presented the *House of Fame* soon after, if not before, the *Parliament of Fowls*, and probably no later than 1385.[16] Its first audience – whether a court of listeners or a coterie of readers – probably conceived of itself as much more than just "Chaucer's first audience." And they themselves often provided far more significant and entertaining scandals to discuss than Chaucer's somewhat stale peccadillo. But the poem's initial presentation refocused that audience's attention on Chaucer's fictionalized "I." The primary topic of the *House of Fame* is the very nature of ephemeral honor and perdurable gossip. Thus it is difficult not to imagine Chaucer anticipating that his inaugural performance would be charged by his audience's awareness of the dream-vision's self-referentiality. The *House of Fame* portrays a panorama of the court itself, at the center of which is the ego of the narrator.

Reading a table of brass (142) which records infamous affairs of yore, Chaucer simultaneously presents his own reactions to this received text of *fama.* Facing a sounding board of personally involved and deeply biased listeners, Chaucer insists that, though Aeneas was a heroic cad, wretched Dido also did amiss (269). So did the women who loved the likes of Theseus. The gender-indifferent moral that Chaucer extracts from this ekphrasis is "Therfore be no wyght so nyce / To take a love oonly for chere" (276–77). The idiom condemn-

[16] See John M. Fyler's analysis of the chronological evidence in *The Riverside Chaucer*, 978a.

ing such *taking* obscures any clear distinction between seduction and rape. Transferring the idiom of *ravishment* from bride-taking to fiancé-slaying, Chaucer also notes that Aeneas later "reft" (*HF*, 457) Turnus of his life and so won Lavinia as his wife. The engraved text within the *House of Fame* presents *ravishment* as a semantic field of ambiguous play wherein the boundaries between real rape, seduction and the taking of a spouse become extremely blurred. The very presence of Chaucer as the playful text's alleged rapist-reciter recalls the dark seriousness of *raptus* as a legal term. In such a tonally and thematically dynamic performance context, the second book's initial image of "Geffrey" being taken "in a swap" (543) plays as much more than just a contrived allusion. The poet presents a scene in which he is himself ravished by a bird of ravine.

In Book 3 of the *House of Fame*, Chaucer presents a universalized but hardly obscure mirroring of his interpretive milieu. The most personally pertinent aspect of Chaucer's portrayal of *fama* is its representation of gossip as the affair of court. Particularly relevant to the business at hand is Chaucer's portrayal of a sixth company of petitioners who appear before Lady Fame and ask that they be granted the completely undeserved reputation "That wommen loven us for wod" (1747). These courtiers are, like Fals-Semblant before them and the Pardoner after, candid hypocrites:

> Thogh we may not the body have
> Of wymmen, yet, so God yow save,
> Leet men gliwe on us the name –
> Sufficeth that we han the fame. (1759–62)

During the first recitation of these lines, Chaucer's direct quotation mandated impersonation. In his own voice, Chaucer's minor distortion of Ovid's phrasing – "fama ... crimen habet" (*Ars amatoria*, 2.632–34; cf. *Roman de la Rose*, 9855–58) – effects a major tonal shift. Ovid had severely criticized such braggarts whose slander is a form of verbal rape. Chaucer domesticates the "we" of male braggadocio. Fame's whimsy may create many an *amans gloriosus*, proud to be falsely accused, but Chaucer's admission that such an amorous *fama* is often mere veneer also subverts the actual guilt of such a charge.

The very next set of courtiers who ask Fame for the very same undeserved reputation are publicly ridiculed. Fame, being Dame Fortune's sister (1547), now mocks the patent absurdity of such a request. Though these men might boast that Isolde herself could not resist their advances, they are dismissed as unworthy of a common maid's attentions: "she that grynt at a querne / Ys al to good" (1798–99). A blushing entendre or two may can still be attached to Chaucer's colloquialism. But Chaucer's now oddly vague pronominal reference to "she that grinds at a hand-mill" may have also once had an immediately apparent though unstated antecedent (that is, Cecilia Chaumpaigne, the baker's daughter).

Chaucer allegedly presented some version of *Troilus and Criseyde* not long after the Cecilia Chaumpaigne affair.[17] In the poem, Chaucer makes nine explicit and, as such, contextually charged references to real rape. The ever-ambiguous rape of Helen had brought all the otherwise contentious Greeks together (1.61–62 and 5.895); yet, Chaucer's Helen seems quite comfortable and comforting among her Trojans. She actually abets, albeit unwittingly (2.1665), Pandarus's plot. Criseyde likewise makes a virtue of the necessity of being taken. And Diomede later boasts (even as he takes Criseyde's bridle) that the imminent fall of Troy will warn mankind to abstain from any future "fecchynge" (5.890). Chaucer, as the reciter of all this matter, would have once seemed encircled, like Troy itself, by a controversy over the very meaning of *raptus*.

Chaucer's single most extended discussion of rape occurs in Book 4 of *Troilus and Criseyde*. A debate is initiated when Pandarus rather bluntly suggests that Troilus simply "Go ravysshe" (4.530) Criseyde. Such a *raptus* would, after all, be the Trojan thing to do (4.533). Pandarus basically advises Troilus to be a man about it – to have, that is, both the "corage" and the "myght" (4.619) to take Criseyde. If Criseyde consents to being so taken, then her elopement is no rape (4.596). If she refuses, then her love was false and forgettable. When Troilus protests that he would rather die than risk ravishing Criseyde against her will (4.637), Pandarus claims that he intended no such thing. Yet, Pandarus's specific wording, "It is no rape, in my dom, ne no vice" (4.596), represents Chaucer's sole use of the word "rape" itself to mean *raptus*.[18] Its very bluntness contrasts with Pandarus's more suave interpretation that such a rape merely entails that Criseyde be "witholden" (4.597). Inverting the semantics of force and freedom, Pandarus goads Troilus by suggesting that Criseyde will "holde" him "nyce" should he "late hire go" (4.598–99). Subsequently, however, despite all glosses, there remains something very smarmy about Pandarus's suggestion "That nost nat that she wol ben yvele appayed / To ravysshe hire" (4.642–43).

Having rejected Pandarus's stratagems, Troilus must then abide Criseyde's scheme to escape her being taken from Troy. She promises a rendezvous that Troilus, though overruled by her powers of persuasion, clearly doubts at first hearing. Troilus mistrusts primarily Criseyde's ability to resist being rhetorically raped while among the Greeks. Calkas, in particular, knows too well how to ravish his daughter from her good intentions (4.1474). And, even if her father fails to win her consent, he can keep Criseyde "by force" (4.1475). In the person

[17] Stephen A. Barney dates the composition of *Troilus and Criseyde* to "[b]efore 1388, probably in the early 1380s" (*The Riverside Chaucer*, 471a).

[18] A syntactically rather confusing reference to "rape" in the *Canon Yeoman's Tale* (1422) is glossed as "seize" by John Reidy in *The Riverside Chaucer* (951a, n1422). In its alchemical context, the text suggests "haste makes waste." Chaucer's three other uses of "rape" (including the *Romaunt*, 1929 and 6516) similarly denote simple haste, though Carolyn Dinshaw has suggested that its use in line 7 of "To Adam Scriveyn" comprises a pun (*Sexual Poetics*, 9–10).

of Troilus, Chaucer here voices the commonplace denial of a clear distinction between persuasion and compulsion, between force and salesmanship. And from this fundamental ambiguity devolve all controversies regarding the issue of *raptus*.

If anyone is truly forced to love in *Troilus and Criseyde*, it is Troilus. Some read Chaucer's description of the loss of Troilus's maidenhead in Book 3 as bordering on farce: "For this or that" (3.1097). Pandarus himself had mocked the rape of the scorner Troilus's imagination by Love (1.300, 308). And Cupid's vengeance for Troilus's initial scorn starts the whole story with a rather matter-of-fact bit of erotic violence. The god of Love simply shoots and then field-dresses his quarry, "For sodeynly he hitte hym atte fulle – / And yet as proud a pekok kan he pulle" (1.209–10). Ignorant and innocent, Criseyde has merely served as Love's lure. As victims of circumstance, both Criseyde and Troilus are serially raped by the imperatives of love. Love first "refte" Troilus of his sleep (1.484). Subsequent despair ravishes both Criseyde and Troilus of the ability to speak (4.249). Criseyde is ultimately bereft of her pain (5.1258) and her name. Troilus is deprived of all his "plesaunce" (5.1260), and then his life, and finally his mundane vanity (5.1817).

On trial for abusing Love in general and Criseyde in particular, Chaucer next presents himself in court pretending to repent. As the poet's attorney in the Prologue to the *Legend of Good Women*, Alceste initially concedes that many a courtier is a braggart liar (as witnessed by the *House of Fame*). She even considers the remote possibility that Chaucer might actually be innocent: "This man to yow may falsly ben accused / That as by right him oughte ben excused" (F, 350–51). But Alceste does not pursue this improbable defense. Like all men in Chaucer's palinode to *Troilus and Criseyde*, the poet-performer is actually presumed guilty. And it was in such a milieu (as parodied by the court trial enacted in the Prologue itself) that Chaucer first recited the legends of Lucrece and Procne, his only two compositions that may properly be termed "rape narratives." Chaucer is forced by his sources to report two relatively detailed accounts of real rape for the first time in his career. For Jill Mann, these two legends constitute "the clearest indications of Chaucer's underlying defence of women." The case of Lucrece in particular exemplifies "the brutal extinction of personality that constitutes the invisible horror of rape."[19] Chaucer's apparent disservice to the inherent pathos of his fifth and seventh legends seems therefore all the more disturbing.

The tone of the *Legend* in general often resists recall. There have been several noble, but largely frustrated, efforts to read these two particularly gruesome narratives as sincere and successfully pathetic tales. But Chaucer's voice de-

[19] Jill Mann, *Geoffrey Chaucer* (Atlantic Highlands, N. J.: Humanities Press International, 1991), 43–44.

flects too much attention from the fictional victims to his own person.[20] His retelling of Livy's *exemplum*, for example, attends more to the ravished imagination of Tarquin's "recordynge" (1760) than to the crime that Lucrece so inspired. The pathos of the rape itself is suppressed by a digression (1812), an apostrophe (1819) and a transition (1825). In retaliation, Stoic Lucrece takes center stage to commit suicide (1855) – and thereby is damned as well as raped. The subsequent expulsion of Tarquin the Proud is indeed reported by Chaucer (1680, 1862), but the tale's anti-regal implications are renounced by this particular court reporter (1684). Meanwhile, the denouement of Lucrece's tragedy is not adequately dramatized to effect any sufficient sympathy or outrage.

Only four lines of the legend of Philomela actually recount her rape. The rest of Chaucer's telling consists of a series of digressions and a complete obfuscation of Ovid's resolution. After Tereus mutilates Philomela, Chaucer adjourns her case as quickly as possible: "Now is it tyme I make an ende sone" (2341). No mention is made of the retribution taken by the sisters against Tereus. Nor has any real compassion been voiced by Chaucer, who only minimally enacts "Allas! The wo, the compleynt, and the mone" (2379) of Procne: "The remenaunt is no charge for to telle" (2383). If read sincerely as an imposed penance, the *Legend* is a study in frustration – a grudging declaration made during the mid-1380s that Chaucer had little to declare.

After 1386, Chaucer's seemingly random references to rape often appear to be more genuinely repulsed or more oddly amused or more callously cavalier than before. After his dedication of a copy of the *Legend* to the Queen "at Eltham or at Sheene" (F, 497), it is also difficult to imagine Chaucer's actually being summoned again to court to perform *in propria persona*. His texts would henceforth be written (or rewritten) for a much broader, but in some ways a much less sophisticated reading public. The resulting distance anticipated between author and text both liberated and problematized Chaucer's subsequent references to rape by disengaging the tone of a manuscript from the interpretive control of his own voice. It is only at this moment of separation, when the persona of the narrative "I" ceases to be a role conceived for the author himself to enact in person, that Fr. Ong's famous dictum that "The Writer's 'Audience' Is Always a Fiction" also comes fully into play.[21] Henceforth, Chaucer can write about rape as a fiction contained within the self-referentiality of the stand-alone text.

[20] In *Chaucer's Rehersynges: The Performability of the Legend of Good Women* (Washington, D.C.: Catholic Univ. Press, 1994), I attempt to explain the comic distortions of the legends of Lucrece (125–39) and of Philomela (159–70) in terms of the entire *Legend*'s comically distorting performance setting.

[21] Walter J. Ong, S.J., "The Writer's Audience is Always a Fiction," *PMLA* 90 (1975): 9–22.

Under investigation, the issue of *raptus* proves to be surprisingly salient throughout the *Canterbury Tales*. A background check reminds the reader that Thomas à Becket was martyred for trying to maintain his episcopal jurisdiction over a rapist priest. Furthermore, the return of spring celebrated at the start of the *General Prologue* represents a settlement achieved between Ceres and Pluto for the rape of Proserpina. A highly ceremonialized *raptus* initiates the *Knight's Tale* when Theseus takes Hippolita as his wife after conquering "al the regne of Femenye" (866).

But the most familiar and provocative reference to rape in Chaucer's entire canon occurs at the start of the *Wife of Bath's Tale*. Released from the tonal burden of immediate self-referentiality, Chaucer has Alison of Bath (who knows so well how the *debitum* proper to marriage can be both extorted and exploited in a variety of fashions) define an unmitigated rape:

> He saugh a mayde walkynge hym biforn,
> Of which mayde anon, maugree hir heed,
> By verray force, he rafte hire maydenhed. (886–88)

King Arthur promptly finds this knight guilty of an "oppressioun" and sentences him to death, the maximum (though seldom enforced) penalty prescribed by English law for either sexual assault or abduction.[22] Margaret Hallissy emphasizes that the Wife of Bath's testimony describes a *raptus* that comprises "a personal injury directed against a woman, not a property crime directed against her husband or father"[23] – precisely the charge from which Chaucer once needed to distance himself absolutely. But H. Marshall Leicester, Jr., would deconstruct any determinate referentiality to the "special case" of rape reported in the *Wife of Bath's Tale*. Within a field of interpretive play that would obliterate the boundaries between reader and text, the "inextricably entangled" issue of rape may be carried

> back to the dream in the prologue, where, we remember, marriage itself is experienced and projected by the Wife as a form of institutionalized rape, one, moreover, whose statutory consequences include the lawful transfer of property to the advantage, in her case, of the violated party.[24]

[22] Joseph A. Hornsby, *Chaucer and the Law* (Norman, Okla.: Pilgrim Books, 1988), 119–20.

[23] Margaret Hallissy, *Clean Maids, True Wives, Steadfast Widows: Chaucer's Women and Medieval Codes of Conduct* (Westport, Conn.: Greenwood Press, 1993), 180.

[24] H. Marshall Leicester, Jr., "'My bed was full of veray blood': Subject, Dream, and Rape in the *Wife of Bath's Prologue and Tale*," in *The Wife of Bath*, ed. Peter G. Beidler, Case Studies in Contemporary Criticism (Boston: St. Martin's Press, 1996), 248.

Cecilia Chaumpaigne did receive the equivalent of Chaucer's annual income. But the swift justice of Arthur's court of law is just as swiftly overruled upon appeal to Guenevere's more merciful (or arbitrary) *court d'amour*.

The never-named victim is then simply forgotten. After a year's respite (like that awarded to the formel in the *House of Fame*), Alison's equally never-named "lusty bacheler" (883) completely "beats the rap."[25] The interposition of the Wife of Bath's voice grants Chaucer license to refer to *raptus* in a heretofore unspeakably comic way. And only such a fully realized persona as Alison of Bath, "by blending wish-fulfillment and legal theory, as well as fiction and fact,"[26] can set the author free to fabricate a quasi-anonymous text so utterly indifferent to his own sensibilities about one particularly real, precedent case.

Indeed, the majority of narrators in the *Tales* acknowledge *raptus* – most inclusively defined as any involuntary *taking* (i.e., *cupiditas*) – though few do so as blithely as Alison of Bath. The bride-taking of Emily, for example, which neither Diana nor Venus can prevent, drives the plot of the *Knight's Tale*. In the *Miller's Tale*, young Alison is essentially harassed by Nicholas, Absolon, and her own husband, John; though the acquisitiveness of each man is repaid quite differently, all three receive an appropriate *contrapasso* in the end. In the *Reeve's Tale*, a miller's wife is taken in the dark. She does not consent to this adultery, but neither does she file a complaint during her "fit" (4230).

Though accused and then abused throughout the *Man of Law's Tale*, Queen Custance seems invulnerable to real rape (914–52). But from the start she was "bounden under subjeccioun" (270) – that is, engaged – for "'Wommen are born to thraldom and penance, / And to been under mannes governance'" (286–87). In the *Clerk's Tale*, the Marquis Walter imposes a premarital contract upon Griselda that demands no less than her unconditional surrender to his abusive possession. Rape, thus, comprises a substantial subcategory of the Marriage Group.

The inherent ambiguity of *raptus* – that is, the legitimacy of any *taking* of the person – is sequentially tested in the *Canterbury Tales* against an expanding lexicon of possible synonyms which include arrest, extortion, prostitution, and even adultery. In the *Friar's Tale*, a summoner fails to blackmail a country wife. But, in the *Shipman's Tale*, a monk more successfully defrauds first a wife of one debt, and then her husband of two. In the *Franklin's Tale*, Dorigen be-

[25] Sheila Delany, *The Naked Text* (Berkeley: Univ. of California Press, 1994), 164. On an archetypal plane, it is possible to see the Loathly Lady as a crone manifestation of the victim maiden herself (both being projections of the Wife's psyche). In which case, the lusty bachelor's final surrender to marriage can be interpreted as ironically satisfying the *lex talionis*. Indeed, the *Old Testament* allows for this plea bargain only if the victim herself is innocent and available for marriage (Deut. 22:28–29).

[26] R. J. Blanch, "'Al Was This Land Fulfild of Fayerye': The Thematic Employment of Force, Willfulness, and Legal Conventions in Chaucer's 'Wife of Bath's Tale,'" *Studia Neophilologica* 57 (1985): 48.

comes obligated to Aurelius's claim upon her truth (primarily because he takes her sarcastic proposition so legalistically). In the *Merchant's Tale*, ravishment either explicitly (1750) or by analogy (1774) comprises a motif "invoked again as a kind of wishful thinking ... to remind us that men are (they hope) capable of it."[27] Proserpina, whose rape is briefly annotated (2230–33) and apparently not fully recompensed, undertakes (2317) to give all women success in sophistry – "suffisant answere, / ... though they be in any gilt ytake" (2266–68). And so on.[28]

In reports from London to Canterbury, we read that men (try to) use force or fraud to coerce the compliance of women. The *Physician's Tale*, however, best represents the *Canterbury Tales*'s worst treatment of rape even though its conspiracy of lechery (149–50) against Virginia is in fact aborted. This tale seems to float in an interpretive limbo of thematic indeterminacy precisely because it has been stripped of Chaucer's recitative tone but has not yet been fully invested with the fictive perspective of a fully realized persona. One of this tale's most disturbing features is that the court of Roman law is itself abused by judge Apius in his attempt to take Virginia. Perversely, Virginia's father is the one accused of her *raptus*. More perversely still, Virginius invokes both patriarchal law and paternal love to prevent this miscarriage of justice and to justify his own execution of Virginia. Whether sincerely melodramatic or darkly satiric, the *Physician's Tale* tale provokes no light laughter.

The *Manciple's Tale* exemplifies yet another mistrial, submitted as an admonitory tale. It is occasioned by the Host's good legal counsel warning the Manciple to refrain from libel lest he be reclaimed by the Cook (72). Cuckold Apollo takes stereotypical vengeance against his wife, but then regrets too late that he denied her due process (284–88). So the minstrel god (113) *quits* (293) the accuser crow as well. Not only does Apollo make this once-white impersonator (243) black as ink; he rapes the thief (292) of his song-making too (305).

[27] Elaine Tuttle Hansen, *Chaucer and the Fictions of Gender* (Berkeley: Univ. of California Press, 1992), 262.

[28] Throughout the *Canterbury Tales*, Chaucer uses the verb "reven" ("to take") in a fashion that seems tonally insignificant. No anxiety regarding the implications of *raptus* can be heard in such occurrences as a description of the sunset in the *Franklin's Tale* (1017), or two listings in the *Monk's Tale* of the trophies won by Hercules (2098, 3001). Possibly, Hercules took yet a third item by force (2106, taking "rafte" as a variant for "brak").

More provocative cognates of a ravishment-motif in the *Canterbury Tales* include the Summoner's satiric comment about the familiar tale of a friar being ravished to hell (Prologue to the *Summoner's Tale*, 1676), the betrayed falcon's description of the bigamist tercelet's seeming to have been ravished for joy in the *Squire's Tale* (547), and Madame Eglantyne's confusingly rhapsodic description of *figurae* ravishing down from God (Prologue to the *Prioress's Tale*, 469). A less explicit but clearer image of ravishment may also be attributed to the golden bondage that imprisons the virago Zenobia in the *Monk's Tale* (2364). The *Nun's Priest's Tale* alone presents a male (albeit not a human) victim of *raptus*. Chauntecleer, taken under "areest" (2900), is "ravysshed with his flaterie" (3324).

Whatever dark implications this *exemplum* had for Chaucer in private, its pertinence to a public tale-teller is stated all too clearly: to avoid self-recrimination in court, the only safety is silence (347, 359). The Manciple, like Ovid, is curiously silent regarding the "man of litel reputacioun" (199) who seduced Apollo's wife and so could be charged with *raptus*; nevertheless, this "oon of litel reputacioun" (253) escapes the tale unpunished as well as unnamed.

Rape *per se* is not named aloud in Chaucer's final homily, but its radical significance is not simply overlooked. Whereas the Man of Law had stipulated that rape is theft (*Man of Law's Tale*, 915, 923) motivated by the "foule lust of luxurie" (925), the Parson explains that all lust ("luxuria") entails some manner of forced deprivation: "This synne is eek a thefte, for thefte generally is for to reve a wight his thyng agayns his wille" (*Parson's Tale*, 877). The gender of "his" is common, and the significance of "thing" is all-inclusive. The Parson extends this conception of cupidity as rape to chastise both adulteresses (878) and pimps ("putours") who "constreyne wommen to yelden hem a certeyn rente" (886). Adultery is placed sixth among the Ten Commandments to show that it bridges theft and manslaughter (887). The relevance of the Parson's teachings is presented as universal and, as such, not irrelevant to the individual case of Geoffrey Chaucer, accused rapist and, *per force*, adulterer.

The most neglected victim of the whole Cecilia Chaumpaigne affair and the most enigmatic respondent to all of Chaucer's subsequent rape references remains his wife. "Let us hope Philippa Chaucer bore the scandal with as much philosophy as Dame Prudence."[29] The fact that such speculation often proves unverifiable does not make it avoidable as a tonally significant factor affecting each reader's response; one's predisposition to Chaucer contextualizes one's response to *Chaucer*, and vice versa. I would like to suggest in retrospect, therefore, that Chaucer's enduring concerns regarding the Cecilia Chaumpaigne episode may have occasioned his composition of at least three works: the *Tale of Melibee*, the *Second Nun's Tale*, and the *Treatise on the Astrolabe*. None of these texts is considered especially entertaining today, yet all three resonate with far more dramatic integrity if read as Chaucer's self-imposed penitential tasks.

Chaucer probably composed a proto-version of his legend of St. Cecilia after 1380 but before 1386.[30] Translating a "lyf ... of Seynt Cecile" (*LGW*, F 426) would have served Chaucer's conscience especially well as a *satisfactio* – a penitential recompense made by the poet's hand offered in honor of Cecilia Chaumpaigne's namesake. Likewise, perhaps nearer to 1380 than 1390, Chau-

[29] Nevill Coghill, *The Poet Chaucer* (London: Oxford Univ. Press, 1967), 115. Philippa Chaucer presumably died in 1387. I think it highly unlikely that Chaucer anticipated performing himself in public after this date.

[30] The proposition that the tale was composed as early as 1373 has been rejected by Florence H. Ridley in favor of "a date in the mid- rather than the early period" (*The Riverside Chaucer*, 942a).

cer translated Renaud de Louens's *Livre de Melibée et de Dame Prudence.*[31] Chaucer explicitly recognizes the labor of translating as a moral discipline (Prologue to the *Second Nun's Tale*, 22–25, and the Retraction, 1088–89). Even though he subsequently contextualized both the *life* and the *livre* within the fictionally distancing frame of the *Canterbury Tales*, Chaucer retained recitation of the *Tale of Melibee* as his own persona's (or personal) obligation (965–66).

The assault that initiates Chaucer's *Tale of Melibee* recalls the start of the *Wife of Bath's Tale*, albeit at an allegorical distance. Sophie's claims as victim are almost as neglected as those of Alison's "mayde." And Prudence, like the Loathly Lady, eventually wins her own will from her husband (1724–25) because such a plaintiff's goodly words can ravish all who hear (1733). But the post-rape reconciliation achieved by Prudence is not based upon the narrator's blithe amnesia regarding the initial crime itself.

Both the *Tale of Melibee* and the *Second Nun's Tale* portray court hearings in which a female litigant surely holds the right. Both prioritize the promulgation of general "doctryne" over immediate "myrthe" (935). And both, therefore, seem to lack a Chaucerian flavor. Yet Chaucer himself felt obliged to retract neither of these two projects. As products, neither seems particularly personalized; as processes, however, both mandated the author's fully contextualized review of conscience. Ten years after his legal affairs with Cecilia Chaumpaigne had supposedly been resolved – and probably as many as five years after retiring from court performance – Chaucer presented *A Treatise on the Astrolabe* to "Lyte Lowys my sone" (1) – that is, to his presumed bastard.[32] Although neither reading nor writing this treatise entails a review of conscience, Chaucer does explicitly state his motives for its transcription. He offers the text as a gift produced with magisterial friendship (6–8) and intends it to be studied in isolation – that is, as the boy's private possession to be read in the author's (if not his father's) absence (41).[33]

Although Cecilia Chaumpaigne had officially released Geoffrey Chaucer from the charge of rape and "aliqua alia" in 1380, and although she had promised him "imperpetuum quietum," he never afterwards seems to have thought of

[31] Although Sharon Hiltz DeLong finally suggests that a "date early in the Canterbury period (1386–90) seems most likely," she concedes that the "date of the Melibee is uncertain" (*The Riverside Chaucer*, 923b).

[32] The evidence that Chaucer fathered Lewis by Cecilia Chaumpaigne "is merely circumstantial" (Pearsall, 138). But her pregnancy "would substantially have reduced her claim" (Howard, 320). Sheila Delany notes that a woman's own "semination" proved her consent and "annihilated her legal case" ("Strategies of Silence in the Wife of Bath's Recital," *Exemplaria* 2 [1990]: 49–69; reprinted in Sheila Delany, *Medieval Literary Politics* [Manchester: Manchester Univ. Press, 1990], 128).

[33] In the first half of the fourteenth century, Renaud de Louens had translated three moral treatises (including the *Livre de Melibée*), one for each of his sons as a coming-of-age present (*The Riverside Chaucer*, 923b).

himself as simply innocent. Chaucer never presumed to hold himself fully released, until finally absolved (Retraction, 1090). Both his public and his private references to rape after 1380 still resonate with a discernible, if not precisely definable range of personal investment. Only actual voicing specifies the particular nuances attachable to each isolated passage. Whereas one reader hears vague embarrassment, another hears grudging regret, another intuits shame, or laughing anxiety or tragic remorse. Critical consideration of such histrionically viable if not historically determinable interpretations remains both irresolvable and mandatory. To insist, however, that the self-referential overtones of Chaucer's texts must be silenced because of our mute uncertainty regarding their potential as performance scripts would be like asserting that all medieval drama remain in the closet.

Chaucer's *Second Nun's Tale*: Record of a Dying World

MARIANNE BØRCH, *Odense University*

Chaucer is an accommodating author: for six centuries "our contemporary," he has responded well to the historicist turn of recent decades. While universalist critics were still congratulating the author on his indifference to historical events taking place on his doorstep, a vanguard headed by scholars like Morton W. Bloomfield noted in Chaucer's works a sense of historical process that made the absence of specific historical references appear less significant.[1] Chaucer's "modernity" has increasingly been challenged, while the focus of interpretation has turned toward the methodological problems of reading literature from a closed, distant, and in many ways alien past.[2]

Chaucer is, indeed, acutely aware of the dynamics of history, and conveys his sense of the past by depicting and remarking on the alien quality even of conventions that express universal human phenomena such as love (e.g., *Troilus and Criseyde*, 2.29–42). The poet writes at a time of rapid change in ideology and sign theory, a time which coincides with the transition between oral and written literature. These changes inevitably affected the validity of conventional modes, genres, and narrative voices, as, indeed, we know from Chaucer's own experiments. The present essay will argue that the *Second Nun's Tale* constitutes a particularly subtle response to changes in late-medieval culture. It will test the hypothesis that Chaucer wrote the *Second Nun's Tale* upon an epistemological premise whose axiomatic status was crumbling. The poet's departures from his sources with respect to both style and substance suggest that the tale may have been, or begun as, an exercise in writing a simple saint's life, a genre which may be said to embody in naive narrative form the philosophical premise that the cosmos is the manifest expression of God's purpose. With the

[1] E.g., in "Chaucer's Sense of History," *JEGP* 51 (1952): 301–13.

[2] See Paul Zumthor's meditation on the medievalist's epistemological exclusion from his subject in *Speaking of the Middle Ages*, trans. Sarah White (Lincoln: Univ. of Nebraska Press, 1986).

gradual erosion of belief in *manifestatio*, however, modes of discourse and genres that rested upon the principle began to lose authority. When Chaucer included the *Second Nun's Tale* in the *Canterbury Tales*, he provided the work with a literary context that would make a new tale even of a work otherwise unrevised; its narrative might now stand forth as simplistic and naive, perhaps even downright subversive of the religious effect that the language of *manifestatio* – analogy – would originally have been devised to achieve. Prefacing his tale with the "Invocacio ad Mariam," Chaucer further appears to question a traditional poetic, for the invocation's figurative language in fact problematizes figural representation. Having thus painted himself into a corner, Chaucer had to abandon work on the tale. Still, it remains as part of the *Canterbury Tales*, and in that context the *Second Nun's Tale* attracts interest for the way its mixed poetic points to both past and future (Chaucerian) practices; and for its significant contribution to what, deferring to David Lawton's definition of the term, I venture to call the "unity" of the *Canterbury Tales*.[3]

Problems of Critical Method

The tenet that all aspects of a text should be accounted for in an interpretation, and that any system these may form should override the authority of systems requiring extratextual complementation, has now lost its once axiomatic status. That status was always challenged by medieval literature with its notoriously unstable texts and pragmatic aesthetic, and interpretational problems in Chaucer criticism have frequently been resolved through reference to homogenizing contexts. Even where extratextual factors are clearly relevant, a quarrel remains over the degree and nature of the control they exert over internal features. The question is to a large extent one of reader or listener response, another extremely elusive factor: the historicization of the modern critic has condemned her to glimpsing the past through the solid bars of time's prison, while studies of Chaucer's contemporary audience may define a "horizon of expectation," i.e., areas of hermeneutical possibility, but no more.[4] In relation to the saint's life, for instance, no analysis of cultural context can finally determine whether a medieval audience would perceive tensions in the generic pattern of one particular specimen as a threat to the work's ideological premises, or would curb intratextual problems by means of extratextual factors.

[3] David Lawton, distinguishes between two kinds of unity; rejecting the hunt for a "harmony of parts," he recommends the notion of "hermeneutic unity," which can accommodate "contradictions, tensions, and disjunctions" ("Chaucer's Two Ways: The Pilgrimage Frame of *The Canterbury Tales*," *Studies in the Age of Chaucer* 9 [1987]: 6).

[4] The term "horizon of expectation" is taken from Hans Robert Jauss's discussion in "The Alterity and Modernity of Medieval Literature," *Modern Language Notes* 10 (1978–79): 182–83.

Whatever the critic's position on its *effect* in individual cases, the criterion for an extratextual feature's *relevance* is always its ability to clear up intransigent meanings and manuscript muddles. Such "face-saving" operation, however, may indicate that the critic, whilst steering clear of a New Critical Scylla, is heading for a Historicist Charybdis, namely that of "the fallacy of the homogeneous past."[5] While the search for unity is inseparable from criticism, the pitfalls of overemphasis, distortion, ironization, or neglect of discrepant detail are especially hard to avoid in studying texts from a culture whose scantily preserved contexts weave around it only the "thinnest" possible cultural fabric. There may, in other words, be few criteria for critique of unifying readings. Nor are these much deplored when it comes to interpreting Chaucer's religious tales. Here, the unity invoked – that furnished by the Christian creed – is made the validating framework for all interpretation, while the attempt to affect the validity of that unifying framework becomes by prior definition ahistorical, i.e., methodologically naive.[6] However, the reading that places religion outside the sphere of textual critique has the weakness – even when accommodating the complexity of cultural practices at any one time – of being unable to register and account for cultural change. To cruise safely between the critical Scylla and Charybdis, then, the student of the past *must* as a matter of principle be suspicious of apparent unity, *however consonant with historical probability*. This strategy will, moreover, steer clear of another potential fallacy, that of viewing a text as passive, a "reflection" of an illuminating "context," when in fact a text is an active force, "contextualizing," and thus commenting upon, its "context." On this assumption, textual tension should even be tested as the cultural marker that may identify a text as a "vehicle for the change of that which it reflects,"[7] i.e., as a locus for both challenging and accommodating a heterogenous audience – an audience capable, for instance, of a variety of responses to a saint's life. In the following, analysis of the *Second Nun's Tale* will demonstrate how *this* saint's life, *narrated in this particular way*, at *this particular moment in time*, and *in this particular context,* problematizes aspects of religious thinking and discourse in Chaucer's time, and that the incongruities which debar unifying interpretation may well reflect the author's inability to assume, and thus play confidently to, a homogeneous "horizon of expectations."[8]

[5] E. D. Hirsch, *The Aims of Interpretation* (New Haven: Yale Univ. Press, 1976), 41.

[6] For a discussion of New Historicism as "incapable of self-criticism" (in relation to Steven Greenblatt's oeuvre), see Paul Hamilton, *Historicism*, The New Critical Idiom Series (London: Longman, 1996), 150 ff.

[7] R. Howard Bloch on the vernacular literature of the High Middle Ages, *Etymologies and Genealogies: A Literary Anthropology of the French Middle Ages* (Chicago: Univ. of Chicago Press, 1983), 15.

[8] The present article has no wish to quarrel with those who read the *Second Nun's Tale* as a sincere religious work, e.g., P. M. Kean, who characterizes the tale as "Chaucer's simplest and most wholehearted treatment of a saint's legend" (*Chaucer and the Making of English Poetry*

Narrative as "Manifestatio"

To question the legitimacy of harmonizing textual meaning by invoking a homogeneous religious context may appear particularly perverse in connection with the *Second Nun's Tale*, which expressly enjoins a reader to do precisely that.[9] A narrative voice points out that Cecilie's life represents cosmic reality in miniature, making that reality available to us as a text – Cecilie's "lif *seith*" (120).[10] The word "lif," then, refers to two speech acts, one divine, the other human. The story, the "life" as a genre, is a supporting mechanism through which the *human* narrator preserves for posterity the primary speech act: the *divine* text of the saint's earthly "lif." What makes the world and the human word truly profitable reading is the assumption of an analogy between various elements in the created order, and even between created and Creator. God's will may be read in and understood from the things that are seen, as well as from names for those things. Thus the etymological reading of Cecilie's name which prefaces the tale tells the same story as her life, only at a different level and in a different form:

> First wolde I yow the name of Seint Cecilie
> Expowne, *as men may in hir storie see.* (85–86)

Cecilie's name signifies her essential qualities, and her qualities in turn articulate themselves in her acts. Both her disposition and her acts find analo-

[London: Routledge & Kegan Paul, 1972], 2.201); and V. A. Kolve, who calls it the "finest [saint's life] to survive in Middle English verse" ("Chaucer's *Second Nun's Tale* and the Iconography of Saint Cecilia," *New Perspectives in Chaucer Criticism*, ed. Donald M. Rose [Norman, Okla.: Pilgrim Books, 1981], 139). Such contributions helped reverse "humanist" misunderstanding and neglect of both religious works and contexts (see C. David Benson's "Introduction" to *Chaucer's Religious Tales*, ed. C. David Benson and Elizabeth Robertson [Cambridge: D. S. Brewer, 1990], 2–3, and, in the same book, Derek Pearsall's "Chaucer's Religious Tales: A Question of Genre," 17). This article addresses the danger of removing "context" from textual critique by making it a premise of valid criticism. Thus Carolyn Collette, otherwise recommending New Historicist critics for breaking down "such monolithic conceptions as 'Christianity'" and seeking to "identify the strains and competing elements in society," bypasses David Aers's thoughtful analysis (in *Chaucer* [Brighton: Harvester Press, 1986], 51–53) with the disqualifying remark that Aers forgets about Chaucer writing for "a culture in which, unlike our own, Christian theology, philosophy, and liturgy are internalized" ("Critical Approaches to the *Prioress' Tale* and the *Second Nun's Tale*," *Chaucer's Religious Tales*, 103).

[9] On the Prologue as an authoritative interpretation of the ensuing narrative, see Paul Clogan, "The Figural Style and Meaning of the Second Nun's Prologue and Tale," *Medievalia et Humanistica*, n.s., 3, (1972): 213–15; and Roger Ellis, *Patterns of Religious Narrative in the Canterbury Tales* (London: Croom Helm, 1986), 85–86.

[10] Citations of Chaucer's works are from *The Riverside Chaucer*, ed. Larry D. Benson, 3d ed. (Oxford: Oxford Univ. Press, 1987). Italics throughout indicate words I wish to emphasize.

gous expression at other levels (available through words though not direct experience) – as for example, the cosmological, in which the Empyrean, the Sun, and the Moon represent moral qualities such as the magnanimity of faith and works (109–12). Etymology thus establishes the ontological and moral unity of all creation the way allegorical narrative tends toward universality and coherence.[11] Indeed, Cecilie *is* a kind of allegory, a *figura*; and not just an allegory of the poets, where the literal level is fictive and contingent, but an allegory of the theologians, or rather, of God, an allegory whose literal level is the saint's presence in history. Cecilie, like Dante's Beatrice, is a miracle manifest.[12]

Since the secular order could be read as a text, analogical thinking legitimized the use of unadorned historical narrative as "an ideal structure for moralization."[13] History might be construed for its moral lesson, its interpretation being controlled not only by the basic notion of *manifestatio*, but also by written texts – the Bible, the *commentatores*, the liturgy, or religious lyrics – that all spin around worldly event and worldly object a net of words expounding, and emulating in coherence, a unified and immanent divine purpose. Cecilie's historical fate thus confirms at every level her meaning, a meaning that is stable and independent of its human reader. To make Cecilie the perfect "ensample" (93, 105), a poet merely needs to "declare," i.e., lay open, what is already there: "Now have I yow declared what she highte" (119).

With history a mirror of the divine will, the events of a saint's life ought, literally, to speak for themselves. So why should not Chaucer, fascinated as he is with the possibilities of a "naked" text (*Legend of Good Women*, G 86),[14] let Cecilie's "lif" speak (for) itself? His wish to do so, and perhaps trust that this was possible (or at least curiosity as to whether it was), may explain a redaction

[11] E. R. Curtius, "Etymology as a Category of Thought," *European Literature and the Latin Middle Ages*, trans. Willard R. Trask (1953; London: Routledge & Kegan Paul, 1979), 495–500; Maureen Quilligan, *The Language of Allegory: Defining the Genre* (Ithaca: Cornell Univ. Press, 1979), esp. chap. 3, "The Context," 156 ff.

[12] The distinction between allegory of the poets and allegory of the theologians is borrowed from the letter to Can Grande attributed to Dante.

[13] Jesse Gellrich, *The Idea of the Book in the Middle Ages: Language Theory, Mythology, and Fiction* (Ithaca: Cornell Univ. Press, 1985), 22. Cf. Judson B. Allen and Theresa A. Moritz, *A Distinction of Stories: The Medieval Unity of Chaucer's Fair Chain of Narratives for Canterbury* (Columbus: Ohio State Univ. Press, 1981), 71–73.

[14] Even in his earliest work, Chaucer has persons who find it difficult to communicate discover that narrative with its "what wyse, how, why, and wherfore" (*BD*, 474) will bridge the gap between them. The *Legend of Good Women* can be seen as an (abortive) attempt to tell stories stripped of most of their traditional apparatus of (moralizing) commentary, a possibility mentioned, but left largely unexplored in Marianne Børch, *Chaucer's Poetics: Seeing and Asking* (Odense: Odense Univ., 1993), 49–50. Since then has appeared Sheila Delany's brilliant and exhaustive analysis of the *Legend* as a project which despite its "minimalism of aesthetic topos" and "aesthetic procedure," nevertheless demonstrates the "impossibility of nakedness" (*The Naked Text: Chaucer's Legend of Good Women* [Berkeley: Univ. of California Press, 1994], 1–2).

of his sources that has surprised critics; namely, a pruning of the material which leaves the narrative shorn of moral commentary and references to the saint's longing for God.[15]

While Chaucer's treatment of his sources is consistent with his interest in narrative, his pared-down version relinquishes hermeneutical controls to make his simple saint's life rely almost entirely, and thus make heavy demands, upon its "horizon of expectation." This makes it crucial to determine how sure Chaucer could be of meeting with the proper response, and also to speculate what would happen if he did not: in that circumstance, can his narrative stand alone as a vehicle for encouraging religious devotion?

Chaucer did more than simply cut and select. In translating his sources, he adopted an orally oriented style and organizing mode that remain a characteristic feature of all his writings, but is especially marked in the early works such as the tale of Cecilie.[16] As it stands in the *Canterbury Tales*, Chaucer's last work made to include some of his earliest, the *Second Nun's Tale* hovers uncertainly between oral and written: as an orally performed tale in a written work told in a partly oral style, and referring to itself as both written to be read (35, 78) and told to be heard (360, 294). Oral and written narrative discourse, however, are significantly different: for instance, attention to causality, ontological distinctions, and complexity of moral purpose will be a low priority in the former mode, but range much higher in the latter. Any transfer from oral to written or vice versa is therefore problematic; in the following analysis of the literary-epistemological difficulties created by Chaucer's pared-down narrative, those difficulties will repeatedly be seen to be compounded by features of an oral style.

The Tale as Analogy

Not only the narrative voice, but also Cecilie herself is eager to "declare" the meaning of signs so as to make "al open and pleyn" (284). The saint's preaching is uncompromisingly straight and demystifying as she uses conceptual explication to clarify religious mysteries that confound prospective converts: she explains the Trinity by analogy with human faculties (336–41), and analyzes a moral state – Almachius's puffed-up pride – by reference to a physical object, a bauble (437–41).

[15] Sherry L. Reames, "The Cecilia Legend as Chaucer Inherited and Retold It: The Disappearance of an Augustinian Ideal," *Speculum*, 55 (1980): 38–57; and her "The Sources of the Second Nun's Tale," *Modern Philology* 76 (1978): 111–35. A different reading of Chaucer's deletions is offered by John Hirsh, "The Politics of Spirituality: The Second Nun and the Manciple," *Chaucer Review* 12 (1977): 599–624.

[16] Derek Brewer, "Chaucer's Poetic Style," *The Cambridge Chaucer Companion*, ed. Piero Boitani and Jill Mann (Cambridge: Cambridge Univ. Press, 1986), 229–30.

Cecilie not only explains, but also creates signs for others to read: Chastity displays, and so signifies, her purity; conversion requires acts no less than faith, baptism no less than belief (170–71). The supremely eloquent sign of her "lif" – one that provokes an avalanche of converts to Christianity – is Cecilie's martyrdom, which she brings about in spite of Almachius's conciliatory suggestion that she believe whatever she likes, as long as she sacrifices to his God. Cecilie must, indeed, signify her scorn *openly*: first, her "busynesse" provides the text that, read by others, will do God's business, but even more crucially, her sign system does not allow a separation of sign and signified, as she demonstrates in rejecting Almachius's distinction between her "religioun" and her "bileeve" (427). The confrontation between pagan Almachius and Christian Cecilie dramatizes radically different notions of the connection between signs and what they signify. Almachius believes in token acts in the modern political sense, acknowledging an arbitrary, potentially oblique relation between sign and signified, whereas Cecilie insists upon a single, unambiguous, and verbalizable affinity between sign and signified. That Almachius's distinction between letter and spirit is false and foolish is corroborated by the highest possible authority when Cecilie's guardian angel stretches his protection beyond the saint's spiritual well-being to the physical integrity that is its necessary adjunct. The material order is not just symbolic of, but ontologically implicated in, the spiritual.

Cecilie, then, is a sign, an interpreter of signs, and a creator of signs. Although the pagans Cecilie addresses render her *explication de texte* dramatically and theologically appropriate, these would, as already pointed out, appear redundant for a Christian audience. Secular data tell God's story, and, although usually indirectly evoked, traditional association will come into play to forestall negative associations (for instance of chastity with frigidity) and instead privilege desirable ones. To see an angel is equivalent to possessing grace, and when a saint loses his life, this death not only promises, but is analogously coincident with, birth in the hereafter.

The identification of *death here* with *life hereafter* illustrates the tale's negative signifying mode. The analogues that illustrate the affinity between heaven and earth consistently discourage attachment to the secular order: spiritual purity precludes physical consummation; a hairshirt subverts the values signaled by a bridal dress; a pagan organ is neutralized by God's music. Analogy is thus harnessed to contempt of the world, not, one notes, a theologically inevitable emphasis, but certainly one consistent with the saint's unemotionally analytic approach to worldly experience.

Even as analogical thought underlies action, exposition, and signifying mode, so one may detect a feature of an "analogous style" at the level of syntax. In the following paratactic arrangement of single lines, style maintains a hairline distinction between analogy and identification. Valerian and Tiburce

losten bothe hir hevedes in the place.
Hir soules wenten to the Kyng of grace. (398–99)

Distinct, complete sentences indicate the separation of co-incidental events; rhyme and parallel construction signify their absolute connection. Thus all levels of the narrative are devised to support the notion – also directly expounded in the text – that empirical surfaces form a text that invites only one kind of response. Other features, however, complicate the issue.

Analogy, Narrative, and Oral Stylistics

An oral style typically provides numerous and conspicuous signposts for easy orientation. Narratorial comments occur regularly, as in "Now wol I speken of my fourthe housbonde" (Prologue to the *Wife of Bath's Tale*, 452), or "Now wol I turne to Arcite ageyn" (*Knight's Tale*, 1488). Narrative signposts characteristically refer to time and space, and beyond clarifying plot, they conveniently fill lines so as to avoid a confusing density of information.[17] In the *Second Nun's Tale* there are many such references:

Whan Maximus had herd the seintes loore,
He gat hym of the tormentoures leve,
And ladde hem to his hous *withoute moore,*
And with hir prechyng, *er that it were eve ....* (372–75)

Cecile cam, *whan it was woxen nyght,*
With preestes that hem cristned alle yfeere;
And *afterward, whan day was woxen light ....* (379–81)

The Second Nun's narrative meticulously adheres to time as its organizing mode, and space as its necessary adjunct.[18] Religious experience occurs within the temporal order, as when Tiburce sees God's angel "in tyme and space" (355). Moreover, if history speaks literally, sequence must be significant, hence

[17] On the necessary "diffuseness" of much medieval literature, see A. C. Spearing, *Criticism and Medieval Poetry* (London: Edward Arnold, 1972), 18.

[18] Spatial relations in the *Second Nun's Tale* rely on the precise localization of events, creating an impression that people are hurrying about among various sites. Valerian moves from his bedchamber to Pope Urban and back again; Tiburce repeats this itinerary. Later, all the Christians are taken to Almachius's court, from there to a place of "tormentoures" (373, 376), then on to Maximus's house and thence to a place of execution, after which the souls of the dead depart for the sky, while Cecilie buries their remains along with Maximus's "Withinne hire buriyng place, under the stoon" (409). Subsequently, Cecilie is taken to a place of "sacrifice" (413), and after her dispute with Almachius to the flame bath in her house, where she is beheaded and left half-dead until her dead body can be carried to its grave. Later, Cecilie's house is inaugurated as a church.

perhaps the regretful "It were ful hard *by ordre* for to seyn / How manye wondres Jhesus for hem wroghte" (358–59). The reference to time and space, and the difficulty of reporting events in their proper order, are Chaucerian additions; while their presence is dictated by meter, their nature emphasizes the story's secular dimension.

Within this temporal framework, Cecilie defines the conditions under which grace is attainable, and for that speaks conditionally: "if that ... if so ... so that." However, with spiritual motivation de-emphasized, and with the proliferation of references to temporal sequence, aided by a tendency for an oral style to downplay analysis,[19] the narrative calls attention to the secular order for its own sake, overriding Cecilie's conditional discourse. An effective leveling of conditional and temporal occurs even at the level of style, in the variation between the conditional "if" and the temporal "when":

> *If* that yow list, the angel shul ye see,
> *So that* ye trowe on Crist and yow baptize. (170–71)

> And *whan* that he hath purged yow fro synne,
> Thanne shul ye se that angel, er ye twynne. (181–82)

Subjected to the scrutiny of leisurely reading, the theological implications of both passages are no doubt problematic. In the former passage, the conditional "if" suggests that human desire is a dominant trigger of divine action, while the theologically weightier conditional of "So that" not only occupies a weaker position, but appears nearly redundant after the first "if" – and is, at all events, ambiguous, meaning alternatively "if that" and "in order that." In the latter couplet, man seems to control otherworldly response by the laws of simple causality: cause, purity; effect, sight of angel. The translation of analogy's timelessness into time-bound causality is theoretically consistent with the idea of history as the temporal enactment of the timeless. But, in writing, the *Second Nun's Tale*'s style underpins the causal orientation of narrative events, by which what is placed first will naturally be understood as a cause, what follows as its effect.

Throughout the tale, man's acts – acts rather than love – precede divine response to suggest that God and His agents are at humanity's beck and call. The angelic messengers even seem to respond with magical swiftness to human impulses:

> for thow so soone
> Assentedest to good conseil also,
> Sey what thee list, and thou shalt han thy boone. (232–34)

[19] Brewer, "Chaucer's Poetic Style," 234.

every maner boone
That he God axed, it was sped ful soone. (356–57)

Again, by analogous logic, impulse *is* response, but simultaneity, subjected to narrative sequentiality, becomes causality. This makes God a kind of spirit of the lamp, or even a projected image of man's omnipotence, which may be one reason for David Aers to pronounce the tale an "infantile fantasy."[20]

The mechanization of grace corresponds to the mechanization of intentionality that follows from Chaucer's revisions. As in other quasi-allegorical genres, the saint's life portrays human perfection in terms of election, an idea which in itself diminishes interest in motivation. Unsupported by descriptions of the saint's love of God, and in a written context that may disastrously call attention to features acceptable in oral narrative, the saint's pursuit of preordained perfection appears mindless, nearly robotic.[21] And by a domino effect, another typical generic feature of the saint's life is affected: the assurance, undaunted militancy, and taunting answers of the prospective martyr. Cumulatively with the tale's automatic link between human demand and divine supply, and the focus upon acts (predominantly the non-acts of rejection and scorn), Cecilie's otherwise properly militant tone and derisive laughter acquire a positively Thatcheresque ring. This unfortunate effect, finally, is further underscored by oral-colloquial line-fillers such as "ful soone," "right there," "out of drede," "right feyn," and "ful faste"; these, from being prosodic padding with little semantic impact, come strongly to reinforce the impression of effortless human control over divine agency. The clinching lapse of stylistic decorum occurs in the description of the declaratory event (331) of God's self-manifestation in the secular realm:

By wórd and bỳ myrácle heigh Góddes Sóne .... (330)

Tone is affected as the last syllable of "miracle" is telescoped with the phonetically long "heigh" to fit within the space of a single weak stress. Strident in the face of her listeners, Cecilie is offhand and complacent about her Divine Connection. Is this really Chaucer's fine religious style?

To sum up: Sequential narrative will concentrate attention upon the secular order; in a written text, especially, description of that order will obscure simulta-

[20] *Chaucer*, 53.

[21] Cf. Angus Fletcher, *Allegory* (Ithaca: Cornell Univ. Press, 1964), who compares the protagonists of allegorical or quasi-allegorical forms to obsessional maniacs or other neurotics, since both are controlled by symbolic forces and therefore behave more or less mechanically (chap. 6, "Psychoanalytic Analogues: Obsession and Compulsion"). Sheila Delany believes Chaucer was generally so little interested in allegory because the mode excludes the "capricious" element of human motivation ("Undoing Substantial Connection: The Late-Medieval Attack on Analogical Thought," *Mosaic* 5 [1972]: 50).

neity to evoke causality, and render problematic silences that are natural in oral poetry; finally, features of an oral style will compound problems thus created.

The difficulty in making historical narrative suggest a spiritual order is particularly clear from the *Second Nun's Tales*'s treatment of bodily experience and its use of the human senses as a criterion of verification.[22] The tale's use of sight at both a literal and a figurative level has strong roots in Christian tradition.[23] The saint's battleground is the empirical world, which is perceived through sight, or *eye*sight; sight also, however, denotes spiritual sight, or *in*sight, something reserved for Christians, who see otherwise invisible angels, flower garlands, and martyred souls ascending to heaven. By an extension of the principle, physically blind Urban can "see," while spiritually blind Almachius has only literal sight. Simple narrative, however, has no means of distinguishing between symbolic and concrete, or, in other words, of indicating which sight we are dealing with at any one moment. Chaucer retains an old plot device for suggesting the difference; namely, the touchstone witness who fails to see what is seen by the elect. Nevertheless, Valerian's failure to perceive the difference between man and angel underscores at the level of plot the problem that narrative representation collapses different ontological categories and cognitive modes. Moreover, in the climactic confrontation of the tale, Cecilie herself conflates the two modes of sight when she relies upon sense evidence to argue that pagan gods have neither being nor power:

> Ther lakketh no thyng to thyne outter yen
> That thou n'art blynd; for thyng that we seen alle
> That it is stoon – that men may wel espyen –
> That ilke stoon a god thow wolt it calle.
> I rede thee, lat thyn hand upon it falle
> And taste it wel, and stoon thou shalt it fynde,
> Syn that thou seest nat with thyne eyen blynde. (498–504)

In the rest of the tale, Christians, "seeing" more than pagans, have insight. There is, however, a difference between seeing more than others and, when seeing less, denying others' claim to see more! Cecilie rejects Almachius's symbolic reading of empirical phenomena by referring to visual evidence available for common verification ("we seen alle" – "men may wel espyen"): a stone is *visibly only* a stone, can be *felt* to be *only* a stone ("taste it wel"), an object

[22] Critics who have perceived a tricky twist of the tale's traditional employment of sense experience are, for example, Aers, *Chaucer*, 53, and Robert Longsworth in "Privileged Knowledge: Cecilia and the Alchemist in the *Canterbury Tales*," *Chaucer Review* 17 (1992): 87–96.

[23] Expounded in Carolyn Collette's "A Closer Look at Seint Cecilie's Special Vision," in *Chaucer's Religious Tales*.

signifying nothing. Her argument caters to pagan materialism[24] and undoubtedly produces a dramatic confrontation, but it also blurs symbolic clarity, since in the rest of the tale sense perception is depreciated, repressed, or spirited away: Pagans are foolish for fearing pain; Cecilie's one specially developed sense is the noblest of the five in requiring no tactile contact with the object perceived, while her typical saint's inability to feel pain, heat, or sexual excitement translates the supersensory, intellectual control of the genuine paragon. It is therefore surprising to find sense evidence invoked in a contest of truth – especially as Cecilie goes on to measure the value of a creed by it. Always herself able to call down the speedy "boons" of her accommodating God, she mocks the pagan gods as deaf and dumb – something even a pagan may "espye" – and consequently unable to hear or answer prayers (284–86):

> To thee ne to hemself mowen noght profite,
> For in effect they been nat worth a myte. (510–11)

Symbolic confusion spells epistemological chaos. With Cecilie's appeal to the senses and the necessary effectiveness of divine agency in the empirical order, the concept "God" becomes meaningless. As Northrop Frye points out, "Once epistemology is founded on a sense-apprehended distinction between objects that are there and objects that are not, 'God' can go only in the illusory class."[25] The empirical has become the real, the "other" the shadow.

The danger of a collapse of ontologically different categories as the empirical sign refuses to transcend itself will always threaten in analogical discourse. For while analogy highlights the *sameness* of different orders, *difference* goes unexplored or is directly suppressed.[26]

Analogy – whether the medieval type founded in *manifestatio* or its demythologized descendent, the poetic simile – calls upon a predominantly intellec-

[24] Aquinas in *Summa Contra Gentiles* argues that for didactic purposes, pagans should be approached through rational argumentation based upon natural reason; see Marcia Colish, *A Mirror of Language* (New Haven: Yale Univ. Press, 1968), 192–94.

[25] *The Great Code* (London: Routledge & Kegan Paul, 1982), 17.

[26] Thomas Aquinas, who employs analogy in the attempt to describe God, comments at length on the dangers of this form of representation. For Aquinas's views of analogue, his use of "analogy by proportion" to suggest the difference that "analogy by attribution" obscures, and review of available alternatives to analogue such as metaphor, see Marcia Colish, *The Mirror of Language*, chap. 3. For a discussion of the danger of collapsing ontological categories in humanity's imitation of *manifestatio*, see Gellrich, who states that "the *interpretans* easily came to be seen as the *interpretandum*" (*The Idea of the Book*, 68); and Quilligan, who perceives behind the allegorical mode the "magic phenomenality" of realist discourse (*The Language of Allegory*, 156 ff.).

tual inquiry into the nature of the similarity proposed.[27] Furthermore, the analogical vehicle belongs to the literal realm, i.e., must be construed at face value: "my love is like a red, red rose" compares two literal entities; in the context of medieval analogy, the choice and construction of the vehicle is determined by a definition of the literal that refers not only to the empirical order, but to both the total cosmological scheme that correlates all signification and traditional texts expounding that scheme. While both tenor and vehicle remain *literal*, as in "Cecilie is the Empyrean," their frame of reference insures a highly *exclusive* reading, which will often be further controlled through clarifying commentary. When the Trinity is compared to a man's mind, mystical implications of the Trinitarian paradox are suppressed in a concise explication of likeness. The exact nature of the similarity between Almachius's pride and a bladder of wind is precisely explained rather than left to the listener's imagination. When Urban calls Valerian a "fiers leon," he seems to violate the previous narrative image of a lamblike, rather than lionlike, husband, but Valerian's behavior being less significant than his function, Urban jubilantly recodes him to fit a proper Christian conversion story that requires him to be pagan predatory lion before he can become Christian sacrificial lamb. Even more emphatically than the poetic simile, the analogy of *manifestatio* elides difference and mystery to highlight sameness, finding, or if necessary inscribing, in the object a literal meaning that accords with its place in the total scheme.

The possibility that analogue turn into identity – to some medieval thinkers not a danger, but a joyful fact[28] – is actualized in the narrative of the *Second Nun's Tale*, which certainly suggests a "substantial connection" between sign and signified.[29] Cecilie's angel is seen "in tyme and space" (355), and, although invisible to some, perceptible to all, for as Cecilie's purity cannot exist apart from her undefiled body, any attempt to violate her body warrants harm to the perpetrator. With the angel so palpably there, one understands Valerian's suspicion that there is a rival in his "chambre." Further, the style, incorporating colloquialisms such as "gan" and "fynt," underscores the Christian's easy intercourse

[27] For my views of analogy, simile, and metaphor I am indebted to Stephen Mannyng, "Analogy and Imagery," in *Middle English Survey: Critical Essays*, ed. Edward Vasta (Notre Dame: Univ. of Notre Dame Press, 1965); Terence Hawkes, *Metaphor*, Critical Idiom Series (London: Methuen, 1972); W. H. Leatherdale, *The Role of Analogy, Model and Metaphor in Science* (Amsterdam: North-Holland Publishing Company, 1974); Northrop Frye, *The Great Code*; Allen and Moritz, *A Distinction of Stories*; Delany, "Undoing Substantial Connection," and *Chaucer's House of Fame: The Poetics of Skeptical Fideism* (Chicago: Chicago Univ. Press, 1972); and Quilligan, *Allegory*.

[28] According to C. Walters, adherents to the "via positiva" held the difference between human and divine "quantitative rather than qualitative"; *The Cloud of Unknowing* (Harmondsworth: Penguin, 1961), 15.

[29] The term "substantial connection" is borrowed from Sheila Delany's "Undoing Substantial Connection: The Late-Medieval Attack on Analogical Thought."

with heavenly harbingers: Valerian "gooth hoom and *fynt* Cecilie / Withinne his chambre with an angel stonde" (218–19); an angel which, having first handed a crown to Cecilie, "after *gan* ... take" (223) another to Valerian. The sense of a "substantial connection" is cemented when the bodily tissue of a Christian proves too strong for a pagan axe, and is incapable of exuding a drop of sweat when placed in pagan flames. Finally, when Cecilie declares the Trinitarian paradox easily understandable from an analogy with the human mind, analogy's danger of creating God in man's image is articulated even by the saint herself.

In the *Second Nun's Tale*, then, signs are presented as openly and plainly indicative of God's order; however, as narrative and style bring about a leveling of letter and spirit, or even privilege the literal level, they highlight the basic problem of the analogical sign. Analogy can, indeed, *analogize*: "this" *is* (like) that; it can also *polarize*: this *is not* (is unlike) that. It cannot, however, "*otherize*," i.e., suggest transcendence. Thus, in the *Second Nun's Tale*, angels and lovers must be the same; and even the insistently negative construction (as in "life is death") will merely confirm the category of being or value it proposes to deny. Cecilie can promise a *better* life in another place – "bettre lif in oother place" (323) – but not an *other* life. She may deny that there is a god in a stone, but when she places God in heaven instead, she takes over what she mistakenly holds the prefect's categories to be, talking in terms of geography rather than metaphysics (508). Again, Cecilie, with her rationalist discourse and legal language (e.g., 389–90), fails to suggest a specifically Christian experience – indeed, she seems a genuine threat to Roman law precisely because her categories of justice and rationality correspond to those of her opponents. With the coalescence of what are essentially different categories, reasoning and rationalization are indistinguishable. If their difference is to be clarified by "criteria external to words, the first of these has to be that of 'things'" – an epistemological tactic with the unfortunate effect, however, of rendering God both epistemologically and linguistically "unfunctional."[30] And (oral) narrative, already privileging the literal level, undoubtedly accentuates the materialistic and man-centered implications of analogy, perhaps even blocks progression beyond the literal, so that if the events of the *Second Nun's Tale* do, in fact, speak for themselves, they also seem to speak mainly *about* themselves.

Hermeneutical Possibility

Against my analysis it may no doubt be averred that Chaucer is speaking to believers, and working within a simple genre and a popular mode that evoke uncomplicated, deeply embedded responses to the familiar and joyfully appreciated in a manner that would easily override textual reflexivity. Moreover, the

[30] *The Great Code*, 12–13, 15.

popular saint's life, for all its otherworldly implications, seeks merely to evoke admiration for, and emulation of, God's soldiery in a practical way. It is not mystical. Its mode is literal, and (oral) narrative's reifying influence only a problem for theologians. One should not ask such critical questions of this intentionally simple text.

Still, returning to the methodological discussion above, if a work by an otherwise self-conscious poet displays formal-epistemological problems, may not this be evidence of "problems of addressivity,"[31] a response to a cultural situation of some complexity? Presented with the tale's mismatch between style, narrative, and analogical thought, could Chaucer's audience have helped asking the questions asked in this article?

In England, the processes that led to the end of the Middle Ages took real speed in the late fourteenth century. Among its principal changes one notes the declining faith in the idea of *manifestatio* in the struggle between nominalism and philosophical realism. The epistemological (indeed, epistemic) crisis reverberates in literature, where notably Chaucer's encounter with Dante in the *House of Fame* culminates in a show-down with the notion of analogy; and throughout his works one can follow Chaucer's process of transferring meaning from text to reader, and, in his depiction of human life, from events to experience.[32] Given the change in intellectual environment, it is doubtful that Chaucer would have the *necessary* audience for this tale, even assuming that genre might curb his own skepticism about analogy. Proper reception would have been doubtful in 1373, the likely date of the *House of Fame* and the earliest suggested date for the *Second Nun's Tale*,[33] and it would have been more doubtful still when, after perhaps thirty years, the work was included in Chaucer's last work, full of tales that place meaning in individual "entente" rather than "thyng that we seen alle." I suggest, therefore, that this tale, as composed and later edited as well as contextualized by Chaucer, identifies a point in history when the saint's life and its epistemological framework could no longer be certain of a proper and homogeneous response, a time when analogy's dangers would consequently assert

[31] Steven Connor, *The English Novel in History: 1950–1995* (London: Routledge, 1996), 10.

[32] Chaucer's break with analogy is analyzed at length by Sheila Delany, *Chaucer's House of Fame: The Poetics of Skeptical Fideism*, and Gellrich, *Idea of the Book*, who detects the "epistemic shift" also in Dante.

[33] The scant factual data available makes the dating of Chaucer's works a slippery affair. Traditionally, "immaturity" of style is associated with early composition, whereas complexity of vision or style will place the tale as late. Even Chaucer's first, and fairly reliably dated, work is sophisticated by any standard, however; moreover, critics increasingly appreciate that maturity is a far from stable cultural concept. As for the *Second Nun's Tale*, it antedates both the *Canterbury Tales* and the *Legend of Good Women*. Possibly a historical reference pushes it back to ca. 1381. The tale can be dated early not because it is bad, but because it represents a thought and a style already under critical review at the time of Chaucer's encounter with Dante, and definitely discounted when the poet compiled and composed the *Canterbury Tales*.

themselves, so that a naked text whose effectiveness presupposes an expressive empirical order declares instead the ineluctable self-containment of that order.

The case for making Chaucer (rather than the modern critic) responsible for problematizing the tale's meaning finds support in the tale's text no less than its context, and not only in the form, already discussed, of a tension between formal-generic and ideological features. In fact, one passage in the Prologue rests upon assumptions that challenge the notion of the world as a text with a conceptualizable meaning available at the literal level. Before analyzing this passage, however, I will very briefly sketch my assumption about the way the incongruous elements of the *Second Nun's Tale* might have come together: When Chaucer incorporated his early saint's life in the *Canterbury Tales*, he added the thematically appropriate "Invocacio ad Mariam," most of which is adapted from Dante's St. Bernard.[34] Dante, whose poetry evinces a rational epistemology and analogical methodology, finely catches St. Bernard's different, mystical, and highly emotional tone. Bernard's metaphorical strategy, however, is inconsistent with the *Second Nun's Tale*'s governing principle of analogy, and in effect makes it impossible to establish unity of any sort in the complete Second Nun's text. The unfinished state of the tale naturally raises speculations as to what Chaucer would have done, had he lived longer. As it stands, the piece seems unfinishable.

The "Invocacio"

Like the tale, the "Invocacio" freely employs the empirical to signify the transcendental, with the difference, however, that no respect is shown for the logic that controls earthly phenomena (time, physical probability) or normal usage. Where analogy coordinates parallel systems in which each sign evokes the whole, while its meaning is reflexively established within the boundaries set by the total hierarchy and rational analysis, the "Invocacio" suspends analogy's literalism and limited repertoire of connotations. Allowing words to develop meanings that are unique and purely verbal, indeed nonsensical if defined within a rational or empirical context, it suggests the inability of the signified "other" to be contained in conceptual, even tradition-determined, human discourse. Instead

[34] The Prologue, the "Invocacio," and Prologue and Tale as a unit, have each been pulled apart by some critics, put together by others. I naturally side with Skeat, who proposed later inclusion of the passage from Dante, and share Robert Burlin's feeling that the "Invocacio" fits the rest badly: it is "unfocused on what is to follow" and provides an "excess of pious information" (*Chaucerian Fiction* [Princeton: New Jersey, Princeton Univ. Press, 1977], 278). Thomas C. Kennedy, in "The Translator's Voice in the Second Nun's *Invocacio*: Gender, Influence, and Textuality," *Medievalia & Humanistica* 22 (1995): 95–110, distinguishes between a written prologue and a spoken tale, and views the former as Chaucer's attempt to manipulate reception of the latter. For further debate, consult Florence Ridley's notes in *The Riverside Chaucer*, 942 ff.

of analogy, metaphor and paradox dominate the passage: love becomes a man, a body a cloister, a virgin is a mother, and a son his mother's father. Where Cecilie rationalizes and naturalizes paradox to offer an alternative to the pagan law, the "Invocacio" delights in the paradox of the law-court of Heaven as an extremely odd place where the "advocat" (68) presents his case among songs of "Osanne" (69), and where the time dimension dissolves into an order where love, humility, nobility, and desire are coincidental with grace, while grace, rather than responding to human dictation, anticipates a petitioner's plea in a violation of logic which precludes causality (53–56). The Incarnation is the crowning paradox of love, uniting human and divine, making a church of the body, transforming the spirit of love and peace into flesh, and in engendering its own nonlogical discourse looks to an order beyond, and essentially different from, material and verbal categories. The "Invocacio" does not, of course, reject traditional images to rely on new ones; it is the *use* of images that is different. Analogical language may suggest likeness, but conceals *un*likeness; metaphorical language insists upon likeness *and* unlikeness. Analogy conceptualizes the ineffable; metaphorical meanings exist only in the space between the sign and the ineffable signified. And since new and untranslatable third meanings are created purely in the area of tension between tenor and vehicle, the conjunction of categories entails no danger of conflation. Metaphor avoids the pitfall of analogy – that of turning God into a construct of the human mind – precisely because it can be construed neither literally nor conceptually.

In the "Invocacio," the sign has torn away from the order of creation to become dependent upon the speaker, a speaker's excited emotions rather than intellect. Such discourse provides an exploration of the speaker's feelings about divine mystery rather than an explication of it. What is "declared" here is not immanence, but pious urgency, precisely the human element excised from the sources. Traditional images remain, but freed from analogy's exclusive repertoire of connotation. They even make space for what is perhaps now rather a reader's than a listener's collaborative privilege: the sign may be variably construed.

Furthermore, the literal sign is no longer a disposable vehicle, valuable only as the ladder to be kicked away in the send-up to another world, but a valuable place to stand. The "Invocacio" does not denounce secular values, but uses them to explore and consolidate man's relation to God. For Cecilie, the body is there to be mortified, even as the Prologue depicts the body as "contagioun" (72) weighed down by "erthely lust and fals affeccioun" (74). In the "Invocacio," however, it is an earthly body that carries God, a redemptive privilege suggested by the metaphor of the virgin's body as a sacred space ("cloistre"). For Cecilie, human relationships are part of the obstacle course to Heaven, although they furnish her with a conveniently captive audience for her apostolic mission. In the "Invocacio," it is a family relationship and its fruits which build a conceptual bridge between man and God to convey an affective dimension of that relationship, even as the central cluster of paradoxes and images draws upon family relationships to explore divine mystery:

> Thow mayde and Mooder, doghter of thy Sone
> ... the Makere ...
> His Sone ...
> Withinne the cloistre blisful of thy sydis
> Took mannes shap the eterneel love and pees
> ... Virgine wemmelees,
> Baar of thy body – and dweltest mayden pure –
> The Creatour of every creature
> ... I, unworthy sone of Eve ...
> Thow Cristes mooder, doghter deere of Anne! (36–70)

Even as verbal play may turn the inadequacy of language into a means of conveying the ineffable, so the human dimension – man's unwieldy physicality and his nonsensically capricious emotions – may find a legitimate place in evoking perfection. The sinful human referent ("sone of Eve") has a meaningful connection with the perfect (the second Eve, Mary). Simultaneously, these remain "playful" words, not words of power; they never compete with the Word, nor do they effect the least epistemological confusion.[35]

Since metaphor establishes meaning through internal textual relations rather than implied context, it is less vulnerable than analogy to changes in cultural climate. As analogy dwindles from *imitatio* to comparison and simile, so does the reading habit required by analogical discourse, the habit through which the detail will evoke the cosmic whole and thus *countervail* the materialistic ethos of narrative. While analogy appeals only to fully acculturated believers, metaphor, playing more freely with cultural signifiers, and using words "abnormally" to evoke a nonverbalizable dimension of reality, can subvert rational disbelief to appeal to the nonbeliever or skeptic as analogy cannot. It is characteristically the tale's pagans who, with their materialistic orientation, best perceive a difference between secular and religious experience, an awareness that allows a person to cherish both worlds and yet prefer one over the other. Valerian can register a sense of otherness by which the world becomes only a dream (262). Tiburce, not yet converted, perceives the transforming quality of heavenly lilies and roses by referring to the real, wonderful lilies and roses of summer:

> I wondre, this tyme of the yeer,
> Whennes that soote savour cometh so

[35] The present argument may invoke support from Thomas Kennedy's analysis of Chaucer's revision of his sources (Dante modified by Aquinas, Alain de Lille, and Macrobius) in "The Translator's Voice," which demonstrates in Chaucer's text a shift from abstract and impersonal to particular and personal.

> Of rose and lilies that I smelle heer.
> For though I hadde hem in myne handes two,
> The savour myghte in me no depper go.
> The sweete smel that in myn herte I fynde
> Hath chaunged me al in another kynde. (246–52)

Almachius, moreover, can accept that a stone may be a stone and yet possess spiritual significance, whereas the saint provides a crushing rejection of the symbolic meaning of the empirical sign when she ridicules Almachius for perceiving a god where eyes see only a stone. Almachius further proposes that a person's "bileeve" may have an arbitrary, possibly oblique relation to her "religion," where Cecilie, both representing and defending that "substantial connection," insists upon a one-to-one reading according to which religious practice equals belief. The meeting between Cecilie and Almachius, then, dramatizes not only the encounter between Christian and pagan, but also the clash between incompatible epistemologies and poetics.[36]

Almachius relates the stone's meaning to personal "entente," which is allowed free play in responding to metaphor – and given special latitude in lyrical, rather than narrative, discourse. The "Invocacio" is, of course, a *lyric*. So is, indeed, the biblical Psalm 115 from which Cecilie borrows her climactic attack on Almachius's stone. The lyric with its primarily affective-emotional emphasis allows things denied in popular narrative.

Problems of Addressivity and the Hermeneutical Unity of the Canterbury Tales

The present essay has argued that Chaucer's epistemologically broken-backed and unfinished tale is a sincere tale told at a time when its epistemological foundation was eroding. The very consistency of the poet's approach to sources, genre, and style suggests that the *Second Nun's Tale* was a generic experiment, and the nature of an experiment is to test what it explores. Incorporating his early work into a late, problematizing context, inserting St. Bernard's prayer, abandoning work on the tale (if not in fact dying whilst working on it), and, finally, displacing it from himself to a *persona*, Chaucer indicates that the experiment disturbed him. At his historical moment, and in written narrative, the analogical text of the world speaks of matter rather than spirit. As an interrogation of appearances, the *Second Nun's Tale* thus takes its place with, for instance, the *Franklin's Tale*, the *Manciple's Tale*, and the *Clerk's Tale*, and with the last it participates in the poet's interrogation of religious discourse:

[36] On the incompatibility of analogue and metaphor, see C. Heffernan, "The Use of Simile in Dante's *Divine Comedy* and Chaucer's *Canterbury Tales*," *Canadian Journal of Italian Studies* 3 (1980): 72–80.

> Most popular religious, didactic language functions to inculcate acceptance of religious belief by assimilating it even more simplistically and uncritically with the idiom of the culture. But for that very reason both the language and the belief, by an irresistable undertow, keep losing their meaning, like dead metaphors.[37]

Elizabeth Kirk argues that the *Clerk's Tale* is one of Chaucer's attempts to restore the "strangeness, the radicalness, the vitality and mystery to religious language."[38] The *Second Nun's Tale*, on the other hand, arguably explores a convention that is losing its "meaning, like a dead metaphor," and is past redemption. A changing philosophical climate and the difference that writing makes highlight as problematic those features of the saint's life which in popular oral narrative would pass unnoticed.

The other side of the epistemological flux reflected in the tale would almost necessarily be an audience Chaucer could neither fully control nor "imply."[39] Whether in revenge, capitulation, or acceptance (though one may suspect the last), Chaucer left the problem for his audience to solve. Pointing in two directions, the tale offered itself to different readings according to the expectations readers brought to their reading. Some might accept its premises and respond with piety, perhaps stabilize the text further by including it in a devotional anthology, as we know happened.[40] Others, those "new men" perhaps,[41] under the influence of debates over epistemology, of the changing mode of reception (*reading* habits replacing *aural* ones), and/or of Chaucer's increasing empowerment of his reader in other contexts, may have responded with mixed or skeptical feelings.

In allowing varied responses from its "users," the *Second Nun's Tale* responds to the dynamics of historical change and to the interplay between medieval codes and practices. The phenomenon of "one tale, contrasting readings"

[37] Elizabeth Kirk, "Nominalism and the Dynamics of the *Clerk's Tale*: *Homo Viator* as Woman," in *Chaucer's Religious Tales*, 116.

[38] Kirk, "Nominalism," 116.

[39] The term "implied reader" refers to a narrative communication model developed on the basis of French structuralism and Wayne C. Booth's theories by Seymour Chatman in *Story and Discourse: Narrative Structure in Fiction and Film* (Ithaca: Cornell Univ. Press, 1978). Chatman identifies three groups: "narratees" (the audience inside a work (e.g., the Canterbury pilgrims), the "implied audience" (those for whom the work is written, e.g., the administration and royal members of the medieval English court), and the "real audience" (those who in fact read or listen to a work). The epistemological and narrative instability of Chaucer's text reflects the author's inability to "imply" a homogeneous audience. This account of Chatman's model is indebted to Ebbe Klitgaard, who discusses its usefulness for the critic of medieval literature in *Chaucer's Narrative Voice in The Knight's Tale* (Copenhagen: Copenhagen Univ. Press, 1995).

[40] See Helen Cooper, *The Canterbury Tales*, Oxford Guides to Chaucer (Oxford: Oxford Univ. Press, 1989), 359.

[41] Collette, "Critical Approaches," 103.

seems to reproduce itself in modern criticism, and, now as then, a harmonizing interpretation requires suppression of textual complexity. A gap, however, opens between medieval and modern readers in assessing the hermeneutical violence required: the former would know, as the latter cannot, whether the blindness to textual signs that will harmonize the *Second Nun's Tale* would have been a "natural" response. The modern critic, denied certainty on this point, must assume that which alone makes criticism meaningful; namely, that context will crucially affect, but not finally control meaning to the extent of contradicting a text's formal gestures. On that assumption, unity bought at the price of disregarding "difficult" parts of a text is clearly illegitimate. And on this assumption, again, one may continue to explore the only broad road of access into a very distant past, for texts are surely the only extensive and most subtle demonstration we have of the way medieval cultural practices would interrogate cultural axioms and institutionalized discourse. Text and context are mutually illuminating, but a text is still its own best interrogator, if only we remember to "take up that dialogic critical discourse of which Roland Barthes spoke, one that grasps the points of rupture and identifies the places where the real breaks forth."[42]

The nature of its hermeneutical instability certainly identifies the *Second Nun's Tale* as a site for the interrogation of cultural conventions.[43] The tale's *literary* context adds to the inquiry. In its view of language and reality, the tale differs from most other *Canterbury Tales* (although the *Knight's Tale* shows traces of the same mode of thought). Its very peculiarity, however, gives the *Second Nun's Tale* the important function of contributing to the often noted representative character of the *Canterbury Tales*. I wish to add to the many unifying readings that have been offered between Dryden's admiring (and deservedly admired) remark on the *Canterbury Tales* as "God's Plenty" (1700) and Derek Pearsall's equally admirable compendium of genres (1985),[44] the unifying notion that the work is Chaucer's record of a multicultural, and at least bi-epistemological, society in rapid transition, a hypothesis which provides a hermeneutical framework for reading the tales without denying their heterogeneity. Chaucer's society saw the simultaneous existence of nearly contrasting ideas about

[42] Paul Zumthor, *Speaking of the Middle Ages*, 89.

[43] "[W]here the ritual of the anthropologist is an essentially conservative force of social cohesion, literature stands at a crossroads of medieval social practice and ideology; ... the poetic performance stands as a ratification of the ideals of the community and as a forum for the articulation of responses to shared dilemmas, and thus, as an instrument of change" (Bloch, *Etymologies and Genealogies*, 15).

[44] Dryden, *A Preface to the Fables* (1700); Pearsall, *The Canterbury Tales* (London: Allen & Unwin, 1985), xi. Pearsall sensibly has his cake and eats it too in making exploration of genre the unifying principle of a work deliberately created in a form that will "defy systematic interpretation, and which will preserve a maximum of provisionality and openness" (x). I offer a similar scheme for approaching without confining the complexity of the *Canterbury Tales*.

the connection between language and reality, God and creation, story and truth, intentionality and meaning, each idea struggling for dominance, each a potential winner in the race toward the future. New modes of discourse would be used by "new men," while a representative of official truths – a knight, for example, or a member of the clergy, such as a nun – would most likely maintain convention rather longer than most. Chaucer saw, heard, and registered these trends, his admired historical sense clearly including a flair for the complex dynamics of the cultural moment. Among estates, genres, and characters, and modes of discourse so daringly juxtaposed that his indisputable Gothicism has evoked associations with the Postmodern,[45] the poet has included the tale of Cecilie, a tottering monument over a crumbling world picture and its miracle manifest: language with a meaning.

[45] Phyllis Portnoy, "Beyond the Gothic Cathedral: Post-modern Reflections in the *Canterbury Tales*, *Chaucer Review* 28 (1994): 279–92.

The Culpability of Chaucer's Prioress

MARY A. MALESKI, *Le Moyne College*

Chaucer's Prioress, Madame Eglentyne, risks distracting her audience from the most miraculous moments of her tale when she digresses with a brief and apparently gratuitous sideswipe at the monk(s):

> This abbot, which that was an hooly man,
> As monkes been – or elles oghte be – (642–43)[1]

Her four-word aside here might variously seem self-righteous, gently instructive, or even, at an extreme, as venomous as her denigration of the Jews. But as Judith Ferster observes, "Nowhere else, on no other subject, does she inject herself into the story, interrupting in this way."[2] This narrative peculiarity invites attention, then, and I submit that its focus suggests a fruitful hermeneutical direction or at least an interesting interpretive perspective. Whether the Prioress means to chide the Abbot of her tale, the Monk on the pilgrimage, or the Monk of the previous tale (the Shipman's Daun John) matters significantly less than what she divulges about herself in making such a pronouncement. In revealing her awareness that a monk should be holy and that indeed he ought to *be*, and to *behave*, in accord with his religious vocation, Madame Eglentyne informs her audience that she may well know exactly what that means and that she may therefore bear responsibility for her "innocent" (translate that "all-too-ignorant") words, demeanor, and behavior. If she does not know, then like the monk(s) in the lines quoted above, she *ought* to.

The Ellesmere Portrait, the *General Prologue*'s reference to Stratford-at-Bowe, and historical evidence all suggest that the Prioress belongs to the Ben-

[1] All citations of Chaucer's work are from *The Riverside Chaucer*, ed. Larry D. Benson, 3d ed. (Boston: Houghton Mifflin, 1987). (I presented a brief version of this paper in October of 1992 at the 26th annual conference of the Center for Medieval and Early Renaissance Studies at the State University of New York at Binghamton. I am grateful to my colleague Neil Novelli for his helpful suggestions about this essay and to the Research and Development Committee of Le Moyne College for its generous support.)

[2] Judith Ferster, "'Your Praise Is Performed by Men and Children': Language and Gender in the *Prioress's Prologue and Tale*," *Exemplaria* 2 (1990): 155.

edictine order. Likewise, the outriding Monk who cares not for the Rule of Seint Beneit is presumably also a Benedictine. Robert B. White, Jr., measured Daun Piers's activities and attitude against his avowed Rule and concluded that this Monk "violated all seven points of discipline to which his vows obligated him; he has compromised both the *tria substantialis* of obedience, poverty, and chastity, and the four major pillars of support: labor, claustration, diet, and propertylessness."[3] Chaucer's *General Prologue* description leaves no doubt that this Monk deliberately ignores his Rule:

> The reule of Seint Maure or of Seint Beneit –
> By cause that it was old and somdel streit
> This ilke Monk leet olde thynges pace,
> And heeld after the newe world the space. (173–76)

Readers might reasonably, therefore, see his sad inability or unwillingness to heed first the Knight's call to stop his tragic tales and then the Host's admonition that he tell instead some comic story, a consequence of his culpable negligence: the Monk has "no lust to pleye" (2806) because he embraces a definition of tragedy as a fall from Fortune rather than a fall from God's grace. Had he familiarized himself with his Rule and other "olde thynges" appropriate to his vocation, rather than "the newe world," he might understand that his freewheeling life constitutes a Boethian tragedy in that he has forgotten who he is, both as a man and as a monk. He ought to know better. In any case, in pointing toward the monks' obligations, the Prioress furthermore betrays that she must know something about what she as a religious of the Benedictine order ought to be, or at least she knows that she should know something about the duties of her state of life according to the Rule she shares with the monk(s) she directly maligns.

And so to to the point of this essay: it remains as commonplace as it is necessary for readers of this tale to consider what this superior of her convent should *be*. But rightly to render judgment on her behavior (and we can judge her moral acts with impunity since she is a woman of fiction rather than reality), it seems crucial – in light of her own illuminating comment about the monk(s) – to ascertain what she must or should *know*. Moral responsibility necessitates an *informed* consent; her awareness depends, then, on whether the appropriate information remains available to her. I will therefore raise and attempt to answer epistemological questions so that we can better understand whether Chaucer presents the Prioress as deserving blame, and if so, why: is the innocence that she so conspicuously professes a euphemism, a respectable veil for unexcusable ignorance? Does Madame Eglentyne unwittingly display grown-up culpability rather than childlike virtue? Sherman Hawkins has called her faults "childish"

[3] Robert B. White, Jr., "Chaucer's Daun Piers and the Rule of St. Benedict: The Failure of an Ideal," *JEGP* 70 (1971): 29.

and thus venial.[4] But given her commitment to the life of perfection as counseled by Paul (the Wife of Bath playfully recalls the passage), one might expect the Prioress to know that the Bible counsels her to be childlike, relying on the father (mother) who is God, rather than childish, that is, undeveloped in her spiritual life (see Matt. 18:1–4, Mark 10:15, and Luke 18:17). A mature and knowing reliance on God does not, of course, preclude responsibility.

Muriel Bowden characterizes Madame Eglentyne as "gentle, demure, aristocratic in her worldly and culpably indifferent outlook on life."[5] And in his analysis of her portrait, Chauncey Wood quotes Augustine's *On Christian Doctrine* concerning the "many and varied obscurities and ambiguities [that] deceive those who read casually, understanding one thing instead of another" to support his conclusion that "there is a culpable ignorance in the Prioress."[6] I discovered Wood's article after independently reaching that same conclusion, but my emphases have been epistemological, questioning the Prioress's ability to know, as I have noted above. Depending on recent historical and feminist scholarship, as well as theology and literary analyses, I offer my thinking here as a contribution to our continuing critical discourse about the Prioress and her fourteenth-century contexts.

Medieval theology informs the idea of culpability operative in the present analysis: each person has an obligation to develop an informed conscience. The formation of a right conscience depends on the accessibility of necessary knowledge, that which accords, for example, with one's vocation. In book 3 of *De Libero Arbitrio* Augustine states that "the soul is not accountable for the things of which it is ignorant by nature and which, by its nature, it cannot do. But it must be held to account for what it has not tried to know, and for what it has not taken proper care in preparing itself to perform rightly."[7] In the *Summa Theologiae*, Thomas Aquinas maintains his patristic mentor's teaching in this regard as he differentiates between what he terms vincible and invincible ignorance when he discusses a person's responsibility for sin. He makes it quite clear that if a person *should* know something about the nature of an act and does not because he or she chooses to neglect informing the self, then that person is culpable, that is, guilty of sin. As Aquinas puts it, "all men are obliged to know the basic truths of faith and the general principles of right and wrong, while each man is obliged to know the duties of his state in life .... It is evident that the man who

[4] Sherman Hawkins, "Chaucer's Prioress and the Sacrifice of Praise," *JEGP* 63 (1964): 600.

[5] Muriel Bowden, *A Commentary on the General Prologue to the Canterbury Tales* (New York: Macmillan, 1948), 103.

[6] Chauncey Wood, "Chaucer's Use of Signs in His Portrait of the Prioress," in *Signs and Symbols in Chaucer's Poetry*, ed. John P. Hermann and John J. Burke, Jr. (University, Alab.: Univ. of Alabama Press, 1981), 99.

[7] Augustine, *On Free Choice of the Will*, trans. Anna S. Benjamin and L. H. Hackstaff (Indianapolis: Bobbs-Merrill, 1964), 138.

fails to accomplish something he is obliged to do commits a sin of omission. Hence, the man who because of negligence is ignorant of something he ought to know commits a sin" (I.II.76.2).[8] This, he explains, is vincible ignorance because it can (and should be) conquered, if one will. Negligence, Chaucer will amply demonstrate in his *Tale of Melibee*, exacts the high cost of the loss of Sophie, of Wisdom.

What would, should, and could a Benedictine prioress, or for that matter an abbot, in fourteenth-century England have known about the duties of her vocation? Would Chaucer have known what she should have or could have known? Furthermore, can a (very) late twentieth-century reader have more than speculative knowledge of the answer to either of the previous two questions? Fortunately, recent historical and feminist scholarship has clarified and augmented responses to these queries, some of which had been shrouded by a veil of male-privileged investigations for all too long (given the previous culture, and given standards for guilt presented here, we can probably safely pronounce those critical errors nonculpable).

Chaucer may have had some direct contact with convent life through his friends and relatives, or perhaps even through meeting some of the uncloistered souls out and about town, wandering by the way. Possibly, as the *Life-Records* seems to indicate, Chaucer had a daughter (some would say sister) named Elizabeth who took vows either at St. Helen's Priory in London or at Barking Abbey just outside of London, and very close to Stratford-at-Bowe.[9] In his biography of Chaucer, Donald Howard states that Elizabeth "was first sent to the Black Nuns, in Bishopgate Street, London" (a correct, if somewhat odd, way of putting it: like Barking and Stratford, St. Helen's/Bishopgate was Benedictine; traditional Benedictine men were called Black Monks, as distinguished from Cistercians, White Monks).[10] Derek Pearsall chides Howard: "the supposition that they [Elizabeth and Agnes] are Chaucer's daughters ... rests on no more than the coincidence of the common surname."[11] Benson, Manly, Bowden, Olson, and others nevertheless refer both to Elizabeth and to Chaucer's other connections with convent life. In his 1926 *Some New Light on Chaucer*, John Manly translated the 1375 will of Queen Philippa's sister Elizabeth who apparently lived at St. Leonard's for several years. (I suspect she may have been one of the *conver-*

[8] Thomas Aquinas, *Summa Theologiae*, Latin text and English trans., vol. 25 (1a2ae. 71–80), *Sin*, ed. and trans. John Fearon, O.P. (New York: McGraw-Hill; London: Eyre & Spottiswoode, 1969), 147–49.

[9] *Chaucer Life-Records*, ed. Martin M. Crow and Clair C. Olson, (Oxford: Clarendon Press, 1966), 545–46.

[10] Donald R. Howard, *Chaucer: His Life, His Works, His World* (New York: E. P. Dutton, 1987), 93.

[11] Derek Pearsall, *The Life of Geoffrey Chaucer: A Critical Biography* (Oxford: Blackwell, 1992), 204. See also Pearsall's review of Howard, *Studies in the Age of Chaucer* 13 (1991): 201.

sae, a convent's lay sisters;[12] that status would explain all the possessions she had to bequeath). Chaucer probably visited there as a youth in the company of his employer Prince Lionel of Ulster's wife, Elizabeth.[13] Supplementing Manly's find, Paul Olson says, "It [Stratford] attracted court people such as Elizabeth of Hainault and Philippa of Ulster (the daughter of Chaucer's early patron, Lionel of Clarence) who took up residence there, and the royal family who visited it on occasion."[14] However tenuous, the above information does at least point to Chaucer's direct knowledge of religious women. Be that as it may, he did somehow have access to the idea that the Prioress should follow her rule and scripture and ecclesiastical decrees. The *General Prologue* description and her tale present internal evidence to that effect.

What, then, do or can we latter-day readers know about what a late fourteenth-century prioress should and could have known? Let me admit first of a terrible difficulty in presenting a complete response since so many doors for research on religious women continue to open. Early scholars Lina Eckenstein and Eileen Power broke new ground when they published their massive and impressive studies on medieval women monastics – Eckenstein (1896) focusing broadly on women religious in Western Europe, Power (1922) specifically on "English Nunneries."[15] Used extensively for decades, their work has now been refined, expanded, and in some cases corrected by historians such as Jo Ann McNamara and Sally Thompson, and archaeologist Roberta Gilchrist.[16]

Symptomatic of the marginalization of female monastics in religious history written by men, volume 2 of Dom David Knowles's important 1955 study, *The Religious Orders in England*, has little to say about nuns and does not even list Power or Eckenstein in its bibliography. In addition, he includes an appendix on Chaucer's Monk, but none on the Prioress.[17] "Reasoning that women do not

[12] For more on *conversae*, see Jo Ann Kay McNamara, *Sisters in Arms: Catholic Nuns through Two Millennia* (Cambridge, Mass.: Harvard Univ. Press, 1996), 262–63.

[13] John M. Manly, *Some New Light on Chaucer: Lectures Delivered at the Lowell Institute* (1926; reprint: New York: Peter Smith, 1951), 204–9.

[14] Paul A. Olson, *The Canterbury Tales and the Good Society* (Princeton.: Princeton Univ. Press, 1986), 133.

[15] Lina Eckenstein, *Woman under Monasticism: Chapters on Saint-Lore and Convent Life between A.D. 500 and A.D. 1500* (1896; reprint: New York: Russell & Russell, 1963); Eileen Power, *Medieval English Nunneries, 1275 to 1535* (Cambridge: Cambridge Univ. Press, 1922).

[16] See especially Jo Ann Kay McNamara, *Sisters in Arms* (Cambridge, Mass.: Harvard Univ. Press, 1996); Sally Thompson, "Why English Nunneries Had No History: A Study of the Problems of the English Nunneries Founded After the Conquest," in *Distant Echoes*, vol. 1 of *Medieval Religious Women*, ed. John A. Nichols and Lillian Thomas Shank (Kalamazoo, Mich.: Cistercian Publications, 1984); and Roberta Gilchrist, *Gender and Material Culture: The Archaeology of Religious Women* (London: Routledge, 1994).

[17] Dom David Knowles, *The Religious Orders in England*, vol. 2, *The End of the Middle Ages* (Cambridge: Cambridge Univ. Press, 1955). Judith M. Bennett points out Knowles's omission of Power in her "Medievalism and Feminism," in *Studying Medieval Women: Sex,*

build institutions or conquer new worlds or make history, the scribes who shape the past have ignored their untidy existence or simply accorded it a hasty nod before pressing forward with the more readily accessible history of male institutions."[18] Exceptions occur, of course, like Jean Leclercq who in a 1981 essay recounts some of the errors made about medieval nuns and advocates using "new methods and means" of research.[19] Honest and probing study of the history of medieval women religious has come of age though: even Hans Küng, a Roman Catholic theologian (albeit one at odds with the Vatican), unabashedly and refreshingly admits the patriarchal dominance of the Church: "Now there was a **repression of women** (in part also legal) which has remained a characteristic of the Roman Catholic paradigm to the present day."[20] With the Second Lateran Council, 1139, celibacy became an absolute requisite for the Roman clergy;[21] nuns were celibate by choice rather than papal dictate, but as women they remained the "other," necessarily dependent on the male-only clergy to minister the sacraments to them. While medieval Church officials held nuns up as an example of those living the perfect life (as far as they believed women could), even abbesses, "who also had spiritual authority, were restricted to their jurisdictional authority."[22] Women's religious ministry was subverted by an exclusively male sacramental and sacerdotal system and then submerged by male historiographers. But even medieval women found answers to the authoritarianism of the Roman Church: surely, for instance, women sidestepped the powerful hierarchy through refuge in mysticism, an individual communion with the deity apart and aside from official church law.[23]

In 1979, Jane Tibbetts Schulenburg decried scholarship that relies solely on history recorded by medieval "celibate clerics [who] were the articulate sector of society."[24] Listing sources of medieval women's voices – prosopographical, iconographic, hagiographic – she estimated that "an immense amount of creative

Gender, Feminism, ed. Nancy F. Partner (Cambridge, Mass.: Medieval Academy of America, 1993), 19, first published as the April 1993 issue of *Speculum*.

[18] McNamara, *Sisters in Arms*, 2–3.

[19] Jean Leclercq, "Medieval Feminine Monasticism: Reality Versus Romantic Images," in *Benedictus: Studies in Honor of St. Benedict of Nursia*, ed. E. Rozanne Elder (Kalamazoo, Mich.: Cistercian Publications, 1981), 53–70; this at 53.

[20] Hans Küng, *Christianity: Essence, History, and Future*, trans. John Bowden (New York: Continuum, 1996), 443. (The emphasis is Küng's.)

[21] Küng, *Christianity*, 402.

[22] Küng, *Christianity*, 443.

[23] For more, see Caroline Walker Bynum, *Fragmentation and Redemption* (New York: Zone Books, 1991), 134–39; and McNamara, *Sisters in Arms*, 337–52.

[24] Jane Tibbetts Schulenburg, "Clio's European Daughters: Myopic Modes of Perception," in *The Prism of Sex: Essays in the Sociology of Knowledge*, ed. Julia A. Sherman and Evelyn Torton Beck (Madison: Univ. of Wisconsin Press, 1979), 33.

research is needed to fill the blatant lacunae of traditional historiography."[25] In some ways, as noted above, the field has since exploded with a response. Yet medievalists had been slower than others to embrace theoretical and feminist modes of inquiry. One remedy, Thomas Hahn's April 1988 Rochester Conference, gathered prominent Chaucerians working from varying critical, theoretical, and disciplinary stances explicitly to share and so proliferate their experiences;[26] and in 1993, the Medieval Academy of America produced its first issue of *Speculum* devoted to medieval women's studies, wherein Judith M. Bennett makes clear that "feminists, then, are revising the field of medieval studies from three directions: adding new information, answering old questions in new ways, and creating entirely new research agendas."[27]

Yet what does any of this new attention contribute to a reading of the Prioress? Simply this: when we understand the bias that has affected our collective vision of medieval nuns, we can ask better questions about Chaucer's portrayal. Could Chaucer have understood and even sympathized with the religious woman's plight through his presentation of the Prioress? If he could give his feisty Wife of Bath words cognizant of women's oppression (see her Prologue, 691–96), why ever should we doubt that he could draw a portrait of a Prioress as complex as the (real or imagined) religious women of the time? None of what we have learned of late indicates that fourteenth-century religious women were less intelligent than men, simply less privileged. Once we have read Jo Ann McNamara's *Sisters in Arms*, together with her and others' essays correcting our perspective on women's history,[28] can we doubt that Chaucer could at least have been aware of the ways in which a Prioress could play games with the truth of her vocation? Could he not even invent a nun who would subvert the dominant system by a masked behavior?

Derek Pearsall rightly questions "the exceptionally prominent role" of women in Chaucer's religious tales, and he responds with insight: "one answer is that their relative lack of power in the social and domestic real world makes them apt representatives of a spirituality which goes out of its way to embrace powerlessness."[29] To his credit, Pearsall sees that both women and religion are thereby marginalized: "The recognition of the special spiritual witness afforded

[25] Schulenburg, "Clio's European Daughters," 49. See, too, Janet Todd's study that succinctly traces the rise and development of *Feminist Literary History* (New York: Routledge, 1988).

[26] Papers from that conference are collected, edited and introduced by Hahn as the Spring 1990 issue of *Exemplaria*.

[27] Bennett, "Medievalism and Feminism," 25.

[28] See, e.g., McNamara's "*De Quibusdam Mulieribus*: Reading Women's History from Hostile Sources," in *Medieval Women and the Sources of Medieval History*, ed. Joel T. Rosenthal (Athens: Univ. of Georgia Press, 1990), 237–58; and "Muffled Voices: The Lives of Consecrated Women in the Fourth Century," in *Distant Echoes*, 11–29.

[29] Pearsall, *The Life of Geoffrey Chaucer*, 265.

women is not protected from the further recognition of the special satisfaction that men may take in granting them such a role. To identify the narrative of faith with the narrative of women's lives marginalizes faith in the measure that women are already marginalized."[30] To approach comprehension of the medieval nun's situation, it might be useful to consider nuns, or just women, in the Roman Catholic Church today. The hierarchy still excludes women from its highest rank, the priesthood; yet in general the Christian, and in particular the monastic, ideal continues to attract extraordinary women such as Sister Helen Prejean of *Dead Man Walking* fame to valiant service.

As for the knowledge available to Chaucer's Prioress, first and foremost she would have had sure and easy access to her Rule. An unmitigated reality endures for both male and female Benedictines: community life is a fundamental aspect of their monastic charism. Their constant togetherness remains possible, despite human differences, because of the central faith-filled purpose to which each person commits her/himself through the vows. In chapter 58 of his Rule, St. Benedict states the specific promises each shall make: "In the oratory, in the presence of all, [s]he shall promise stability, conversion of his [her] life, and obedience; and this before God and his Saints, so that [s]he may know that should [s]he ever do otherwise [s]he will be condemned by him whom [s]he mocks" (131).[31] Simply put, the vow of stability binds the nun to her convent, the vow of obedience to her Rule, and the vow of conversion (*conversatione morum suorum*), a turning toward the monastic and away from the secular life.[32] The monastic life embraces the three evangelical counsels, and so the promise of conversion includes both chastity and poverty, obedience already specifically vowed. Initially, the Rule assures poverty by its prescription that the novice come to the profession ceremony only after fulfilling the gospel counsel which forms the basis for the vow: "Jesus said to him, 'If thou wilt be perfect, go sell what thou hast, and give to the poor, and thou shalt have treasure in heaven; and come, follow me'" (Matt 19:21). And so Benedict advises, "if he [the entrant] possess any property, let him either give it beforehand to the poor, or make a formal donation bestowing it on the monastery" (58.133).

At its start, Madame Eglentyne's avowed Rule classifies types of monks (nuns): first the category to which Benedictines belong, the Cenobites, "who live in monasteries, serving under a rule and an abbot"; then Anchorites, solitaries; Sarabaites, whose "law is their own good pleasure" (1.15); and finally Gyrovagues, wanderers who are "worse in all respects than the Sarabaites" (1.17). Adding to that Benedictine swipe at those who have no stability, "in 1298, Boni-

[30] Pearsall, *The Life of Geoffrey Chaucer*, 266.

[31] *The Rule of Saint Benedict, in Latin and English*, ed. and trans. Abbot Justin McCann (London: Burns Oates, 1952). Unless otherwise indicated, all citations of the Rule are from this edition, with references given to chapter and page.

[32] *The Rule*, 204–5 (notes).

face VIII, in his bull *Periculoso*, decreed that all religious women everywhere must be cloistered. He stressed the peril of men's inability to resist raping women and women's natural inability to refrain from tempting men."[33] (Sounds like the theory behind the *Wife of Bath's Tale*!) Although women did not obey, the edict and its extension by Clement V "remained in force and were reinstated at the Council of Trent and again at the First Vatican Council in the nineteenth century."[34]

Before even reading Chaucer's description of her, we might well wonder, therefore, why the Prioress is on a pilgrimage. She bound herself by rule to the priory when she professed her vows. True, as Prioress, she was at times enjoined to entertain visitors and also to go out of her convent when either business or charity so warranted. But what excuse or reason would sanction a pilgrimage? As Eileen Power and countless others point out, the typical pilgrims with their bald ribaldry did not provide suitable traveling companions for a nun.[35] Perhaps more importantly, acting in accord with Papal decrees, bishops consistently forbade their charges to go on pilgrimages. The Prioress was therefore duty-bound not only to obey her ecclesiastical superiors but in turn to enforce their ruling on her sisters. After citing the injunction of the Council of York forbidding nuns to go on pilgrimages, Graciela Daichman additionally reminds us that "besides the morally dangerous consequences risked by anyone going on pilgrimage in the fourteenth century, there were physical perils too, such as highway bandits lurking behind every tree along the road, while illnesses and inadequate lodging also plagued the traveller."[36] For the Wife of Bath to engage in "muchel of wandrynge by the weye" (*General Prologue*, 467) is one thing, but for the Prioress yet another: as head of the house, she had an obligation to set a sterling example for her sisters. Her Rule tells her that. On the other hand, historiographers like McNamara adjust our perspective on traveling nuns: "The simple irony was that nuns may often have been safer outside their cloisters than within them."[37] From "marauding soldiers" to immoral chaplains,[38] threats within the cloister could be fiercer than those outside. Still, the Prioress faced the dilemma posed by the vow of obedience to her Rule; it would seem that she needs a tough rather than a tender conscience to be virtuous, to avoid transgression.

In writing the Rule, St. Benedict foresaw the possibility that some might plead innocence, or ignorance, of their obligations, and so he directs his commu-

[33] McNamara, *Sisters in Arms*, 317.

[34] McNamara, *Sisters in Arms*, 317.

[35] Power, *Medieval English Nunneries*, 371.

[36] Graciela Daichman, *Wayward Nuns in the Middle Ages* (Syracuse: Syracuse Univ. Press, 1986), 137.

[37] McNamara, *Sisters in Arms*, 362.

[38] McNamara, *Sisters in Arms*, 368.

nity (interestingly, this counsel attached to an admonition about wandering): "The monastery should, if possible, be so arranged that all necessary things, such as water, mill, garden, and various crafts may be within the enclosure, so that the monks may not be compelled to wander outside it, for that is not at all expedient for their souls. We desire that this Rule be read aloud often in the community so that no brother may excuse himself on the ground of ignorance" (66.153). Wriggle as she may, Madame Eglentyne cannot easily, if at all, claim "innocence" of her duties. Furthermore, because of her position as Prioress, she has an even more profound obligation than her sisters, among whom she remains an equal despite her position. Benedictines embrace humility as one of their special virtues (7.37–49). In this regard, Madame Eglentyne may be more aptly, if mildly, comparable to the exhibitionist Wife of Bath than to the Second Nun whose absence from the *General Prologue*'s portraits may well signal her self-abnegation, her humility.

An abbess, or a prioress[39] like Madame Eglentyne, embraced the further responsibilities of being the authoritative "voice of God" for her sisters and, to the extent humanly possible, a living exemplar of the Rule (2.19). While in their invaluable work on nuns Eckenstein and Power emphasized that prioresses most often emerged from the aristocracy, neither the Rule itself nor more recent historical investigations well support their conclusions. Chapter 64 of the Rule makes the abbot's qualifications clear: "Let him who is to be appointed be chosen for the merit of his life and his enlightened wisdom, even though [s]he be the last in order of the community" (145). While readers seemed convinced for some time that by the decadent, or at least lax, fourteenth century, women were appointed superior by force of wealth or family status, Marilyn Oliva's recent prosopographical study of "the social status of office holders, and office-holding patterns in the 11 female monasteries of the diocese of Norwich,"[40] supports the existence of meritocracy in convent elections. Using five social ranks, from titled aristocracy to yeoman, Oliva demonstrates that the middle group, the parish or the lower gentry, supplied "64 per cent of all of the known office-holders."[41] It would be faulty to conclude, in any case, that a person's class necessar-

[39] A Prioress, according to the Rule, could be appointed to serve just below an abbess (65.149–51). Stratford-at-Bowe was a priory, i.e., a smaller convent attached to a parish; the superior of such a convent was called a prioress (a second use of the term). The wealthier and larger convent at Barking was a free-standing monastery, an abbey, ruled by an abbess. During the eleventh-century monastic expansion, Abbot Hugh of Cluny declared houses other than his own "priories," dependent on his abbey: "all Cluniac monks, wherever they lived, were in theory members of the community of Cluny itself" (C. H. Lawrence, *Medieval Monasticism*, 2d ed. [London: Longman, 1989], 96).

[40] Marilyn Oliva, "Aristocracy or Meritocracy? Office-Holding Patterns in Late Medieval English Nunneries," in *Women in the Church*, ed. W. J. Sheils and Diana Wood (Oxford: Basil Blackwell, 1990), 198.

[41] Oliva, "Aristocracy or Meritocracy?" 201.

ily dictates her behavior, or that because *some* women became nuns for pragmatic or other less-than-lofty reasons, all or even the majority did. Besides, as Margaret Wade Labarge notes, "from the thirteenth century on greater emphasis was put on the free choice of the conventual life by the girls themselves."[42] Oliva also learned that those who became abbess or prioress usually rose to the office through serving first in lesser positions,[43] and that it was the demonstration of "substantial administrative skill"[44] rather than social status that merited a woman the office of prioress. Knowing that, one wonders how "innocent" Chaucer's prioress could or would have been?

In his *Summa Theologiae*, Aquinas asks whether "the importance of the sinner affect[s] the gravity of the sin," and he answers "yes" on four counts, the most pertinent being the fourth: "bad example and scandal may result" (I.II.73.10).[45] And in II.II.186 on "the essential elements of the religious state," the ninth article examines "whether a religious always sins mortally in transgressing the rule?" After stating that sins against various precepts may not be grievously sinful, he continues: "Now, the vow of profession chiefly concerns the three things mentioned, i.e., poverty, continence and obedience; everything else is ordained to these. Therefore a transgression of these three involves mortal sin, but a transgression of the others is not a mortal sin, unless there is contempt of the rule ... or it involves a precept, given orally by the superior or expressed in the rule, for this would be to act against the vow of obedience."[46] And finally in the tenth article, "whether a religious sins more gravely than a layman by the same kind of sin," he answers "yes," in these three ways: (1) if the religious breaks a vow, (2) "if [s]he sins out of contempt," or (3) if she thereby gives scandal.[47] Considering the fourteenth-century religious milieu, I do not wish to argue that the Prioress's pilgrim companions were scandalized either by her presence or her tale, although the sober response of that audience and especially of the ground-staring character Chaucer do invite such a consideration. But I do maintain that her sisters in community must have been somehow affected, even scandalized by their superior's behavior. After all, in chapter 2 of the Benedictine Rule, the abbess is instructed to show her charges "by deeds more than words, what is good and holy. To those who understand [s]he may

[42] Margaret Wade Labarge, *A Small Sound of the Trumpet: Women in Medieval Life* (Boston: Beacon Press, 1986), 100.

[43] Oliva, "Aristocracy or Meritocracy?" 206.

[44] Oliva, "Aristocracy or Meritocracy?" 207. See also McNamara, *Sisters in Arms*, 272–74.

[45] Aquinas, *Summa Theologiae*, vol. 25, *Sin*, 91, 93.

[46] Thomas Aquinas, *Summa Theologiae*, vol. 47 (2a2ae.183–89), *The Pastoral and Religious Lives*, ed. and trans. Jordan Aumann, O.P. (New York: McGraw-Hill; London: Eyre & Spottiswoode, 1973), 135–37.

[47] Aquinas, *Summa Theologiae*, vol. 47, *The Pastoral and Religious Lives*, 139–41.

expound verbally the Lord's directions: but to the stubborn and dull, [s]he must exhibit the Divine commandments by his [her] actions in everyday life."[48]

Carolyn Eckhardt's annotated bibliography for the *General Prologue*, as well as the Variorum editions of that prologue and of the *Prioress's Tale*, summarizes the many essays that have thoroughly studied her dress and demeanor with sometimes wildly differing conclusions about the nature or even the existence of her infractions.[49] Wearing her band too high, pinching that wimple, keeping those dogs, being elegantly cloaked, counterfeiting courtly behavior, sporting gold baubles and displaying fastidious table manners: all seem to accord more with the prescriptions of the Duenna in the *Roman de la Rose*[50] than with the counsels of St. Benedict. Chauncey Wood has pointed out that the adverb "ful" meaning "very" is used eleven times in the portrait of the Prioress and that "the net result is, if you will pardon the pun, fulsome."[51] Her being out on this pilgrimage and so exhibiting herself against ecclesiastical admonitions simply does not fit the station of a nun, let alone the superior of a priory – and Madame Eglentyne should know that.

Not all readers agree with this assessment of the Prioress. Henry Ansgar Kelly recently wrote to correct misconceptions in our view of medieval religious which have been bred by historians whose sympathies were Protestant; despite all the important factual information he provides, I believe he swings the critical pendulum yet too far in the opposite direction when he urges readers "to take more seriously the favorable judgment about Chaucer's nuns arrived at by Sister Mary Madeleva, who was not only a working medievalist, ... but also a working nun, whose insights into living the common religious life should carry real weight."[52] As argument, that position seriously falters when confronted with

[48] *The Rule of St. Benedict*, trans. and ed. Anthony C. Meisel and M. L. del Mastro (Garden City, N.Y.: Doubleday, 1975), 48. For the passage cited, this translation is more easily understood than McCann's.

[49] Caroline D. Eckhardt, *Chaucer's General Prologue to the Canterbury Tales: An Annotated Bibliography, 1900 to 1982* (Toronto: Univ. of Toronto Press, 1990); *A Variorum Edition of the Works of Geoffrey Chaucer*, vol. 2.1A, *The Canterbury Tales: The General Prologue*, comm. and ed. Malcolm Andrew, Charles Moorman, and Daniel J. Ransom, and vol. 2.1B, notes by Malcolm Andrew (Norman: Univ. of Oklahoma Press, 1993); *A Variorum Edition of the Works of Geoffrey Chaucer*, vol. 2.20, *The Canterbury Tales: The Prioress's Tale*, ed. Beverly Boyd (Norman: Univ. of Oklahoma Press, 1987). See also Florence H. Ridley *The Prioress and the Critics* (Berkeley: Univ. of California Press, 1965).

[50] See Guillaume de Lorris and Jean de Meun, *The Romance of the Rose*, trans. Charles Dahlberg (Princeton: Princeton Univ. Press, 1971), esp. 231–33. See also Daichman, *Wayward Nuns*, 141–44; and Emerson Brown, Jr., "Chaucer and the European Literary Tradition," in *Geoffrey Chaucer: A Collection of Original Articles*, ed. George Economou (New York: McGraw-Hill, 1976), 47–48, 51.

[51] Wood, "Chaucer's Use of Signs," 90.

[52] Henry Ansgar Kelly, "A Neo-Revisionist Look at Chaucer's Nuns," *Chaucer Review* 31 (1996): 126.

Sister Mary Hostia's essay that finds the Prioress sorely wanting in humility, temperance, sincerity, and true charity.[53] With a touch of humor, though, Donald Howard asserts that "everyone has always been charmed by the portrait of the Prioress – her ladylike daintiness, her affectations, and her negligible infractions against the usual rules of convents ...." He complains that "a few prigs fuss at her 'sentimentality' and her failure to be a good nun in the strictest sense. But nuns have never been any fun if something of the woman doesn't manage to squeeze through the headdress and petticoats. It takes someone without any personal experience of nuns to be scornful of the Lady Prioress in that initial description of her."[54] Truth be told, even a few days in a religious community where the sisters stayed home fulfilling their obligations to work, pray, and study while their superior flitted about traveling, partying or both, would likely compel a visitor to acknowledge the dissension such conduct might engender! Speaking again to the point of what Madame Eglentyne should know, Daichman, evidently a "prig" like me, reminds us that "as much as disobedience, overindulgence was in violation of the Benedictine Rule which cautioned: '*delicias non amplecti*' (not to seek soft living)."[55] Thomas Hahn argues that the Prioress wears the appropriate feminine mask, conforming to what her male-dominant society might expect of her, "to ensure that she receives the highest valuation from others that her rank may warrant."[56] We cannot ascertain whether or not she comes from nobility, but even if she does, she lives – or she *should* live – first and foremost, not according to societal expectations but according to her Rule.

Perhaps that concern for societal approval motivated her to learn French from a noble woman like Elizabeth of Hainault. Although the *General Prologue* intimates that Chaucer's Prioress has a working knowledge of French, we observe only that she uses Latin, not whether she understands it. She fulfills her Rule by reciting (probably) the Little Office of the Virgin Mary in Latin, but detractors would insist she could have done this only by pronouncing the words without comprehension – a very low level of language usage. Beyond the recitation or singing of the office though, the well-discussed motto on her brooch, *Amor vincit omnia*, adds a bit to the possibility that she may have known *some* Latin. If she understands that in a secular manner, she strays from her calling; if she takes it as a reference to her love of God, she may yet again be intimating

[53] Sister Mary Hostia, "The Prioress and Her Companion," *College English* 14 (1953): 351–52.

[54] Donald R. Howard, *The Idea of the Canterbury Tales* (Berkeley: Univ. of California Press, 1976), 276. Howard goes on to demonstrate the horror of the Prioress's mindset in her tale.

[55] Daichman, *Wayward Nuns*, 155.

[56] Thomas Hahn, "The Performance of Gender in the Prioress," *Chaucer Yearbook* 1 (1992): 116. See also Anne Laskaya, *Chaucer's Approach to Gender in the Canterbury Tales* (Cambridge: D. S. Brewer, 1995), 172–75.

that she knows more about what that signifies according to her vocation. Furthermore, her clergeon sings the anthem *Alma Redemptoris Mater*, perhaps without knowing its full meaning, but he was given a summary sense when he asked his peer-teacher:

> His felawe, which that elder was than he,
> Answerde hym thus: "This song, I have herd seye,
> Was maked of our blisful Lady free,
> Hire to salue, and eek hire for to preye
> To been oure help and socour whan we deye." (530–34)

If indeed the Prioress *can* translate those words of that song which prays for mercy (she certainly lets the older boy speak the gist of it), she shows little understanding of them in her merciless attitude toward the Jews of her tale – something again she *ought* to know.

We might well wonder, however: does the emphasis we sometimes place on w hether late medieval nuns understood Latin smack of the same superficiality, the same concern for externals attributed to the Prioress in the *General Prologue*? Might we better focus on the substance behind the Prioress's words than on whether she is learned in the language of scholars? That is to say, is it not most important that she be aware of the substance of the spirit? Nice to have both substantial matter and form, but, while she might have learned Latin through other venues, a university education was simply not then available to women. In his history of early Oxford and Cambridge, Alan B. Cobban attests that "attitudes towards women on the part of the English university authorities were permeated by the belief that women and universities should be kept apart as much as was conveniently possible."[57]

Ironically, nuns may well be thought in some sense *avant-garde* if indeed they read important texts in English rather than Latin since, by the late fourteenth century, the vernacular had become the language not only of the common person but of the arts (witness Chaucer), and it was fast becoming that of the law as well. William Holdsworth cites Edward III's 1362 statute mandating English: "all pleas pleaded in the king's courts or in any other courts 'shall be pleaded, shewed, defended, answered, debated, and judged in the English tongue, and that they be entered and inrolled in Latin'; but it provides 'that the laws and customs of the same realm, terms and processes be holden and kept as they be and have been before this time.'"[58] English did not yet prevail; nevertheless, the vernacular grew in importance. Since formal education in Latin likely remained un-

[57] Alan B. Cobban, *The Medieval English Universities: Oxford and Cambridge to c. 1500* (1988; reprint: Berkeley: Univ. of California Press, 1990), 378.

[58] William Holdsworth, *A History of English Law*, 4th ed., 16 vols. (1903; reprint: London: Methuen, 1936), 2.477–78. See also David N. Bell, *What Nuns Read: Books and Libraries in Medieval English Nunneries* (Kalamazoo, Mich.: Cistercian Publications, 1995), 71.

available to the Prioress, then, perhaps she can rightly be admired for the knowledge she does have and indeed be held innocent, that is, not culpable on this linguistic issue.

Several sections of Benedict's Rule enjoin its followers to read and to meditate. Earliest among these in the nun's spiritual development, each novice must listen to the Rule itself read in its entirety several times and at prescribed intervals as part of the process of discerning her vocation (58.131). As noted above, Benedictines are required to chant the office, a practice through which the Prioress would have repeatedly sung or recited the Psalms and various hymns. St. Benedict directed a concomitant "reading of lessons": "the books to be read at Matins shall be the inspired Scriptures of the Old and New Testaments and also the commentaries on them which have been made by well-known and orthodox Catholic Fathers" (9.51). After supper, a sister would read aloud "the Conferences of Cassian or the Lives of the Fathers, or something else that may edify the hearers" (42.101). A reader also provided spiritual sustenance with meals (38.93). Lent exacted yet another intellectual obligation: privately to read a book "through consecutively" (48.113). It seems that were the Prioress earnestly to perform even a tenth of her duties regarding learning, she should know quite enough to enable her to make moral judgments consonant with the religious life, the high calling, she professed.

All this prescribed reading predicates the existence of libraries. Relying on the research of Ker and Watson[59] together with his own reading of wills and various other records, and acknowledging a huge debt to Eileen Power, David N. Bell has gathered and analyzed lists of extant books from medieval English nunneries.[60] We now have a fuller sense of what the Prioress could have known and so can better discern what she should have known. According to Bell, her convent St. Leonard's, Stratford-at-Bowe, is one of the priories hard hit both by fire, and even, as Roy Midmer notes, by flood.[61] For that reason, and no doubt also because of the dissolution of the monasteries under Henry VIII, none of the references noted above includes extant manuscripts from Stratford-at-Bowe. Not so surprisingly, a monastery's books were sometimes stolen, often loaned, and at times not returned. But Latin, French, and English manuscripts have nevertheless survived from Barking, Stratford-at-Bowe's wealthier sister abbey;

[59] N. R. Ker, *Medieval Libraries of Great Britain: A List of Surviving Books*, 2d ed. (London: Royal Historical Society, 1964); N. R. Ker, *Medieval Libraries*, suppl. to 2d ed., ed. Andrew G. Watson (London: Royal Historical Society, 1987).

[60] David N. Bell, *What Nuns Read*; see also R. Sharpe et al., *English Benedictine Libraries: The Shorter Catalogues* (London: The British Library, 1996); and Anne Clark Bartlett, "A Descriptive List of Extant Books Owned by Medieval English Nuns and Convents," in her *Male Authors, Female Readers: Representation and Subjectivity in Middle English Devotional Literature* (Ithaca: Cornell Univ. Press, 1995), 149–71.

[61] Bell, *What Nuns Read*, 46; Roy Midmer, *English Mediaeval Monasteries (1066–1540): A Summary* (Athens: Univ. of Georgia Press, 1979), 297.

these include devotional works, a hymnal, theological tracts, prayers, books of the Bible, and other manuscripts – even perhaps, as the will of William Pownsett suggests, works such as the *opera omnia* of Virgil.[62] Bell wisely warns against concluding that the presence of a book proves that it was read, and Power likewise cautions that "it is never safe to argue from silence and some nuns may still have busied themselves over books."[63] My point here is simply that devotional and theological texts were indeed available to the nuns of fourteenth-century England, and by implication, then, to Chaucer's Prioress.[64]

Internal evidence does suggest that the Prioress knows things essential to her vocation: whatever the reality of the proper method for entuning her office, the *General Prologue* does verify that "she soong the service dyvyne" (122). While the prologue also credits her conscience as tender in charity and compassion (142–50), examples of her spending those virtues on mice and dogs in a time of widespread poverty and plague somehow do not either engender admiration or compel imitation (like her, Chaucer's wayward Monk travels with dogs). She demonstrates too that she grasps enough scripture to cite exemplars such as Rachel and Moses in her tale; she also knows prayers, hymns, and hagiography, i.e., devotional literature. Besides the saintly clergeon, she refers to Saint Nicholas (514), Saint John (581), and Hugh of Lincoln (684). Presumably, too, she would be able to recite the story of the patron of her parish, St. Leonard, an exemplar of mercy especially to prisoners of whom he was commonly considered the patron saint.[65] But the Prioress's special patron, whose life she no doubt best knew, was Mary, the virginal mother of God – the ideal woman.

Judith Ferster chooses a psychoanalytic perspective as she analyzes the Prioress's/the Clergeon's Marian devotion, and with interesting results. She argues, for instance, that Madame Eglentyne substitutes the feminine in place of the masculine "divine."[66] From a religious perspective, however, the Prioress's portrayal of Mary sidesteps what could, in Ferster's reading, be bold indeed, probably in fact heretical. Fourteenth-century Roman Catholic theology makes it clear that adoration (*latria*), the worship due God, belongs to no one else; *dulia* designates the veneration properly rendered the saints – the triumphant ones in heaven, of course, not the militant others still making their way through an earthly pilgrimage. Mary, the mediatrix of all grace, the mother figure who intercedes for humans to her Son, the second person of the Trinity, merits yet a

[62] Bell, *What Nuns Read*, 46–47, 116–20.

[63] Power, *Medieval English Nunneries*, 237–38.

[64] For information on women's oral culture and their sharing of and willing of texts, see Felicity Riddy, "'Women talking about the things of God': A late medieval sub-culture," in *Women and Literature in Britain, 1150–1500*, ed. Carol M. Meale (Cambridge: Cambridge Univ. Press, 1993), 104–27.

[65] Jacobus de Voragine, *The Golden Legend*, trans. Granger Ryan and Helmut Ripperger (New York: Longmans, Green and Co., 1941), 657–61.

[66] Ferster, "'Your Praise Is Performed by Men and Children,'" 155.

more special worship, *hyperdulia*, something far less than that owed God, but more than that reserved for ordinary saints.[67] The Prioress's language in both her prologue and tale manifests her awareness of Mary's special role: before beseeching her help, Madame Eglentyne addresses and praises Christ, "O Lord, oure Lord" (453). She places Mary "next hir Sone" (466), arguably "next" meaning just below him as well as nigh, and she acknowledges the mother's role as mediatrix:

> For somtyme, Lady, er men praye to thee,
> Thou goost biforn of thy benyngnytee,
> And getest us the lyght, of thy preyere,
> To gyden us unto thy Sone so deere. (477–80)

Clearly Christ is the port to which Mary, at times called Star of the Sea, will guide the petitioner. Likewise, *Alma Redemptoris Mater*, the anthem which the tale's Clergeon risks all to learn, hails Mary as the mother of the Redeemer. Rather than further multiply instances of the Prioress's apt Mariology though, let me make the point: this woman exhibits an intelligence *somehow* theologically aware in that she keeps Mary in her proper place vis-à-vis the Godhead. Knowing that fact helps us to think more astutely about her culpability.

Ironically, the Prioress, expert in sweet cries for mercy, is anything but yielding in the treatment of the Jews in her little miracle of the Virgin. Yet again, Chaucer allows her to reveal herself through her merciless and scandalously thorough punishment of the saintly clergeon's murderer(s):

> With torment and with shameful deeth echon,
> This provost dooth thise Jewes for to sterve
> That of this mordre wiste, and that anon.
> He nolde no swich cursednesse observe.
> "Yvele shal have that yvele wol deserve";
> Therfore with wilde hors he dide hem drawe,
> And after that he heng hem by the lawe. (628–34)

Such an ending, of course, mimics one common version of this story; what interests me is that Chaucer chooses *this* version rather than one wherein the Jews are converted.[68] The Second Nun, who in contrast to the Prioress is not described in

[67] See Jaroslav Pelikan, *Mary through the Centuries: Her Place in the History of Culture* (New Haven: Yale Univ. Press, 1996), 100–102, as well as his *The Growth of Medieval Theology (600–1300)*, vol. 3 of *The Christian Tradition: A History of the Development of Doctrine* (Chicago: Univ. of Chicago Press, 1978), 160–71.

[68] "Though conversion, when not a major issue, could always be a welcome consequence, at the heart of the greater number of anti-Semitic miracles is a personal hostility, a hatred of Mary by the Jews, and, simultaneously, the power of Mary to triumph over their hostility" (Robert Worth Frank, Jr., "Miracles of the Virgin, Medieval Anti-Semitism, and the 'Prioress's

the *General Prologue*, gets to tell the tale of a different sort of saintly music-maker – indeed later called the patron saint of music – Cecilia, whose enemies are constantly translated, converted through her holiness. Quite an instructive difference. But the Second Nun's saintliness cuts two ways: the Prioress's transgressions seem not to have adversely affected her chaplain.

While it would be salutary for Madame Eglentyne to reverse order and learn from her sister, instead she aligns herself with the innocent little Clergeon of her tale. Given the lady's age and her station, a reader might better perceive her lack of knowledge as culpable ignorance rather than this self-flattering innocence. We might even suppose that the boy is not really as worthy of imitation as the Prioress seems to believe; he does, after all, know but nevertheless shirk his obligation to study. But then again, he is only seven years old. One might easily expect the Prioress to reach beyond the puerile for educational inspiration, but her skewed perspective on the obligations of her own vocation seem somehow echoed in the Clergeon's choice to neglect his assigned studies.

But can we not cite the religious decadence of fourteenth-century England as the reason why the Prioress could not possibly quite understand that which she seems to or needs to know? Not really. In addition to sources already specified, regular visitations by the bishops served as constant reminders of spiritual obligation, as did sacramental confession. Furthermore, either by studying them herself or through the instruction of her bishop, she would be aware of papal bulls. Bishops, men high in the hierarchy of the patriarchal Roman church, wrote registers, reports of their visitations that detailed the sisters' faults and complaints. These continue to be an important source of information; nevertheless, our current understanding of ecclesiastical attitudes toward women makes it wise at least to question the correctness of the bishops' perceptions regarding women religious.

While the medieval Church deserves blame for fostering prejudice toward Jews early on, papal and episcopal injunctions often and consistently admonished Christians against such prejudice. Jacob Marcus perceptively notes that "the continuous stream of papal decrees from about 1120 to 1763, however, would lead one to believe that they were of little lasting avail in coping with prejudice."[69] In his valuable essay, "Chaucer and the Jews," Richard Rex furthermore cites numerous examples of sermons, tracts and even poetry contemporary to Chaucer which not only counsel tolerance for Jews, but, better yet, pro-

Tale,'" in *The Wisdom of Poetry: Essays in Early English Literature in honor of Morton W. Bloomfield*, ed. Larry D. Benson and Siegfried Wenzel [Kalamazoo, Mich.: Medieval Institute, 1982], 184). See also Carleton Brown, *A Study of the Miracle of Our Lady Told by Chaucer's Prioress* (London: Chaucer Society, 1910).

[69] Jacob R. Marcus, "A Bull of Pope Gregory X, October 7, 1272," in his *The Jew in the Medieval World: A Source Book, 315–1791* (New York: Atheneum, 1938), 152.

claim their moral superiority.[70] So even though the Jews had been expelled from England since 1290, Chaucer surely heard in his own land as well as through his travels quite enough to make him aware of the effect he created by choosing to have the Prioress demonstrate as she does. As Louise Fradenburg says, "the *Prioress's Tale* registers its anxieties and desires – its fear of internal differences, its desire for union – through a phobic narrative about the threat posed by the 'outside' (learning, criticism, Jews) to the 'inside.'"[71] Let me note too that the Prioress gives evidence that she understands the role of knowledge in the commission of a moral (or immoral) act when she has all the Jews who *knew* of the murder of the clergeon tortured and executed (628–30). While the Church issued mixed messages about the Jews, the Prioress's view is persistently and cruelly anti-Semitic: she remains adamant and aggressive in her condemnation.

Like Sister Madeleva, we latter-day reader-responders might prefer a kinder, gentler analysis of the Prioress's state of soul, but in the light of medieval theology, Chaucer's text suggests otherwise. I keep thinking of a comparison which I have not room to explore here, but let me at least pose it: the gentlemanly narrator of *Troilus and Criseyde* might seem to excuse that gentlewoman too lightly when in Book 5 he describes her as "Tendre-herted, slydynge of corage" (825), but her words in Book 4 reverberate in Book 5. She indeed condemns herself there when she says to Troilus:

> For thilke day that I for cherisynge
> Or drede of fader, or for other wight,
> Or for estat, delit, or for weddynge,
> Be fals to yow, my Troilus, my knyght,
> Saturnes doughter, Juno, thorugh hire myght,
> As wood as Athamante do me dwelle
> Eternalich in Stix, the put of helle! (1534–40)

Similarly, the Prioress betrays and condemns herself, first in her self-righteous comment on monks and then in all the vincibly ignorant choices she makes. She ought to know better.

Incontrovertibly locked in the present, we know nevertheless a good deal more about the medieval nun's life today than we did yet a decade ago. Good scholarship may even, in some instances, have washed away prejudicial predispositions. Certainly we know now that under normal circumstances, a fourteenth-century nun could and should have known all that was necessary for right moral behavior in accord with her religious vocation. By rendering his Madame Eglentyne responsible for her actions, as he does, Geoffrey Chaucer

[70] Richard Rex, "Chaucer and the Jews," *Modern Language Quarterly* 45 (1984): 107–22.

[71] Louise O. Fradenburg, "Criticism, Anti-Semitism, and the *Prioress's Tale*," *Exemplaria* 1 (1989): 98.

has created a character not so much like the immaculately conceived Mary, but rather more like each and every fault-filled human being. He has thereby lifted the Prioress above the sentimental, wispy status too often afforded her by modern readers.

"Renewing" *Troilus*, 1.890-96: *Si Erravit Scriptor, Debes Corrigere, Lector*[1]

VINCENT DIMARCO, *University of Massachusetts – Amherst*

Chaucer's anxiety over the faithful reproduction of his works is twice a matter of poetic record: toward the end of *Troilus and Criseyde* (5.1793–99) the author, in releasing to his audience (and to posterity) his "litel bok," prays that the integrity of the finished work, now beyond his direct control, be preserved in the face of dialectical variation, while elsewhere, and less piously, Chaucer anathematizes[2] a carelessly indifferent scribe whose previous negligence has involved the poet in a constant effort to *renewe* (i.e., to correct, and hence to make new again and restore) what he had originally written. That the second of these statements, "Chaucers Wordes unto Adam, His Owne Scriveyn," is itself uniquely preserved in manuscript in a production of John Shirley – arguably the most enthusiastic as well as the most idiosyncratic copyist of Chaucer – carries its own irony, of course. Yet, for whatever reasons, Chaucer did not exercise the degree of editorial supervision evidenced, say, by Gower over the *Confessio Amantis*; and while in comparison with the *Canterbury Tales* – an unfinished project of more than a decade's involvement – *Troilus and Criseyde* exhibits a high degree of authorial revision, completion, and polish, Chaucer himself would probably have admitted that for all his rubbing and scraping away of the appalling products of scribal *rape*, the *complete* restoration of the poet's *trewe makyng* could hardly be expected, especially if to do so required the detection of inadvertencies of a less

[1] A fifteenth-century scribal notation, quoted by John Scattergood, "The Jongleur, the Copyist, and the Printer: The Tradition of Chaucer's Wordes unto Adam, His Own Scriveyn," in *Courtly Literature Culture and Context: Selected Papers from the 5th Triennial Congress of the International Courtly Literature Society, Dalfsen, The Netherlands, 9–16 August, 1986*, ed. Keith Busby and Erik Kooper (Amsterdam and Philadelphia: John Benjamins, 1990), 503. Scattergood is here citing W. Wattenbach, *Das Schriftwesen im Mittelalter* (Leipzig: S. Hirzel, 1896), 340; for similar scribal apologies, see Wattenbach, 339–44. (For valuable comments on a draft of this essay I am indebted to the Five College/UConn Chaucer faculty seminar and to Ernest Gallo.)

[2] Chaucer's light and ironic invocations of the formulas of malediction are the subject of James A. Work, "Echoes of the Anathema in Chaucer," *PMLA* 47 (1932): 419–30.

immediately perceptible order than Adam's usual blunders. In that spirit, my purpose in the following pages is to "renewe" a passage from Book 1 of the poem which Adam Scriveyn, perhaps for understandable reasons, got wrong. It is, I suggest, a scribally disarranged passage that, lacking clear and obvious evidence of error or nonsense, likewise escaped Chaucer's attention in his "ofte adaye" review of Adam's work, and for that reason passed undetected into the manuscript tradition represented by all extant texts.

Consider the following familiar lines from Book 1:

And whan that Pandare herde hire name nevene,
Lord, he was glad, and seyde, "Frend so deere,
Now far aright, for Joves name in hevene.
Love hath byset the wel; be of good cheere!
For of good name and wisdom and manere
She hath ynough, and ek of gentilesse.
If she be fayr, thow woost thyself, I gesse,

"Ne nevere saugh a more bountevous
Of hire estat, n'a gladder, ne of speche
A frendlyer, n'a more gracious
For to do wel, ne lasse hadde nede to seche
What for to don; and al this bet to eche,
In honour, to as fer as she may strecche,
A kynges herte semeth by hyrs a wrecche.

"And forthi loke of good comfort thow be;
For certeinly, the ferste poynt is this
Of noble corage and wel ordeyné,
A man to have pees with hymself, ywis.
So oghtist thow, for noht but good it is
To love wel, and in a worthy place;
The oghte not to clepe it hap, but grace.

"And also thynk, and therwith glade the,
That sith thy lady vertuous is al,
So foloweth it that there is some pitee
Amonges alle thise other in general;
And forthi se that thow, in special,
Requere naught that is ayeyns hyre name;
For vertu streccheth naught hymself to shame.

"But wel is me that evere that I was born,
That thow biset art in so good a place;
For by my trouthe, in love I dorste have sworn
The sholde nevere han tid thus fayr a grace.
And wostow why? For thow were wont to chace

At Love in scorn, and for despit him calle
'Seynt Idiot, lord of thise foles alle.'"[3]

My aim is to rehabilitate the status and reputation of lines 1.890–96, a stanza whose genuineness has never been denied, but one whose relevance and appropriateness to Pandarus's argument have been questioned by modern editors and commentators. The lines are found originally in but three manuscripts, PhH^{2}H^4 (two of which, Ph and H^2, for this part of the poem were produced by the same scribe). These three manuscripts,[4] the reader will remember, constitute for Books 1 and 2 the authorities that attest the *alpha* text, long considered that which preserved Chaucer's earliest, unrevised version of *Troilus and Criseyde.* The lines in question are also found in Thynne's edition (1532) – the text of which in Book 1 shows a considerable number of *alpha* readings – as well as in those early prints and editions that derive directly or indirectly from Thynne; namely, the reprint (1545?) of Thynne, the edition of Stow (1561) and those of Speght (1598; 1602), Kynaston's reprint (1635) of Speght, and the edition of Urry (1721).[5] W. S. McCormick had previously noted that the stanza is also found added in a later hand in the margin of MS. J (St. John's College, Cambridge, L.1), though this is not recorded by R. K. Root in his edition.[6]

Lines 890–96 regularly have been viewed as an insertion that interrupts and momentarily suspends Pandarus's arguments. The authoritative statement is that of Root:

> [B]eautiful as the stanza is in itself, it breaks the continuity of thought. Both before and after, Pandarus is speaking primarily of Criseyde, and basing his hope for Troilus on the qualities of his niece's character. In the stanza under discussion, he turns to moralize on the strength which comes from being at

[3] I quote from Stephen A. Barney's edition of the text in *The Riverside Chaucer*, ed. Larry D. Benson, 3d ed. (Boston: Houghton Mifflin, 1987). There are no significant variants in this passage in the editions of Root, Robinson, Donaldson, Baugh, Fisher, and Windeatt.

[4] Huntington Library, HM 114 (formerly Phillips 8252; misnumbered 8250 by both Root and Robinson); British Library, Harley 3943; and British Library, Harley 2392.

[5] Speght's 1598 edition is from Stow; his 1602 edition is "corrected" from that of 1598, but apparently without comparison of manuscripts. Urry's edition is based on the text of Thynne or Speght under correction of three manuscripts, one of which was Ph.

[6] See *The Works of Geoffrey Chaucer* (The Globe Edition), ed. Alfred W. Pollard et al. (London: Macmillan & Co., 1913), 451. At least with regard to 1.890–96 Root is incorrect in tracing such marginal corrections in MS. J to Speght's 1602 edition, for readings in J of 1.893 and 896, which correspond to no earlier printed edition, substantially agree with the unique variants of H^4, as follows: 893. A man] om. J H^4; 896. Thee] *men* J H^4. Cf. Robert Kilburn Root, *The Manuscripts of Chaucer's Troilus*, Chaucer Society, 1st ser., 98 (London: Oxford Univ. Press, 1914 [for 1911]), 34.

> peace with one's self. The excision of the stanza leaves no gap in the thought, but rather consolidates it.[7]

Charles A. Owen, Jr., who accepts Root's textual reconstruction of the poem, sensitively extends this line of argument by noting that *without* the stanza Pandarus's speech is consistently lighthearted and reassuring in tone, with three stanzas (1.876–82, 883–89, 897–903 [immediately sequential if 1.890–96 is omitted]) devoted to Criseyde's virtues, one stanza (1.904–10) serving as a transition in which Pandarus expresses surprise at Troilus's situation (since earlier he had so disparaged love), then three immediately sequential stanzas (1.911–17, 918–24, 925–31) detailing the hero's former mockery and calling for Troilus to repent of such sins. Finally, says Owen, the skillful pedagogue Pandarus "is ready to modulate to a more serious tone and instruct Troilus on the proper deportment of a lover";[8] he elaborates the subject of what had earlier been 1.890–96 in 1.953–59 –

> Now loke that atempre be thi bridel,
> And for the beste ay suffre to the tyde,
> Or elles al oure labour is on ydel:
> He hasteth wel that wisely kan abyde.
> Be diligent and trewe, and ay wel hide;
> Be lusty, fre; persevere in thy servyse,
> And al is wel, if thow werke in this wyse –

and wisely develops it there in a fashion that, by imagining a time when Criseyde will be affected by Troilus's conduct, implies the possibility of the same intimate relationship that Troilus had earlier despaired of attaining.

Root printed 1.890–96 in the body of the text, but in brackets to indicate that "its cancellation would seem to be an authentic revision."[9] Curiously, this is not his procedure regarding lines found after 2.1750 in Bodley MS. Rawlinson Poet. 163 (MS. R):

> For ye must outher chaungen [now?] your face
> That is so ful of mercy and bountee
> Or elles must ye do this man sum grace
> For this thyng folweth of necessytee
> As sothe as god ys in his magestee

[7] *The Book of Troilus and Criseyde by Geoffrey Chaucer*, ed. Robert Kilburn Root (Princeton: Princeton Univ. Press, 1926), 426.

[8] Charles A. Owen, Jr., "Minor Changes in Chaucer's *Troilus and Criseyde*," in *Chaucer and Middle English Studies in Honour of Rossell Hope Robbins*, ed. Beryl Rowland (Kent, Ohio: Kent State Univ. Press, 1974), 309.

[9] *The Book of Troilus and Criseyde*, ed. Root, 426.

That crueltee with so benigne a chier
Ne may not last in o persone yfere.

Root accepted the genuineness of these lines, too, but relegated the stanza to the table of variants below the text proper, as representing what he felt was "an afterthought" by the poet, which had been neglected by the copyist because Chaucer had perhaps written it on "a discarded piece of paper or parchment, at the top of which had already been written the first two lines of stanza 226 [2.1576–77],"[10] where it seemed (rightly) to make no sense. But one may wonder why Root chose not to restore these lines to the body of the poem, especially since they are uniquely found in a manuscript that he felt alone offered throughout the poem Chaucer's final revision, the *beta* version.[11]

Root's theory of revision, in which the *alpha* version, before yielding to the poet's final *beta* text, also parented through a corrupt manuscript an unauthorized, partially revised *gamma* version, has been proven largely untenable by Barry Windeatt,[12] who has shown that most of the distinguishing omissions of the Ph-family manuscripts (Root's *alpha* version) represent merely scribal omissions of passages that, while perhaps composed at different times, were nevertheless necessary to contexts that could never have been considered complete by the poet without them. Now, as opposed, for example, to Troilus's song in 3.1744–71, which was missing in H^2 and added by the scribe in correction of Ph, but preceded in the text by the clear anticipation of its inclusion ("And thanne he wolde synge in this manere" [3.1743]), the lines here under discussion, 1.890–96, cannot be said to be demanded by context. But certainly with the status of the Ph-family shown merely to reflect early *scribal* confusion over Chaucer's working papers, rather than representing a first, unrevised authorial draft of the poem, we cannot simply assume that lines found only in this manuscript family were canceled in revision. Yet Windeatt also brackets 1.890–96, considering it "something of an interpolation" that Chaucer "may have intended to cancel";[13] by so doing this editor may be said to agree with the literary assessment of Root and Owen while denying that assessment's textual underpinnings. The argument that the lines as they stand are an interruption remains a strong one, however, and I readily concede that Owen's is a gracefully argued analysis,

[10] *The Book of Troilus and Criseyde*, ed. Root, 458.

[11] *The Book of Troilus and Criseyde*, ed. Root, lix.

[12] See Barry Windeatt, "The Text of the *Troilus*," in *Essays on Troilus and Criseyde*, ed. Mary Salu, Chaucer Studies, 3 (Cambridge: D. S. Brewer, 1979), 1–22; and *Troilus & Criseyde: A New Edition of The Book of Troilus*, ed. B. A. Windeatt (London: Longman, 1984), 36–53. Windeatt's views have recently been examined by Kevin K. Cureton, "Chaucer's Revision of *Troilus and Criseyde*," *Studies in Bibliography* 42 (1989): 153–84, which cannot be said to offer support for Root's theory that Chaucer "published" the poem in an early version, then subsequently made changes in the publication copy supplied by his scribe.

[13] *Troilus & Criseyde*, ed. Windeatt, 139.

sensitive to the nuances of a characterization of Pandarus in easy and effective control of situations, which is later so much in evidence in his adroit manipulation of Criseyde, regardless of the extent to which she may be more than merely a passive victim of such manipulation.[14] We may well wonder what Chaucer might ever have sought to achieve by inserting 1.890–96 where the manuscripts say he did. I would like, however, to suggest an alternative textual reconstruction that preserves these lines as an understandable, even *necessary* part of Chaucer's conception of the scene. I should say at the outset that it is an explanation that suggested itself in reading the scene aloud, momentarily oblivious to the textual and critical history of the passage; coincidentally, it is an explanation that finds some support on analogy to Root's own comments on that other controversial stanza, the lines found in MS. R after 2.1750.

Root suggested that the lines found after 2.1750 had been scribally misplaced from their intended position after 2.1730–36 because they had been written on a slip inserted by Chaucer in his manuscript. By his argument, the lines should thus have read:

"Aviseth yow what folk ben hire withinne,
And in what plit oon is, God hym amende!"
And inward thus, "Ful softely bygynne,
Nece, I conjure and heighly yow defende,
On his half which that soule us alle sende,
And in the vertu of corones tweyne,
Sle naught this man, that hath for yow this peyne!

"For ye must outher chaungen [now] your face 1736a[15]
That is so ful of mercy and bountee, 1736b
Or elles must ye do this man sum grace; 1736c
For this thyng folweth of necessytee, 1736d
As sothe as God ys in his magestee, 1736e
That crueltee with so benigne a chier 1736f
Ne may not last in o persone yfere. 1736g

"Fy on the devel! Thynk which oon he is,
And in what plit he lith; com of anon!
Thynk al swich taried tyde, but lost it nys.
That wol ye bothe seyn, whan ye ben oon.
Secoundely, ther yet devyneth noon

[14] It might, however, be objected that Pandarus's "recasting" of 1.890–96 (supposedly intended to be canceled) as 1.953–59, where Pandarus counsels the largely practical virtues of diligence and perseverance in order to attain a difficult end, depends for its full effect on our memory of the perfection of the self through love which he had proclaimed in the earlier, more high-minded verses.

[15] The emendation, to repair a metrically deficient line, is Root's.

Upon yow two; come of now, if ye konne!
While folk is blent, lo, al the tyme is wonne."

Such a reordering serves to eliminate what might seem to some readers too sudden an echo of "And in what plit oon is" (2.1731) by "Thynk which oon he is, / And in what plit he lith" (2.1737–38). More positively, however, this reordering suggests how Chaucer's conception of Pandarus's speech is shaped by the poet's earlier *Complaint to Pity*. Mention of the "corones tweyne" (2.1735), invoked by Pandarus as an argument for acting to save the life of the despairing Troilus, recalls the description of Pity in the lyric as the "coroune of vertues alle" and the "corowne of Beaute" (*Pity*, 58, 75). Root reminds us[16] that in the lyric Pity is "annexed ever unto Bounte"; with that in mind, reading the stanza after 2.1736 provides a prompt gloss for the "corones tweyne" of 2.1735, in the mention that "mercy and bountee," united in the beauty of Criseyde's face, must prove that "crueltee" has not usurped their place and unnaturally allied herself with "so benigne a chier." For such has proven to be the case in *Pity* where, with that virtue dead, Cruelty has supplanted her "under colour of womanly Beaute" (*Pity*, 66). The allegory is probably not, as we might at first think, from the *Roman de la Rose*, which regularly features *Pitié* allied with *Franchise* (not *Bonté*) against *Dangier* (rather than *Cruauté*), though *Franchise* and *Bonté* may be said to overlap in a common sense of lavish action, and Cruelty – an uncommon personification in French allegorical love poetry – might be understood as an intense manifestation of *Dangier*, i.e., merciless resistance. But Wimsatt[17] has identified the specific opposition of Pity and Cruelty in two poems of Machaut, the *Dit dou Vergier* (which also features *Dangier*) and the balade "Helas! je suis de si male heure nez"; and the collocation of *Pitié* with *Beauté* and virtues such as correspond with *Bonté*, *Franchise*, etc., is found in other productions of Machaut which Chaucer surely knew, such as *Le Jugement du roy de Behaigne* –

Et d'autre part Bel Acueil m'appelloit,
Son Dous Regart riant m'asseüroit,
Et Dous Espoir doucement me disoit
    En loyauté

[16] *The Book of Troilus and Criseyde*, ed. Root, 456. There is no need to entertain Root's alternative suggestion (based on *ABC*, 137–44) that Chaucer perhaps means Mercy and Justice. For a catalogue of the ingenious, occasionally bizarre explanations of "corones tweyne" which have been put forward (often with scant relevance to the context of 2.1730ff.), see Stephen A. Barney's note in *The Riverside Chaucer*, 1036–37.

[17] James I. Wimsatt, "Guillaume de Machaut and Chaucer's Love Lyrics," *Medium Aevum* 47 (1978): 80–81; cf. Wolfgang Clemen, *Chaucer's Early Poetry*, trans. C. A. M. Sym (New York: Barnes and Noble, 1964), 181.

Et m'affermoit c'onques si grant beauté
Ne pot estre, qu'il n'y eüst pité –

(On the other hand, Fair Welcome summoned me, her smiling Sweet Glance enticed me, and Sweet Hope gently whispered in loyalty to me and assured me that never could there be such great beauty without pity –)[18]

the *Dit dou Vergier* –

Car Esperence, la seüre,
Li promet en bien l'asseüre
Qu'onques biauté si affinee
Ne pot estre sans Pitié ne.
Et puis que douceur est en li,
Franchise y doit bien estre aussi –

(But Hope, the stable one,
Promises and assures him completely
That never could a beauty
So refined be born without Pity.
And since sweetness is hers
Generosity must be too –)[19]

and the *Remede de Fortune*, as we shall see.

Pandarus then (2.1737) reminds Criseyde of Troilus's condition, suggests that her reputation is safe, and predicts a future in which, once she shows pity, all the previous time will seem to her to have been wasted. The *Complaint to Pity* at the corresponding point (96–106) likewise returns to a depiction of the lover's woeful plight after expressing concern for the lady's reputation and renown (86), but then concludes, far less optimistically than does Pandarus, that with Pity buried in the lady's heart, the lover's faithful service – which in spite of all he vows to continue – is doomed to failure and futility.

In this respect, Book 2 of *Troilus and Criseyde* offers us Pandarus expressing a somewhat opportunistic, perhaps even cynical reformulation of ideas that the lover in *Pity* – himself hardly a disinterested participant – has advanced sincerely. Book 5 again sounds these motifs, but there expresses them through the consciousness of Criseyde, as she considers rejoining Troilus. Not only are the same notions subtly played upon, but their exposition unfolds in much the

[18] Guillaume de Machaut, *Le Jugement du roy de Behaigne and Remede de Fortune*, ed. James I. Wimsatt and William W. Kibler; music ed. Rebecca A. Baltzer (Athens, Georgia: Univ. of Georgia Press, 1988), lines 456–62, pp. 82–83.

[19] Guillaume de Machaut, *The Fountain of Love (La Fonteinne Amoureuse) and Two Other Love Vision Poems*, ed. and trans. R. Barton Palmer, Garland Library of Medieval Literature, 54 (New York: Garland, 1993), lines 749–54, pp. 60–61.

same order and development. In Criseyde's important monologue beginning at 5.689 we are presented first with what she fears will be construed as her false (because pitiless) response to Troilus's pleas (5.697–98), then with the image of her beautiful face suddenly altered in appearance, as she seems to acknowledge that present anxieties prevent her "herte trewe" from manifesting itself in action (5.706–14). She then experiences the painful memory (5.715–19) of Troilus's noble service, which passes over imperceptibly into a regret that she has overvalued or misjudged the possible effect on her reputation of fleeing Troy with him. Finally Criseyde, caught as she is "in the snare" of the present, soberly reflects on the futility of hoping to understand or control the future (5.746–49).

I suggest, perhaps because it was also composed on a separate slip inserted by the poet in his manuscript, or written somewhere in the margin, that 1.890–96 was similarly misplaced,[20] and was intended by Chaucer to *follow*, rather than *precede*, 1.897–903 thus:

And also thynk, and therwith glade the,
That sith thy lady vertuous is al,
So foloweth it that there is some pitee
Amonges alle thise other in general;
And forthi se that thow, in special,
Requere naught that is ayeyns hyre name;
For vertu streccheth naught hymself to shame.

And forthi loke of good comfort thow be;
For certeinly, the ferste poynt is this
Of noble corage and wel ordeyné,
A man to have pees with hymself, ywis.
So oghtist thow, for noht but good it is
To love wel, and in a worthy place;
The oghte not to clepe it hap, but grace.

But wel is me that evere that I was born,
That thow biset art in so good a place;
For by my trouthe, in love I dorste have sworn
The sholde nevere han tid thus fayr a grace.
And wostow why? For thow were wont to chace

[20] For an analogous case, see the masterful reconstruction by Robert A. Pratt, "Chaucer and the Pillars of Hercules," *Studies in Honor of Ullman*, ed. Lillian B. Lawler, Dorothy M. Robathon, and William C. Korfmacher (St. Louis: The Classical Bulletin, 1960), 118–25, where Pratt shows that the mysterious marginal gloss to the *Monk's Tale* in the Hengrwt and Ellesmere manuscripts, *Ille vates Chaldeorum Tropheus*, is but a scribal conflation of two glosses, quite possibly Chaucer's own, that were written in the margin as originally separate: *vates Chaldeorum*, to Daniel in the Nabugodonosor section of the tale, and *Tropheus*, to the lines devoted to Hercules.

At Love in scorn, and for despit him calle
"Seynt Idiot, lord of thise foles alle."

Chaucer follows the *Filostrato* closely at the beginning of Pandarus's speech, with 1.876–82 and 1.883–89 quite faithfully rendering *Filostrato* stanzas 21 and 22. But the stanza of Boccaccio's poem immediately following (23) does not at all correspond to 1.890–96; instead it suggests Chaucer's *next* stanza as regularly printed, 1.897–903, albeit, as Windeatt points out,[21] with the argument reversed, for to Pandaro the sole impediment to Troilo's success derives from the fact that Criseida is *onesta*, whereas Pandarus counts on Criseyde's virtue as a cause for hope of Troilus's satisfaction. Indeed, Chaucer is turning away from Boccaccio in 1.897–903 in favor of working directly from Machaut's *Remede de Fortune*, where the argument linking virtue and pity is made *exactly* as Pandarus presents it. Chaucer's close adaptation of the *Remede* in *Troilus and Criseyde* has been demonstrated by Kittredge and, more recently, Wimsatt,[22] who has shown the extent to which Pandarus in his encouragement of Troilus in these scenes in Book 1 corresponds in language and function to Machaut's Lady Esperance, an allegorical representation of what proves to be a crucially important psychological attribute of the unsatisfied lover. Moreover, as the agent who saves Amant from despair by instruction in the means to transcend the effects of Fortune, Esperance clearly imitates Boethius's Lady Philosophy, with the important difference that Esperance identifies true happiness with the virtuous possession of an earthly loved one, rather than in a knowledge of and union with the divine. It would, however, be a mistake to understand the *Remede*'s recasting of Boethian philosophy in an amatory context as a parodic repudiation of the former, for Machaut defines in the poem a virtuous love between man and woman that does not require, nor does it seem even to seek as a *sine qua non*, physical consummation. As such, the *Remede* may be said to recast Boethianism as a courtly alternative to the ethos of the *Roman de la Rose*, at least as that poem is read as the allegorical "history" of a successful seduction. Chaucer must have understood and appreciated Machaut's project in this regard, for as we shall see he uses Pandarus, who occupies a position in the narrative analogous to that of Boethius's Lady Philosophy and her equivalent in the *Remede*, as the representative of a more sensual practicality, reminiscent of the *Roman de la Rose*.

In composing the *Book of the Duchess*, Chaucer chose almost exclusively to treat material found in the first third of the *Remede*, a work of some 4298 lines;[23]

[21] *Troilus & Criseyde*, ed. Windeatt, 139.

[22] George Lyman Kittredge, "Chaucer's *Troilus* and Guillaume de Machaut," *Modern Language Notes* 30 (1915): 69; and James I. Wimsatt, "Guillaume de Machaut and Chaucer's *Troilus and Criseyde*," *Medium Aevum* 45 (1976): 277–93, esp. 282–84.

[23] I quote throughout from the edition and translation of *Le Jugement du roy de Behaigne and Remede de Fortune* by James I. Wimsatt and William W. Kibler (Athens: Univ. of Georgia Press, 1988); the parallel was put forward by Kittredge, "Chaucer's *Troilus* and Guillaume de

the influence of Machaut's poem on Chaucer's earlier composition effectively ceases before Esperance begins her instruction and correction of the sorrowful lover. Here in Book 1 of *Troilus and Criseyde*, however, Chaucer draws on about 700 lines of Esperance's conversation with the lover, from line 1796 to approximately line 2490 of the French poem. And although for the *Book of the Duchess* Chaucer ranged freely among Machaut's lines, not strictly following the order and progression of the *Remede*, in Book 1 of *Troilus and Criseyde* he extracts for Pandarus's speech the argument of Esperance much more closely in the order of its elements as he found them in the French poem. Not only, then, does the proposed reordering 1.897–903, 890–96 reflect Chaucer's sequential use, then temporary abandonment, of the *Filostrato* in favor of another source, but Pandarus's argument, thus reordered, will be seen largely to follow a sequential reading of Chaucer's French source at this point in the poem.

Wimsatt has noted the close verbal parallels between Pandarus's reminding Troilus of the inestimable value of serving his lady (1.813–19) and Esperance's assertion of a similar "reward" to one so unworthy:

> Tu *ne* te *dois pas las clamer*,
> Se tu l'aimes bien, *n'esmaiier*
> Qu'elle ne te doie paiier
> *Plus mille foys que ne desers*
> En ce que tu *l'aimes et sers*.
> Et aussi c'est chose petite
> A li de rendre a toy merite,
> Car tout le mendre *guerredon*
> De qu'ell te puist faire don,
> Dont elle a sans fin et sans nombre,
> *Vaut .v.c. foys, s'a droit le nombre,*
> *Plus que deservir ne porroiez*
> *Se tu l'amoiez et servoiez.* (1636–48)[24]

> What *sholde* he therfore *fallen in dispayr*,
> Or be recreant for his owne tene,
> Or slen hymself, al be his lady fair?
> *Nay, nay*, but evere in oon be fressh and grene

Machaut," 69, and Wimsatt, "Guillaume de Machaut and Chaucer's *Troilus and Criseyde*," 282–83.

[24] See B. A. Windeatt, *Chaucer's Dream Poetry: Sources and Analogues*, Chaucer Studies, 7 (Cambridge: D. S. Brewer, 1982), 58–64, 167–68. "[Y]ou must not pity yourself if you love her well, nor be dismayed that she doesn't pay you a thousand times more than you deserve for loving and serving her. And besides, it's next to nothing for her to repay you, for the very least reward she is able to give you, of which she has endless and numberless ones, is worth, at true reckoning, five hundred times more than you could deserve were you to love and serve her" (trans. Wimsatt and Kibler, 258).

To serve and love his deere hertes queene,
And thynk it is a *guerdon hire to serve,*
A thousand fold moore than he kan deserve. (1.813–19)

Closely following in the *Remede* is a description of the lady's virtues, which becomes to Esperance an argument that she must also possess pity:

Encor dois tu penser aussi
Pour toy meitre hors de soussi, ...
Que puis qu'elle a parfaitement
Tous les biens qu'on puet bonement
Ymaginer, dire, ou penser,
Qui croissent en li sans cesser,
Et qu'elle est des vertus paree
Et de tous vices separee,
Qu'il couvient de neccessité
Qu'en li soit Franchise et Pitié. (1671–82)[25]

So too in Chaucer, in those lines which I suggest ought to be moved back in the text:

And also thynk, and therwith glade the,
That sith thy lady vertuous is al,
So foloweth it that there is some pitee
Amonges alle thise other in general. (1.897–900)

Reading a couple of leaves further, Chaucer would have come upon lines that might have furnished the figure of the concluding line of the misplaced stanza, though the thought is admittedly conventional:

Car elle [Amours] t'a fait *plus de grace*
Que ne pourroiez desservir
En li .v.c. mil ans servir.
Et si te veuil dire comment:
Amours t'a fait loyal amant
A la millour et la plus belle
Qui vive. (1790–96)[26]

[25] Wimsatt, "Guillaume de Machaut and Chaucer's *Troilus and Criseyde*," 283–84. "And also you must believe, in order to stop your worrying, ... that since she possesses perfectly all the qualities one can properly imagine, describe, or conceive, which increase constantly within her, and since she is enriched with virtues and free from all vices, she must of necessity have Sincerity and Pity" (trans. Wimsatt and Kibler, 260).

[26] "[F]or she [Love] has blessed you more than you could earn in serving her five hundred thousand years. I wish to tell you how: Love has made you the loyal lover of the best and most beautiful woman alive" (trans. Wimsatt and Kibler, 266).

So oghtist thow, for noht but good it is
To love wel, and in a worthy place;
The oghte not to clepe it hap, but grace. (1.894–96)

The suffering Amant, embarrassed like Troilus to confess his love and near despair, is told to take hope in the knowledge of the virtues his lady possesses, for such a lady will be certain to recognize and show pity to a virtuous lover. Amant's virtue is to be shown by loyal, faithful service, honorable character and intentions, and the perfection of the self under the influence of love. Because such faithful love is founded on virtue, it will succeed in bringing happiness, for as a *bien a vertue* (2803) it is not subject to Fortune.[27] But this requires self-mastery, as manifested in the rational exercise of patience and "souffissance." As Esperance says:

Or tien donc son pouoir si vil
Qu'aies de toy la seigneurie.
Gardes que Raisons te maistrie
Et qu'aies en toy pacïence
Et la vertu de souffissance,
Car beneürtés vraiement
Vient de souffrir pacïenment. (2484–90)[28]

Or as Chaucer puts it in the mouth of Pandarus:

And forthi loke of good comfort thow be;
For certeinly, the ferste poynt is this
Of noble corage and wel ordeyné,
A man to have pees with hymself, ywis. (1.890–93)

Windeatt is correct in noting the similarity of phrasing here to *Boece*, 2.pr.4.131–38:

> I schal schewe the schortly the poynt of soverayn blisfulnesse .... [Y]if it so be that thow art myghty over thyself (*that is to seyn, by tranquillite of thi soule*), than hastow thyng in thi powere that thow noldest nevere leesen, ne Fortune may nat bynymen it the.

But this echo of Chaucer's own translation of *De consolatione Philosophiae* is almost certainly triggered, I suggest, by Machaut's rendering of 2.pr.4 here and

[27] See the stimulating discussion by Douglas Kelly, *Medieval Imagination: Rhetoric and the Poetry of Courtly Love* (Madison: Univ. of Wisconsin Press, 1978), 130–37.

[28] "Then hold Fortune's power in contempt and be your own master. See that Reason rules you and that you are patient and have the virtue of sufficiency, for happiness comes from enduring patiently" (trans. Wimsatt and Kibler, 304, 306).

elsewhere in the *Remede*.[29] The importance of this concept to Boethius could hardly have been lost on Chaucer. He probably also recalls Boethius's anticipation of the argument in 1.m.4.1–5 –

> Whoso it be that is cleer of vertue, sad and wel ordynat of lyvynge, that hath put under fote the proude wierdes, and loketh upryght upon either fortune, he may holden his chere undesconfited –

which likewise asserts the power of self-mastery over the vicissitudes of changeable Fortune, and may have furnished him with the phrase in Pandarus's speech, "and wel ordeyné," (from Jean de Meun's translation of "composito serenus aevo" ["calm in well ordered life"] as "de aage bien ordené").[30] Chaucer may also have remembered 1.pr.6.71ff., where Lady Philosophy diagnoses Boethius's true ailment as having forgotten what he is, and hence as having exiled himself from true happiness. To Boethius, self-mastery and control show themselves in freedom from both hopes and fears regarding false sources of (earthly) happiness, which serve only to enslave one to Fortune:

> Hope aftir no thyng, ne drede nat; and so schaltow desarmen the ire of thilke unmyghty tiraunt. But whoso that, qwakynge, dredeth or desireth thyng that nys noght stable of his ryght, that man that so dooth hath cast awey his scheeld, and is remoeved from his place, and enlaceth hym in the cheyne with whiche he mai ben drawen. (1.m.4.15–22)

Machaut in the *Remede* seeks to distinguish a compromising, merely physical desire from a more virtuous hope of gaining the woman's love on the basis of the lover's self-possession and patient service, while Pandarus suggests a somewhat similar connection between self-regulation and loving "wel"; but the ellip-

[29] For Machaut's use of Boethius in the *Remede*, see *Oeuvres de Guillaume de Machaut*, ed. Ernest Hoepffner, 3 vols., SATF, 57 (Paris: Firmin Didot, 1908–21), 2.xxi–xxxii. Machaut again draws specifically on *De consolatione* 2.pr.4 in lines 2685–88 (cf. 2.pr.4.27ff.), where Esperance consoles the lover with the fact that Fortune has at least left him that which is most precious, i.e., his life. (Philosophy, while not denying mankind's "special concern to preserve their own lives," seeks to console Boethius by the fact that his father-in-law, wife, and sons live in safety and virtue.)

[30] I quote from V. L. Dedeck-Héry, "Boethius' *De Consolatione* by Jean de Meun," *Mediaeval Studies* 14 (1952): 165–275 (1.m.4.1, [p. 176]). As noted by Kevin Brownlee, *Poetic Identity in Guillaume de Machaut* (Madison: Univ. of Wisconsin Press, 1984), 230n22, Machaut's knowledge of Boethius was possibly mediated by Jean de Meun's prose translation, despite the judgment of Hoepffner, who did not have the benefit of an edition of the translation. When Chaucer in *Boece*, 3.pr.12.40–41, writes "so ordene moevynges" for Boethius's "tam dispositos motus," he is similarly following Jean de Meun's translation of "si ordenéz mouvemens" (Dedeck-Héry, "Boethius' *De Consolatione*," 229). Similarly in *Boece*, 4.pr.1.41–42, where Chaucer's "ryght ordene hous" (cf. Boethius's "dispositissima domo") echoes Jean de Meun's "la tres ordenee maison" (234).

tical quality of the concept as Pandarus expresses it, in comparison with its source in both *De consolatione* and the *Remede*, emphasizes a deeper insufficiency of the situation in Book 1 seen from a broader perspective, for Pandarus here encourages Troilus in his desire for that which Boethius would characterize as an example of false felicity, and Machaut as dishonorable.[31] In Book 3, in response to Pandarus's duplicitous rumor of Criseyde's infidelity, Chaucer has Criseyde quote *De consolatione*, 2.pr.4, regarding first (3.812–19) the anxiety produced by the insufficiency of earthly things (corresponding to 2.pr.4.75–80, 118–27), then (3.821–33) the sad condition of mankind who either does not know that earthly joy is changeable – and hence lives in ignorance – or *does* know it, which renders him perpetually fearful and unhappy (corresponding to 2.pr.4.150–55). What is missing from Criseyde's analysis here is that which forms the *center* of Boethius's argument, and which Machaut was able to redefine in a romantic context: the necessity of that possession and mastery of the self (2.pr.4.131–49) that places an individual serenely beyond the tribulations of mortal things and Fortune's power. Lacking this insight, Criseyde is enslaved to a joy she knows to be "brotel" and "fals"; and she allows herself to be convinced that not to succor Troilus immediately would prove a despicable lack of "bounte" and "gentilesse" (3.881–82). But without self-mastery, for all her pity and generosity of spirit, Criseyde remains unstable, because she is bound to "slydynge Fortune" (1.m.5.34):

> She sobre was, ek symple, and wys withal,
> The best ynorisshed ek that myghte be,
> And goodly of hire speche in general,
> Charitable, estatlich, lusty, fre;
> Ne nevere mo ne lakked hire pite;
> Tendre-herted, slydynge of corage. (5.820–25)

If I have succeeded up to this point in suggesting that the manuscript tradition gives no support for the theory that 1.890–96 was canceled by Chaucer, that the ideas in this stanza are important both to Chaucer's source and to that poem's source (itself a work of profound influence on the English poet), and that Chaucer appears to be working seriatim through Machaut's *Remede* in the construction of Pandarus's speech, I will also want to show that the repositioning of

[31] See *Remede*, lines 2003–11 (ed. Wimsatt and Kibler, 278–79): "Dont cilz qui vit de si douce pasture / Vie d'onnour puet bien et doit mener, / Car de tous biens a comble mesure, / Plus qu'autres cuers n'en saroit desirer; / Ne d'autre merci rouver / N'a desir, cuer, ne beance, / Pour ce qu'il a Souffissance; / Ne je ne sçay nommer cy / Nulle autre merci" (Therefore he who lives on such sweet nourishment / can easily and must live a life of honor, / for he has all blessings in abundance, / more than another heart would dare desire; / nor does he have the heart, desire, or longing / to implore any other reward, / because he has Sufficiency; / nor can I name here / any other reward to ask for).

these lines after what is now 1.897–903 makes good poetic and logical sense. I believe it does, and in a fashion that answers objections raised against the passage in its present position as either an interruption or interpolation. In 1.876–82 and 883–89, Pandarus, having extracted from Troilus the name of his beloved, discourses on Criseyde's virtues of character, conduct, and appearance. Among these attributes is her gracious temperament, which disposes her to virtuous action that will only increase her honor (1.885–88). Then, in the proposed repositioned stanza, Pandarus infers from what he has just asserted, that since the lady is virtuous in this fashion, she naturally can be expected to possess pity (1.898–900). But the honor that Pandarus has just said accrues to Criseyde's conduct must, he goes on to insist, be respected by Troilus once he receives the benefit of such pity (1.902). Indeed, the connection in thought between Criseyde's conduct and that of Troilus is made through the reiteration of a similar diction and figure:

> and al this bet to eche,
> In honour, to as fer as she may strecche,
> A kynges herte semeth by hyrs a wrecche. (1.887–89)
>
> Requere naught that is ayeyns hyre name;
> For vertu streccheth naught hymself to shame. (1.902–3)

The stanza that should then follow, 1.890–96, similarly develops that which has just preceded it; first, by drawing a conclusion from the inevitable existence of Criseyde's pity, "And forthi loke of good comfort thow be" (1.890), and second, by enlarging upon the topic of Troilus's conduct which was introduced in the last three lines of the previous stanza. Readers familiar with the Boethian context will certainly pause over Pandarus's conclusion (1.894–96), which suggests that the best love is in its effects divine, rather than dependent on fortune or chance, but in the stanza immediately following (1.904–10 in the traditional numbering) Pandarus employs the same notion of "grace" – and even the same rhyme of "grace" / "place" – to define the miraculous workings of Love on the undeserving Troilus.[32] The Boethian distinctions are being finessed, as the language of *De consolatione* is accommodated to the fragile idealism of *fin'amor*: in the space of but ten stanzas, as Chaucer leaves Machaut to reengage Boccaccio's poem, Pandarus will explicitly invoke the notion of a "celestial" love, but only to distinguish it from that more natural variety of which he feels his niece is capable. But having invoked the familiar courtly ideals of pity for virtuous service in love, Pandarus already sounds the religious overtones tongue-in-

[32] For the spiritual connotations of pity in an erotic context, see the valuable discussion of Douglas Gray, "Chaucer and 'Pite,'" in *J. R. R. Tolkien, Scholar and Storyteller*, ed. Mary Salu and Robert T. Farrell (Ithaca: Cornell Univ. Press, 1979), 173–203, esp. 173–76, 183–84.

cheek, as he details Troilus's past trangressions against "Seynt Idiot, lord of thise foles alle." Troilus eagerly repents. What Boethius would call the pursuit of false felicity gets underway.

What of Criseyde? It strikes me as significant that at a key moment in her important speech to Troilus (4.1528–96) in which she sufficiently persuades him that they should not flee Troy together before the appointed time of her return to her father, Chaucer constructs a close formal parallel with those stanzas in Book 1 which this essay argues to have been scribally misplaced. Compare the proposed repositioned lines 1.890–903, spoken by Pandarus –

And also thynk, and therwith glade the,
That sith thy lady vertuous is al,
So foloweth it that there is some pitee
Amonges all thise other in general;
And forthi se that thow, in special,
Requere naught that is ayeyns hyre name;
For vertu streccheth naught hymself to shame.

And forthi loke of good comfort thow be;
For certeinly, the ferste poynt is this
Of noble corage and wel ordeyné,
A man to have pees with hymself, ywis.
So oghtist thow, for noht but good it is
To love wel, and in a worthy place;
The oghte not to clepe it hap, but grace –

with Criseyde's remarks –

And also thynketh on myn honeste,
That floureth yet, how foule I sholde it shende,
And with what filth it spotted sholde be,
If in this forme I sholde with yow wende.
Ne though I lyved unto the werldes ende,
My name sholde I nevere ayeynward wynne;
Thus were I lost, and that were routhe and synne.

And forthi sle with resoun al this hete!
Men seyn, "The suffrant overcomith," parde;
Ek "Whoso wol han lief, he lief moot lete."
Thus maketh vertu of necessite
By pacience, and thynk that lord is he
Of Fortune ay that naught wole of hire recche,
And she ne daunteth no wight but a wrecche.

Once again Troilus seeks a boon from Criseyde, though now without the active aid and presence of Pandarus. In stanzas with beginnings remarkably similar to those of Book 1 ("And also thynk[eth]" ... "And forthi [imperative]"), Criseyde phrases her refusal of Troilus's request as an argument of her virtue, which, she contends, could not, and should not, grant what Troilus asks. In effect, something has been required of her "that is ayeyns hyre name," which, were she to grant it, would turn her virtue into shameful vice. Then in the following stanza, which draws, as did Pandarus earlier, on Lady Philosophy's words in *De consolatione* 2.pr.4, an appeal is made to Troilus's desired conduct, that equanimity of spirit founded on reason and control of the self, manifested in patience, that puts one beyond the power of Fortune. To Machaut such conduct is evidence of a deserving and virtuous lover. Here, sadly, such *souffissance* seems to be exhorted by one who, for whatever reasons, does not herself possess it, and as a result will soon come more to resemble Fortuna and the false world's *brotelnesse* than she does Philosophia.[33]

[33] Criseyde's personality traits, redefined in the social circumstances of her being a widow, is the subject of a provocative study by Carolyn Collette, "Criseyde's Honor: Interiority and Public Identity in Chaucer's Courtly Romance," in *Literary Aspects of Courtly Culture: Selected Papers from the Seventh Triennial Congress of the International Courtly Literature Society, University of Massachusetts, Amherst, USA, 27 July–1 August, 1992*, ed. Donald Maddox and Sara Sturm-Maddox (Cambridge: D. S. Brewer, 1994), 47–55. Collette concludes that "Criseyde's need for public identity, the female need for support and status dependent on men and their decisions, triumphs over her free choice to love Troilus."

“Queynte” Arguments: The Ellesmere Order May Be the Most “Satisfactory” But Is It Chaucer’s?

KATHLEEN FORNI, *Loyola College in Maryland*

> It is hard to think of any work ever written, important or unimportant, which was intended as a unit and in which there is anything like so chaotic a condition in the early authorities. This chaotic condition is the conspicuous feature of the MSS. to one familiar with them; it could hardly be worse.[1]

In *The Text of the Canterbury Tales* (1940), the first edition to offer a complete collation and description of fifty-seven manuscripts of the *Canterbury Tales*, John M. Manly and Edith Rickert provided a table exhibiting some twenty-seven different tale orders and concluded that “none of the extant MSS exhibits an arrangement which with any probability can be assigned to Chaucer.”[2] Half a century later several scholars have again concluded that none of the orders found in the extant manuscripts is authorial. For instance, Ralph Hanna asserts that “None of the tale orders we have received necessarily reflects Chaucer’s plan (if indeed he had one) but rather the difficulties of manuscript supervisors trying to make a text left manifestly incomplete at its author’s death look like a continuous whole,” and Charles Owen, retracting his two-way journey theory, has reached the same conclusion: “In this century of manuscript history no evidence connects any ordering of the fragments to Chaucer.”[3] Derek Pearsall goes as far as to suggest that the poem should be packaged as a “partly assembled kit with no directions,” reflecting the fragmented and unfinished condition of the poem:

[1] J. S. P. Tatlock, “The *Canterbury Tales* in 1400,” *PMLA* 50 (1935): 101.

[2] *The Text of the Canterbury Tales on the Basis of All Known Manuscripts*, ed. John M. Manly and Edith Rickert, 8 vols. (Chicago: Univ. of Chicago Press, 1940), 2.489. See also Norman Blake, *The Textual Tradition of the Canterbury Tales* (London: Edward Arnold, 1985), for the orders found in the manuscripts and early editions.

[3] Ralph Hanna III, “The Hengwrt Manuscript and the Canon of the *Canterbury Tales*,” in *English Manuscript Studies 1100–1700* 1 (1989): 79; Charles Owen, *The Manuscripts of the Canterbury Tales* (Cambridge: D. S. Brewer, 1991), 125.

> This is how it should, ideally, be presented, partly as a bound book (the first and last fragments are fixed) and partly as a set of fragments in a folder, with the fragmentary information as to their nature and placement fully displayed. This would not make studies of the structure or design of the Tales impossible or illicit; it would merely ensure that such studies were conducted in a proper context of understanding.[4]

And yet, curiously, many Chaucerians continue to base critical approaches to the *Canterbury Tales* on the assumption that the Ellesmere (El) order is authorial. For instance, most recently, in *An Ars Legendi for Chaucer's Canterbury Tales*, Dolores Frese advances "the claims of the Ellesmere manuscript as the poetic text reflecting Chaucer's final authorial intentions in the matter of narrative ordering for the *Tales*." She reads the *Canon Yeoman's Tale* as Chaucer's own metaphoric critique of Hengwrt's order:

> Presuming a literary-historical event – which Chaucer has conveyed under the trope of the "broken pot" whose contents are "scatered al the floor aboute" – we are furnished with an ingenious reference to the fractious act whereby various elements of a previously ordered literary exemplar could have become deranged; ... the broken "pot" may be interpreted as the breaking of the final looping stitch with which a bookbinder secured his ordered gatherings.[5]

Even more significantly, the editors of the Variorum Chaucer, despite their claim that no order is preferred, and their faith in the unique authority of Hengwrt, have adopted the El order. For instance, Donald Baker introduces the *Squire's Tale* with the Merchant's endlink, following the arrangement in El. In Hengwrt, the *Squire's Tale* follows the *Man of Law's Tale* without the endlink and the Merchant's endlink is used to connect the *Merchant's Tale* to the *Franklin's Tale*. Given this clear preference for the El order, Baker's claim that he is "fortunately not in the position of using one manuscript (Hg) as the base text and another (e.g., El) as the basis for order" is odd.[6]

Below I examine how the El order was canonized as Chaucerian. I argue that Robinson's edition, which effectively canonized this structure, was never intended as the verbal icon in which it is treated. Moreover, I show that despite several highly influential pleas for El's authority, there is no clear textual evidence for the assertion that this order reflects Chaucer's intention. The arguments put forth by Larry Benson, John Gardner, John Fisher, and E. Talbot

[4] Derek Pearsall, "Editing Medieval Texts: Some Developments and Some Problems," in *Textual Criticism and Literary Interpretation*, ed. Jerome McGann (Chicago: Univ. of Chicago Press, 1985), 97.

[5] Dolores Warwick Frese, *An Ars Legendi for Chaucer's Canterbury Tales* (Gainesville: Univ. of Florida Press, 1991), 222.

[6] *A Variorum Edition of the Works of Geoffrey Chaucer*, vol. 2.12, *The Canterbury Tales: The Squire's Tale*, ed. Donald C. Baker (Norman: Univ. of Oklahoma Press, 1990), 38.

Donaldson more than two decades ago have been more influential than warranted. These critics all finally assert that the El order embodies Chaucer's intention because it is the most "satisfactory" or "artistically coherent" structure.[7] Their conception of a "satisfactory" design, however, is clearly shaped by Kittredge's conceptualization of the work as a "Human Comedy." Kittredge's dramatic reading, especially his notion of the Marriage Group, has been so popular that is seems as though many of the arguments for the El order are more concerned with validating his interpretive frame rather than recovering an authorial text. Buttressed by Kittredge's approach, the El order does seem the most plausible design, and the most amenable to unitary studies and undergraduate instruction. But, of course, the real concern should be whether an order is authorial, not whether we like it.

There are many other orders represented in the manuscripts and the early editions, most of which disregard topographical consistency and internal allusions. These early witnesses are ignored because of the pervasive influence of Kittredge's reading, which is too often equated with Chaucer's intention. That scholars with Frese's energy and acumen continue to devote book-length studies to validate the arrangement of El suggests that this important manuscript has imposed an unwarranted tyranny on literary-critical thinking. I am not suggesting that the editorial grail of recovering Chaucer's intended order is misguided; but, given the hegemony one version has imposed on our conception of this poem, more attention should be paid to other versions of the text. Some orders are obviously more plausible than others; for instance, several scribal editors appear to have read the *Canterbury Tales* merely as a collection of stories, placing, for instance, the *Wife of Bath's Tale* after the *Clerk's Tale* and *Merchant's Tale*. The links suggest that, had he lived to finish the work, Chaucer would have provided the tales with a structure; however, because he did not live to finish the project, and no holograph exists, it is impossible to determine in what order Chaucer intended the series of fragments to be read. The different orders represented in the manuscripts and early editions offer an as yet unexamined resource for interpretive studies; but these historical constructions of the *Canterbury Tales* will remain neglected as long as authorial intention is the criterion for authenticity and aesthetic value.

[7] E. T. Donaldson, "The Ordering of the *Canterbury Tales*," in *Medieval Literature and Folklore Studies*, ed. Jerome Mandel and Bruce A. Rosenberg (New Brunswick: Rutgers Univ. Press, 1970), finally argues the El order is Chaucerian because it is "entirely satisfactory" (203); John Gardner, "The Case Against the 'Bradshaw Shift'; or, the Mystery of the Manuscript in the Trunk," *Papers on Literature and Language* 3 (1967), argues that "the Ellesmere order is probably Chaucer's" since it has an "artistic coherence" missing in other arrangements of the tales (106); and Larry D. Benson, "The Order of the *Canterbury Tales*," *Studies in the Age of Chaucer* 3 (1981), believes the order is Chaucer's because it has "considerable artistic merit; ... it is difficult to believe that anyone other than Chaucer could have made so satisfactory an arrangement" (111).

I

In 1775 Thomas Tyrwhitt was the first editor to analyze the proper order of the tales. He began with two premises: (1) the "the work was never finished by the author," and (2) no extant manuscript order is authoritative.[8] Elevating dramatic propriety to an editorial principle, Tyrwhitt relied on internal allusions as well as the evidence of what he considered to be the "best" manuscripts to arrange the tales. Previous editors – Speght (1598, 1602, 1687) and Urry (1721) – had followed Thynne's 1532 arrangement with the *Squire's Tale* following the *Man of Law's Tale*, and the *Merchant's Tale* preceding the *Wife of Bath's Tale*.[9] Tyrwhitt uses the Man of Law's Epilogue with the reading "Shipman" to connect the *Pardoner's Tale* and the *Shipman's Tale*, on the basis that the harsh tone of the passage is "highly improper in the mouth of the '*curteis Squier*,'" and uses what was the Merchant's Prologue in the early editions ("'In feith Squier, thow hast thee wel yquit / And gentilly. I preise wel thy wit,' / Quod the Marchant") to link the *Squire's Tale* to the *Franklin's Tale* because the speaker refers to his grown son, whereas the Merchant has just recently married.[10] Tyrwhitt also moves the *Merchant's Tale* after the *Wife of Bath's Tale* since the Merchant refers to her in his discussion of marriage. Although he did not have access to El, the order he derives is the same as that represented by Manly and Rickert's group *a*, except for his use of the Man of Law's Epilogue to introduce the *Squire's Tale*. He is the first modern editor to create what later became known as the "Marriage Group."

In trying to decide on an order for the Chaucer Society's *Six-Text*, Frederick Furnivall initially felt that Tyrwhitt "had hit on the right order of the Tales."[11] However, if Tyrwhitt did "use his head" in placing the *Wife of Bath's Tale* after the *Man of Law's Tale*, he "didn't use it enough" in neglecting to provide a "chat" to link the tales. Furnivall agreed with Tyrwhitt that the Man of Law's Epilogue suited the Shipman. Yet he believed that since the Epilogue was not in El, Chaucer had omitted it, recognizing "the rudeness shown in it towards the Parish Priest jarred with the respect and reverence that he had shown for the Parson in the Prologue."[12] Henry Bradshaw, however, suggested to Furnivall

[8] *The Canterbury Tales of Chaucer*, ed. Thomas Tyrwhitt, 5 vols. (London, 1721), 4.121.

[9] Thynne's 1532 arrangement: *KT MT RT CT MLT* (*ML* Epilogue reads "Squier") *SqT* (words of the Merchant to the Squire) *MeT WBPT FrT SuT ClT FkT SNT CYPT PhT PdT ShT PrT Thopas Mel MkT NPT MancT ParT* (Rt omitted). The Retraction does not reappear until Urry's 1721 edition. In Thynne's 1542 edition the spurious *Plowman's Tale* follows *ParT*. In the 1550 edition it precedes *ParT*. Urry also inserts *Gamelyn* after *CkT*.

[10] *The Canterbury Tales*, ed. Tyrwhitt, 4.173, 4.162–63.

[11] Frederick J. Furnivall, *A Temporary Preface to the Chaucer Society's Six-Text Edition of Chaucer's Canterbury Tales*, Chaucer Society Publications, ser. 2, pt. 3 (London: Trübner, 1868), 23.

[12] Furnivall, *A Temporary Preface*, 23.

that the Host's observation, "This was a thrifty tale for the nones" (B^1 1165), "inseparably linked" the passage to the Man of Law, who says in his Prologue, "I kan right now no thrifty tale seyn" (B^1 46). In addition, Bradshaw observed that if Fragment B^2 follows the *Man of Law's Tale*, another infelicity in El is ameliorated: the reference to Siddingborne in the Wife of Bath's Prologue correctly precedes the reference to Rochester in the Monk's Prologue. Furnivall adopted the "Bradshaw Shift" – using the Man of Law's Epilogue with the next speaker designated as the Shipman, followed by group B^2 – under the assumption that geographical realism superseded manuscript evidence. Furnivall's conclusion that a "subsequent reviser," rather than Chaucer, had deleted the Man of Law's Epilogue is the origin of the myth that El is an "edited" text, a myth that continues to inform editorial discussion.

Manly (1928) is the first modern editor to adopt the El order (he prints the Man of Law's Epilogue in an appendix). Instead of the letters adopted by Furnivall for his *Six-Text* and by Skeat in his Clarendon edition, he used Roman numerals to designate the individual "fragments."[13] For his 1933 edition F. N. Robinson follows Manly's precedent, making it clear, however, that his decision to follow the order in El is provisional and expedient:

> [Chaucer] not only failed to complete the tales, but he never made a final arrangement of what he had written, or worked out a consistent scheme for the pilgrimage. Under the circumstances an editor must now choose between keeping the arrangement of the best MSS., with all its imperfections, or making the unauthorized adjustment adopted in the Six-Text and several succeeding editions. The former is undoubtedly the sounder procedure.[14]

Robinson uses both letters and Roman numerals in order to acknowledge the classifications used by the Skeat and the Chaucer Society, and, paradoxically, to lessen the confusion "in departing from the system of groups used in references in the prolific Chaucer 'literature' of the past fifty years."[15] Robinson emphasized, however, that it is "not to be supposed ... that this order represents any final decision of the author .... Chaucer had obviously not arrived at any final arrangement."[16] It is noteworthy that his cautionary remarks are deleted from the third edition (*The Riverside Chaucer*). Although neither Tyrwhitt nor Robinson claimed this particular order was Chaucerian, this text has, in Pearsall's words, come to be thought of as "definitive and canonical":

[13] *The Canterbury Tales*, ed. John M. Manly (New York: Holt, 1928).

[14] *The Complete Works of Geoffrey Chaucer*, ed. F. N. Robinson (Boston: Houghton Mifflin, 1933), 889.

[15] *The Complete Works of Geoffrey Chaucer*, ed. Robinson , 889.

[16] *The Complete Works of Geoffrey Chaucer*, ed. Robinson , 696.

> Robinson's text of the *Canterbury Tales* came to be so widely accepted, and so universally employed for citation in scholarly and critical writing, that it got to be thought of as definitive and canonical – not as one among a number of possible editorial choices as to what Chaucer had written; Robinson's ordering of the *Tales*, that is, Ellesmere's ordering, likewise became thought of as what Chaucer had decided. In this way the *Canterbury Tales* became a Book, in the most portentous medieval sense of the word, which is very portentous indeed.[17]

II

Those who maintain the El order is Chaucer's must ascribe to two large assumptions not shared by Tyrwhitt, Furnivall, or Robinson: (1) that Chaucer was in the process of revision when he died, but that he had arranged the tales, and (2) that the sophistication of the arrangement is beyond the ability of any scribe. The issue of authorial revision remains problematic; however, in order to account for the disordered geographical references in El, and, more importantly, for the fact that the Man of Law's Epilogue is absent, advocates of the El order claim that Chaucer was in the course of a substantial revision when he died. For instance, Gardner asserts: "We know that Chaucer was the kind of poet who revised extensively. He made significant changes in the *Troilus*, transformed the original prologue to the *Legend of Good Women*."[18] Similarly, Fisher contends that in "Chaucer's last revision of the Canterbury collection ... dramatic interplay had emerged as a fundamental characteristic of the collection."[19]

Adopting the hypothetical reconstruction which was originally used to support the Bradshaw Shift, both Gardner and Fisher proposed that the Man of Law originally told *Melibee* (a tale in prose) and the Wife of Bath initially told the *Shipman's Tale* (which explains why he refers to himself as a woman). When Chaucer recreated the Wife of Bath and conceived the Marriage Group, he composed the tale of Constance for the Man of Law, and followed this tale of the woe that is in marriage with the *Shipman's Tale* (told by the Wife of Bath), introduced by the Man of Law's Epilogue, designating the speaker as the Wife of Bath. Later, he created the Wife of Bath's Prologue and *Tale*, which more pointedly address the issues of wifely obedience raised in the *Man of Law's Tale*, assigning the *Shipman's Tale* to the materialistic and amoral Shipman: "The result, in terms of the Tales' dramatic principle was this: the sharply contrasting positions of the Man of Law and Wife of Bath set off a debate and com-

[17] Derek Pearsall, "Authorial Revision in Some Late Medieval Texts," in *Crux and Controversy in Middle English Textual Criticism*, ed. A. J. Minnis and Charlotte Brewer (Cambridge: D. S. Brewer, 1992), 40–41.

[18] Gardner, "Case Against the 'Bradshaw Shift,'" 81.

[19] John H. Fisher, "Chaucer's Last Revision of the *Canterbury Tales*," *Modern Language Review* 67 (1972): 243.

promise .... In terms of geography the shift made for havoc, but not in terms of thematic and dramatic order."[20]

Both Gardner and Fisher argued that although Chaucer may have begun by ordering the tales according to geographical markers, the signs of revision, specifically the canceled Man of Law's link, show that he had devised a higher dramatic or thematic purpose:

> that Chaucer's plan may possibly have changed and developed as he worked on the *Canterbury Tales* makes it plausible that the illogical sequence of references to time and place may have resulted not from a scribe's confusion but from Chaucer's having himself shifted tales around for some purpose of his own, intending to correct the sequence of geographical allusions later.[21]

In other words, these critics maintain that Chaucer's creative process imitated twentieth-century hermeneutic approaches: the earlier, and more simplistic plan of ordering the tales according to itinerant realism occurred to Chaucer first; however, as his plan matured, he was moving toward a more sophisticated order, based on thematic contrast. The implication is that we have discovered Chaucer's creative process, but the fact that it imitates our own critical changes is suspect. Transmission variants – the presence or absence of the Man of Law's Epilogue – may indeed reflect authorial revision, but when transmission history becomes a neat allegory for authorial composition we must at least be aware of the possibility that we are substituting our own intentions for the author's.

Because both the El order and the Bradshaw Shift depend upon the Man of Law's Epilogue, this link has probably received more textual-critical scrutiny than any other passage in the *Canterbury Tales*. When the link appears, as it does in thirty-five manuscripts, it always, except in two witnesses, links the *Man of Law's Tale* to the *Squire's Tale*. Twenty-four manuscripts attribute the interruption to the Squire. Six manuscripts designate the speaker as the Summoner, but still follow with the *Squire's Tale*, except Harley 7334, which reads "Summoner" and follows with the *Wife of Bath's Tale*. Selden designates the speaker as the Shipman and follows the *Man of Law's Tale* with the *Shipman's Tale*. Hammond suggested long ago that since all of the variant readings begin with an "s," only an "s" might have been legible in the archetypal manuscript.[22] Therefore, Robert Pratt correctly observes: "No MS. reading – whether 'shipman' or 'squyer' or 'somnour' – is of any authority whatever except as a witness for the archetypal 's.'"[23]

[20] Gardner, "Case Against the 'Bradshaw Shift,'" 90.

[21] Gardner, "Case Against the 'Bradshaw Shift,'" 82.

[22] Eleanor Hammond, "On the Order of the *Canterbury Tales*: Caxton's Two Editions," *Modern Philology* 3 (1905–1906): 163–64.

[23] Robert A. Pratt, "The Order of the *Canterbury Tales*," *PMLA* 66 (1951): 1150.

Although the Man of Law's Epilogue is missing from what are considered the two most authoritative manuscripts – El and Hengwrt – it appears in brackets in *The Riverside Chaucer*, with the reading "Shipman," followed by the Prologue to the *Wife of Bath's Tale* and the tale itself. This peculiar combination, not found in any manuscript, reflects the assumption that Chaucer originally assigned the link to the Wife of Bath to introduce the *Shipman's Tale*, and perhaps represents a vestigial nod to the Bradshaw Shift. Some advocates of the El order argue that the link is "genuine but canceled," primarily on the basis of dramatic impropriety. For instance, Benson claims the speaker's promise to "waken al this compaignye" is "inappropriate in tone":

> It is one thing for a churlish character to object to a long and heavily learned discourse that has apparently put some of the company to sleep and quite another matter for such a character to object so boisterously to a pious tale of Christian suffering. The Man of Law's endlink is tactless as an epilogue to the tale of Custance and so, though it was allowed to stand temporarily in the early version, Chaucer finally canceled it. He was sometimes careless about small details, but his sense of tact was infallible.[24]

However, if the Man of Law's Epilogue is considered tactless as a response to the *Man of Law's Tale*, or inappropriate in the mouth of the Squire (to whom it was attributed in all the black-letter editions), it has come to be viewed as quite appropriate to the Wife of Bath. That is, it conforms to modern notions of Chaucer's aesthetics, particularly the association of sexuality and textuality: "The Wife's analogy between her 'joly body' and the *corpus* of her text invokes a powerful medieval connection between sexuality and reading."[25] Carolyn Dinshaw, although acknowledging in a note that "the ascription of speaker to these lines is uncertain," asserts that the Epilogue voices a kind of feminist manifesto: "The prospect of a suffocating sermon, especially after the *Man* of Law's Tale is too much for the Wife of Bath. Out of this company of 'good men' the voice of the woman bursts .... The Wife opposes her tale to the 'lerned men's' lore: it is her 'joly body' against their oppressive teaching and glossing."[26] But when dramatic propriety replaces textual evidence, almost any reading can be, and has been, argued.[27] Attributing this link to the Wife of Bath both extends the Marriage Group and supports twentieth-century feminist interpretations, but it should not be forgotten that this is a twentieth-century reconstruction.

[24] Benson, "Order," 100–101.

[25] Lee Patterson, "'For the Wyves love of Bathe': Feminine Rhetoric and Poetic Resolution in the *Roman de la Rose* and the *Canterbury Tales*," *Speculum* 58 (1983): 660.

[26] Carolyn Dinshaw, *Chaucer's Sexual Poetics* (Madison: Univ. of Wisconsin Press, 1989), 113.

[27] For instance, Aage Brusendorff, *The Chaucer Tradition* (London: Oxford Univ. Press, 1925), suggests Chaucer intended the link for the Squire's Yeoman (72–73).

The El order may indeed be the most coherent and sophisticated structure, the order most amenable to criticism. But is this order Chaucer's? Advocates of the Bradshaw Shift, while not beyond denigrating scribes, happily accepted El as the best scribal guess. Those scholars who maintain the El order is authorial, however, must assume that the sophistication of the order is beyond any scribe. Benson argues that the El order "represents Chaucer's own final arrangement" and that to attribute the order to an editor or scribe "requires a long series of strained assumptions, ... and in this matter, as in most, Occam's razor must be applied: ... the fewer assumptions necessary to account for the facts, the more probable the validity of the account":[28]

> It is difficult to believe that anyone but Chaucer could have made so satisfactory an arrangement .... If we assume that some one other than Chaucer invented the type *a* order, we must assume the existence of an unknown literary prodigy who has left no other traces of his genius. So improbable an assertion is not necessary; it is much more reasonable to assume that the Type *a* order was the work of the author of the *Canterbury Tales*.[29]

But the only necessary assumption, which is surely not "strained" or "improbable," is that a scribal editor was intelligent enough to derive a satisfactory tale order.

III

Since Benson's "The Order of *The Canterbury Tales*" remains one of the most influential and persuasive pleas for the authority of the El order, his argument deserves close attention. His conclusion, however, that the El arrangement is Chaucer's is based on several untenable assumptions. To support his belief that no scribe could invent this order, and that the Hengwrt scribe bungled his attempt to order the tales correctly, Benson has to argue for the unlikely *in vita* circulation of the *Canterbury Tales* as a whole, which no other scholar has accepted: "*The Canterbury Tales* must have been in circulation very early indeed, perhaps even in Chaucer's own lifetime .... It seems to me most probable that *The Canterbury Tales* were in circulation before 1400, but that remains a probability rather than a certainty."[30] Secondly, Benson maintains that the explicit at the end of El, which states that the work was "compiled" by Chaucer, is evidence that the poet arranged El himself: "Here we have the direct testimony of one of the earliest scribes of the tales, if not the earliest, that Chaucer was not only the 'maker' of the book but the one who 'compiled' it, who gave it its *ordi-*

[28] Benson, "Order," 79–80.
[29] Benson, "Order," 111–12.
[30] Benson, "Order," 109–10.

natio."[31] A. J. Minnis does distinguish a compiler from an *auctor* as someone who writes and gathers together the materials of others, adding "no opinions of his own."[32] Similarly, M. B. Parkes states, "The compiler adds no matter of his own by way of exposition (unlike the commentator) but compared with the scribe he is free to rearrange (*mutando*). What he imposed was a new ordinatio on the materials he extracted from others."[33] Yet both Minnis and Parkes clearly specify that El's colophon does not necessarily mean that Chaucer arranged the tales in a certain order, but that he organized the material in relation to tales and tellers; that is, he organized the "diverse *materiae* by distributing them amongst fictional characters":[34]

> The *Canterbury Tales* is divided according to pilgrims rather than into books and chapters, yet the attitude of the compiler seems to lie behind Chaucer's words in the General Prologue:
>
> Thogh that I pleynly speke in this mateere,
> To telle yow hir wordes and hir cheere,
> Ne thogh I speke hir wordes proprely.
> For this ye knowen al so wel as I,
> Whoso shal telle a tale after a man,
> He moot reherce as ny as evere he kan
> Everich a word, if it be in his charge,
> Al speke he never so rudeliche and large,
> Or ellis he moot telle his tale untrewe
> Or feyne thyng, or fynde wordes newe.[35]

Therefore, the scribal notation indicating that the tales were "compiled" by Chaucer does indicate that he distributed the tales among tellers; it does not mandate, however, that he is responsible for the arrangement in a particular manuscript.

Finally, Benson's argument that the El order is Chaucerian is based on his assumption that Chaucer had completed the poem when he died: "unfinished, unrevised, and imperfect as *The Canterbury Tales* may be, Chaucer was finished with it."[36] For Benson, the Retraction represents "Chaucer's word he was finished with the work":

[31] Benson, "Order," 112.

[32] A. J. Minnis, *Medieval Theory of Authorship* (London: Scolar Press, 1984), 94.

[33] M. B. Parkes, "The Influence on the Concepts of Ordinatio and Compilatio on the Development of the Book," in his *Scribes, Scripts and Readers: Studies in the Communication, Presentation, and Dissemination of Medieval Texts* (London: Hambledon Press, 1991), 59.

[34] Minnis, *Medieval Theory of Authorship*, 202.

[35] Parkes, "Influence," 61–62.

[36] Benson, "Order," 81.

> We have Chaucer's own word, in the *Retraction*, that, unfinished as *The Canterbury Tales* obviously is, he was finished with it. We have, in short, not a work in progress to which Chaucer intended to return and would have, had not death or illness prevented this, but rather Chaucer's final version, as it was when he decided his work on it was ended.[37]

Norman Blake contends, however, that it is questionable whether the Retraction was the last thing Chaucer wrote, or that it necessarily signifies that Chaucer was finished with the poem: "Although the author retracts his secular works, it need not imply that he was going to write nothing else; ... the poem was not written in the order in which it is now usually read, and if genuine [the Retraction] might well have been written before some of the tales which are included in the *Canterbury Tales*."[38] Furthermore, although Benson maintains that the Retraction proves that Chaucer had arrived at a final order, he also argues that there are two different orders that can be assigned to Chaucer, both containing the Retraction: "The mss show that from the very beginning the work circulated in but two orders, both of which can be attributed to Chaucer; one may be an early version, in which case the Type *a*-Ellesmere order is the final arrangement."[39] Thus, Benson himself concedes that composing the Retraction did not inhibit Chaucer from rearranging the tales.

Advocates of the El order are forced into putting too much weight on questionable premises because they begin with unarticulated assumptions about Chaucer's aesthetics, then attempt to manipulate manuscript evidence and historical events so that they will fit these preconceptions. One way out of this impasse may be to make the distinction between the editorial and the critical edition. G. Thomas Tanselle suggests that for some texts, such as an uncompleted manuscript, unprepared by the author for publication, "there is literally no final intention, either because the author never prepared his manuscript for publication or because he wavered in his revisions." He suggests that in such cases "two kinds of edition, rather than a single one, may be desirable: a complete transcription, faithful to the demands of the document, and a reading text (or more than one), faithful to the demands of the work of art."[40] If a critic chooses to work within an aesthetic framework, studying perhaps themes in the *Canterbury Tales*, the order of the tales is irrelevant and a standard critical edition suffices. Critics who choose to study the poem based on its structure, however, should acknowledge that the manuscripts are historically mediated texts, and that El, coherent and aesthetically pleasing as it may be, is probably a scribal

[37] Benson, "Order," 80.

[38] Norman Blake, "On Editing the *Canterbury Tales*," in *Medieval Studies for J. A. W. Bennett*, ed. Peter L. Hayworth (Oxford: Clarendon Press, 1981), 188.

[39] Benson, "Order," 117.

[40] G. Thomas Tanselle, "The Editorial Problem of Final Authorial Intention," in his *Textual Criticism and Scholarly Editing* (Charlottesville: Univ. Press of Virginia, 1990), 67.

arrangement. At the very least it should be acknowledged that *The Riverside Chaucer*, following the order in El, but including the Man of Law's Epilogue, is an editorial reconstruction, a version of the poem that before 1933 did not exist. Whether Chaucer intended this version cannot be determined on any historical, textual-critical, or aesthetic grounds. Since Chaucer's text survives only in manuscript versions, these orders ought to be studied as products of specific material cultures, just as in a few years the *Riverside* itself may be seen as a product of twentieth-century hermeneutics. Perhaps, with the increased availability of these manuscripts on CD-ROM made possible by *The Canterbury Tales Project*, discussions of tale order may switch attention from the paradigm of an authorial, transcendent verbal icon to the orders known to be authorial – even if that author is not Chaucer.

Controversy and Criticism: Lydgate's *Thebes* and the Prologue to *Beryn*

JOHN M. BOWERS, *University of Nevada – Las Vegas*

Recently I received a letter informing me that my 1985 article "Alternative Ideas of *The Canterbury Tales*" had been chosen for reprint in a collection of essays on the Chaucerian tradition in the fifteenth century.[1] Curious to see exactly what I had committed to print over a dozen years ago, I took down from the shelf volume 7 of *Studies in the Age of Chaucer* and began reading: "It is safe to say that few people have read John Lydgate's *Siege of Thebes* or the anonymous *Tale of Beryn* ...." Only halfway through the first sentence, I realized that even the opening statement had been rendered inaccurate by the course of Middle English studies since the early 1980s. Long considered one of the most barren stretches of literary history, the fifteenth century has become one of the richest and most fertile fields for critical discussion. Distinguished medievalists such as Lee Patterson, Derek Pearsall, Tony Spearing, Seth Lerer, David Aers, Larry Scanlon, Gail Gibson, James Simpson and Paul Strohm have pursued a variety of theoretical initiatives to awaken interest in long-neglected and often disdained figures such as Thomas Hoccleve, Margery Kempe and John Lydgate.[2] The time seemed propitious, then, for taking a new critical look at Lydgate's *Thebes*

[1] John M. Bowers, "*The Tale of Beryn* and *The Siege of Thebes*: Alternative Ideas of *The Canterbury Tales*," *Studies in the Age of Chaucer* 7 (1985): 38–50; reprinted in *Writing After Chaucer: Essential Readings on Chaucer and the Fifteenth Century*, ed. Daniel Pinti (New York: Garland, 1997), 201–26.

[2] Exemplary publications not cited in later notes include A. C. Spearing, *Medieval to Renaissance in English Poetry* (Cambridge: Cambridge Univ. Press, 1985); David Aers, *Community, Gender, and Individual Identity: English Writing, 1360–1430* (London: Routledge, 1988); Gail McMurray Gibson, *The Theater of Devotion: East Anglian Drama and Society in the Late Middle Ages* (Chicago: Univ. of Chicago Press, 1989); *The Long Fifteenth Century: Essays for Douglas Gray*, ed. Helen Cooper and Sally Mapstone (Oxford: Clarendon Press, 1997); and *Rewriting Chaucer: Culture, Authority and the Idea of the Authentic Text, 1400–1602*, ed. Thomas A. Prendergast and Barbara Kline (Columbus: Ohio State Univ. Press, 1998).

and the Prologue to *Beryn* (hereafter *The Canterbury Interlude*[3]) within historical contexts more fully responsive to the discursive controversies that helped to bring these texts into being as agents of ideological commitment.

Recognizing the ineluctable contingency of texts and their openness to a multitude of material processes, Paul Strohm has identified signal instances in which brilliant acts of creation such as Chaucer's – even when not deliberately poised for appropriation – could become "subject to revision and eventual effacement through the operations of political agency beyond textual control."[4] It is true enough that many of the earliest editorial efforts involving Chaucer's unfinished *Canterbury Tales* were aimed merely at producing "books" as material objects for commercial copying and for presentation to aristocratic patrons.[5] Yet these practical concerns for material appearance and marketability cannot be isolated as the sole motivations for all of the attempts at continuation. The ill-defined discursiveness of Chaucer's frame-narrative invited the imposition of a variety of interpretations, most notably the two major efforts at supplementation around 1420 – Lydgate's Prologue to *Thebes* and the *Canterbury Interlude* – in which the pilgrims are imagined completing their visit to Canterbury before setting off again toward London, continuing the tale-telling enterprise during the homeward phase of the journey.

Both of these later efforts to write what Chaucer had left unwritten become legible as interventions of a critical nature. And both can be read in terms of "strategies of containment"[6] designed to impose ideological views on specific topics that had generated intense controversy in the opening decades of the fifteenth century. By situating these two poetic projects in their precise historical environments, I hope to show how the energies of cultural contestation steadily informed their discursive contents and rhetorical means. Each in turn stages its own critical initiative at determining, in a more narrowly stipulative manner, the meaning of the *Canterbury Tales* as the foundational classic of a newly formed

[3] This is the title I devised for my edition of the Prologue to *Beryn* in *The Canterbury Tales: Fifteenth-Century Continuations and Additions* (Kalamazoo: Medieval Institute Publications, 1992). In addition to denoting the Canterbury location of the action, the title better acknowledges the ludic quality of the continuation and its central positioning within the Northumberland manuscript where the unique copy of the work survives. I cite my own edition of the *Interlude* and Lydgate's Prologue to *Thebes* throughout the following pages.

[4] Paul Strohm, *Hochon's Arrow: The Social Imagination of Fourteenth-Century Texts* (Princeton: Princeton Univ. Press, 1992), 7.

[5] These were moves already sanctioned in the fifteenth century by a nascent "literate ideology" that suppressed Chaucer's staged spontaneity of oral improvisation. On the impact of a literate ideology on modern editorial practices, see Kathleen O'Brien O'Keeffe, "Texts and Works: Some Historical Questions on the Editing of Old English Verse," in *New Historical Literary Study*, ed. Jeffrey N. Cox and Larry J. Reynolds (Princeton: Princeton Univ. Press, 1993), 54–68.

[6] This phrase comes from Fredric Jameson, *The Political Unconscious: Narrative as a Socially Symbolic Act* (Ithaca: Cornell Univ. Press, 1981), 10.

vernacular tradition and the political identity of Chaucer as the author whose work had been singled out for this textual business.

Lydgate's Prologue to the Siege of Thebes

John Lydgate's *Siege of Thebes* was written midway in his long career, begun sometime after the Treaty of Troyes in May 1420 and completed probably around the time of Henry V's death in August 1422.[7] The relationship between the *Siege* and the king who served as Lydgate's patron has been brilliantly explored by Lee Patterson,[8] and it is my contention that the Prologue, despite its low-style tone and humor, was composed with Henry V even more specifically in mind as its primary audience.[9] Lydgate's continuation draws attention to the radically incomplete state of the pilgrimage-narrative in the very act of literalizing and continuing it. It extends the frame by imagining that Chaucer's original pilgrims had actually arrived at Canterbury, where the monastic poet is drawn into their company by the Host. The continuation is, however, overall a great disappointment. The visit to the shrine in the cathedral is presumed already to have been accomplished, and the original pilgrims are never described as actual presences, only as a jumbled group of characters remembered and sometimes misremembered by the later continuator.[10] After a section praising

[7] *Fifteenth-Century Continuations and Additions*, ed. Bowers, 11–22; see also Walter F. Schirmer, *John Lydgate: A Study in the Culture of the XVth Century*, trans. Ann E. Keep (London: Methuen, 1961), 59–65, and Derek Pearsall, *John Lydgate* (Charlottesville: University Press of Virginia, 1970), 151–59.

[8] Lee Patterson, "Making Identities in Fifteenth-Century England: Henry V and John Lydgate," in *New Historical Literary Studies*, ed. Cox and Reynolds, 69–107, believes *Thebes* was completed before the Henry V's death (74). John M. Ganim, "Mannerism and Moralism in Lydgate's *Siege of Thebes*," in his *Style and Consciousness in Middle English Narrative* (Princeton: Princeton Univ. Press, 1983), 103–22, interprets the monumental style as an attempt to bridge the gap between the cloister and the court. Rosamund S. Allen, "*The Siege of Thebes*: Lydgate's Canterbury Tale," in *Chaucer and Fifteenth-Century Poetry*, ed. Julia Boffey and Janet Cowen, Medieval Studies, 5 (London: King's College, 1991), 122–42, expands the notion of the courtly audience to include "dowager queens, princesses and royal nannies as well" (129).

[9] Derek Pearsall, *John Lydgate (1371–1449): A Bio-bibliography*, English Literary Studies, 71 (Victoria: Univ. of Victoria Press, 1997), 18–23, emphasizes the monk's prized role as "Poet to Henry V, 1413–22." Lydgate's failure to address the poem to Henry V, or to any other aristocratic benefactor, strongly suggests that the poet had lost his royal patron just when completing the work. James Simpson, "'Dysemol Daies and Fatal Houres': Lydgate's *Destruction of Thebes* and Chaucer's *Knight's Tale*," in *The Long Fifteenth Century*, ed. Cooper and Mapstone, 15–16, believes that *Thebes* itself was completed after Henry V's death, when its narrative assumed more pressing significance as Gloucester and Bedford began reenacting the fraternal strife of Ethyocles and Polymyte.

[10] John M. Bowers, "The House of Chaucer & Son: The Business of Lancastrian Canon-Formation," *Medieval Perspectives* 6 (1991): 135–43, suggests that Lydgate did not own a personal copy of Chaucer's poem but had occasional access to it, through his connection with Thomas Chaucer, in the Westminster tenement where the poet's papers remained after his death.

the original poet, Lydgate displaces not only Chaucer but all other pilgrims as well, installing himself as the exclusive focus of the Prologue in a face-off with the Host, whose voice excludes all others, even to a large extent Lydgate's own.[11] The real point of the Prologue becomes a justification, placed in the mouth of this secular authority-figure, of what could easily be construed as the Benedictine monk's irregular lifestyle.

It has long been recognized that Lydgate's self-portrait draws upon the topics and even the precise phrases used by Chaucer to describe his Monk and, more to the point, that this rewriting of the monastic figure largely refutes the accusations of corruption and excess that had formed the basis of Chaucer's caricature.[12] What has seldom been factored into critical assessments, however, is the urgent topicality of these complaints against the monasteries for Lydgate and his confreres. In March 1421 – at precisely the time when Lydgate was working on his *Siege* – Henry V took a sudden interest in the alleged laxity of the Benedictine foundations in England.[13] His first response was to send a letter to the abbot of Bury St. Edmunds, Lydgate's monastery, asking him to convene a General Chapter of the order in Westminster at the beginning of May. The king's representatives formulated his complaints in thirteen articles. These were then referred to monastic committees which answered the charges in two separate responses, one coauthored by William Courtney, the future abbot of Bury St. Edmunds. Henry V then left England for France in June 1421, and by the time the Benedictine commission had completed its final report in July 1423, their royal critic was dead and the government of his infant heir Henry VI had far more pressing affairs to which to attend.[14]

This would account for Lydgate's early knowledge of the work, but his uneven and faltering recollection of particulars. This suggestion was taken up by Derek Pearsall, *The Life of Geoffrey Chaucer* (Oxford: Blackwell, 1992), 280–82.

[11] Paul Strohm, "Fourteenth- and Fifteenth-Century Writers as Readers of Chaucer," in *Genres, Themes, and Images in English Literature from the Fourteenth to the Fifteenth Century*, ed. Piero Boitani and Anna Torti (Tübingen: Gunter Narr Verlag, 1988), 90–104, notes that all later Chaucerian imitators had lost the multiplicity of voices.

[12] D. W. Robertson, Jr., *A Preface to Chaucer* (Princeton: Princeton Univ. Press, 1962), 253–56, made the case that Chaucer's portrait of the Monk was bitterly satirical rather than mildly humorous. See also Kumiko Shikii, "Chaucer's Anti-Clericalism as Seen in the Monk," *The Fleur-de-Lis Review* (25 December 1980): 25–54; John V. Fleming, "Daun Piers and Dom Pier: Waterless Fish and Unholy Hunters," *Chaucer Review* 15 (1981): 287–94; and Patterson, "Making Identities," 100n29.

[13] Reasons for the king's sudden interest in reform are suggested by Patterson, "Making Identities," 93–95. Thomas Walsingham, *Historia Anglicana*, ed. Henry Thomas Riley, 2 vols. (London: Longman, Green, 1863–64), 2.337, put the blame on slanders by certain "false brothers."

[14] All of the relevant materials are assembled in *Documents Illustrating the Activities of the General and Provincial Chapters of the English Black Monks, 1215–1540*, ed. William Abel Pantin, Camden 3d ser., 47 (London: Camden Society, 1933), 2.98–134.

But Lydgate's poetic response was composed amid the heat of this controversy. The opening lines of the *Thebes* Prologue refer to a rare astronomical conjunction that establishes the fictional date as 27 April 1421, just a month after Henry V's letter pressing for the monastic convention at Westminster.[15] The poet's tactics are different from the Benedictine committees, which tended to defend current practices by citing revision of canonist authorities and deferring to the rights of the abbots to set standards within their separate houses. Lydgate seems to side with the king's sentiments, representing in his own textual self-figuration an exemplar adhering to the ancient ideals and practices of St. Benedict's *Rule*. Any apparent irregularities in his livelihood are explicable in terms of exemptions and dispensations carefully spelled out in this authoritative text. These were the very same appeals to original standards which Henry V himself extolled as the pristine religion of the monks (*de pristina religione monachorum*) while condemning the negligence and impiety of modern monks (*modernorum negligentiis et indevotione*) when he attended in person the Westminster convocation in May 1421.[16]

Chaucer had cannily anticipated these criticisms. Because the *Canterbury Tales* quickly became a staple of the literary culture created by the Lancastrian regime, it is even conceivable that his satiric caricature of the Monk contributed to Henry V's sudden concern for laxity among the Benedictines. Chaucer's Monk was described as an outrider who took inordinate pleasure in hunting. Harry Bailey also suggested he possessed a robust masculinity that appealed to the married women with whom he had contact (*General Prologue*, 167; Prologue to the *Monk's Tale*, 1945–61).[17] The eleventh article of the king's criticisms in 1421 targeted these specific abuses, condemning monks who left their cloister to seek outside amusements of exactly the sorts lampooned by Chaucer (*GP*, 190–92).[18] Lydgate counters these charges by depicting himself as a pious pilgrim who has traveled to Canterbury with the utmost humility:[19]

[15] Johnstone Parr, "Astronomical Dating for Some of Lydgate's Poems," *PMLA* 67 (1952): 251–58.

[16] This is the report of Walsingham, *Historia*, 2.337–38. Christopher Allmand, *Henry V* (Berkeley and Los Angeles: Univ. of California Press, 1992), 278, summarizes the proceedings: "it was an appeal for a stricter observance of existing rules, not a call for real change or reform."

[17] All quotations of Chaucer's works come from *The Riverside Chaucer*, ed. Larry D. Benson, 3d ed. (Boston: Houghton Mifflin, 1987).

[18] *Documents*, ed. Pantin, 115: "quod suis prelatis penitus facultas ipsos licenciandi ad comedendum, potandum seu loquendum in ipsis locis preterquam cum multis nobilibus interdicatur, cum ex hoc gravia oriri poterunt scandala et incentiva viciorum." Pearsall, *John Lydgate (1371–1449): A Bio-bibliography*, 21–22, questions the long-standing belief that Lydgate's commissions, payments and social contacts meant that he spent considerable time outside the cloister.

[19] Barbara Harvey, *Living and Dying in England, 1100–1540: The Monastic Experience* (Oxford: Clarendon Press, 1993), 80–82, observes that well-off monks quite commonly made pilgrimages to sites such as Canterbury; for a sick monk, as Lydgate describes himself here, the

That me byfil to entren into toun,
The holy seynt pleynly to visite
Aftere siknesse, my vowes to aquyte,
In a cope of blak and not of grene,
On a palfrey slender, long and lene,
With rusty brydel mad nat for the sale,
My man toforn with a voide male .... (70–76)

These lines work hard at the business of repairing Lydgate's personal reputation as a monk. Whereas the fifth article repeated Chaucer's charge that Benedictines had begun wearing elaborate habits made from expensive dyed cloth (*GP*, 193–97),[20] Lydgate describes himself wearing the standard black habit, and his "wonder thred-bare hood" (90) was much inferior to what a monk was directed to wear while journeying beyond the cloister.[21] Furthermore, Lydgate's skinny nag is no match for the stable of fine thoroughbreds provided for Chaucer's Monk (*GP*, 168). The second article criticized decorations on monastic horses, especially gilt bosses and elaborate bridles like the Monk's that jingles as loud as a chapel bell (*GP*, 169–71).[22] These complaints are answered by Lydgate's description of his "rusty brydel" and later by the Host's observation that the monk's "bridel have neither boos ne belle" (85).

Living like gentry, fifteenth-century Benedictines who belonged to wealthy foundations like Bury St. Edmunds enjoyed a full staff of servants, whose extravagant liveries figured in article two's complaints.[23] Yet Lydgate describes himself traveling with only a single manservant, who is not described as wearing any livery at all and who carries in his lap an empty purse. This is ironic, because a private servant of this sort needed to be paid from the monk's own per-

"therapeutic value of the holiday, however, was not in doubt" (99).

[20] John V. Fleming, "Gospel Asceticism: Some Chaucerian Images of Perfection," in *Chaucer and Scriptural Tradition*, ed. David Lyle Jeffrey (Ottawa: Univ. of Ottawa Press, 1984), 183–95, and Laura F. Hodges, "A Reconsideration of the Monk's Costume," *Chaucer Review* 26 (1991): 133–46, contribute to the scriptural and social contexts for this satire.

[21] *St. Benedict's Rule for Monasteries*, trans. Leonard J. Doyle (Collegeville, Minn.: Liturgical Press, 1948), 76 (chap. 55): "Those who are sent on a journey . . . let their cowls and tunics be somewhat better than what they usually wear."

[22] *Documents*, ed. Pantin, 111: "Item moderetur sumptuosa et nimium ipsorum equitatura scandalosa, tam in vario et irregulari apparatu famulorum, quam in phaleratura equorum; et quod qui maiores sunt inter eos, ultra viginti equos, computatis summariis, et cum frenis deauratis, sub pena gravi temporali camere apostolice applicanda, equitare non presumant."

[23] *Documents*, ed. Pantin, 111. Though Cardinal Gasquet had reckoned ten servants for every monk, Harvey, *Living and Dying*, 146–78, has reduced that ratio to two-to-one at Westminster Abbey (164). Pearsall, *John Lydgate (1371–1449): A Bio-bibliography*, 12, reckons that in 1400 Bury St. Edmunds had 60 to 80 monks with as many as 200 servants of every variety. Harvey notes that personal servants were paid by the individual monk (150–52), and the powerful status of the monastery was proclaimed by the fine liveries provided to its dependents (168–69).

sonal funds. Though easily taken as a plea for more generous patronage, the reference to an empty purse seems meant instead to reply to article four's restrictions on monks having any personal money of their own.[24] And when the Host observes, "To ben a monk, sclender is youre koyse!" (102), the poet refutes the popular belief, expressed in article seven, that monks ignored the obligation for fasting and instead overindulged in all manner of luxury foods, like the Monk's roasted swan (*GP*, 206). Consequently real-life monks were, as Barbara Harvey has concluded, "surely on average rather obese."[25] By contrast, the Host's recommendation for Lydgate to dine on pudding and haggis, followed by an omelette or a pancake, lay well within the approved menu of minced meats and dairy products.[26]

Lydgate's Prologue continues this line of response, shifting the responsibility for any irregularities to the Host's overbearing instructions rather than the monk's self-indulgence. Since he has been sick, Lydgate is told to neglect his Divine Office by not rising at midnight and to improve his rest by sleeping with a pillow and wrapping his head in turbanlike scarves (109–21). These comforts violated the guidelines for proper monastic bedclothes spelled out by the *Rule* as affirmed by Henry V's thirteenth article.[27] Moreover, article nine forbade monks from keeping personal books in their custody, such as the collection of a hundred tragedies that Chaucer's Monk is said to have in his cell (Prologue to the *Monk's Tale*, 1971–72). Because a good monk could have only scriptural writings borrowed from the library by giving a document of indenture to the prior,[28] Lydgate is described as reading piously from a "portoos" or portable breviary (162) in accordance with the requirement of the *Rule* (50) that monks on a journey must not neglect their service.

When instructed by the Host to tell a merry tale, Lydgate offers the 4540-line epic chronicling the disastrous careers of a series of Theban rulers from Oedipus through Creon, ending with events that dovetail with the beginning of Chaucer's *Knight's Tale* and closing the circle of the *Canterbury Tales* by ending where it

[24] *Documents*, ed. Pantin, 111.

[25] Harvey, *Living and Dying*, 71. Her principal site of study is Westminster Abbey; since Chaucer's Monk offers to tell "the lyf of Seint Edward" (Prologue to the *Monk's Tale*, 1970) and St. Edward the Confessor was founder of Westminster, this was probably his monastery, too. For a contrary suggestion, see Glending Olson, "Chaucer's Monk: The Rochester Connection," *Chaucer Review* 21 (1986): 246–56.

[26] Harvey, *Living and Dying*, 51–56 and 61–62. The *Rule*, 55 (chap. 36), permitted meat to the sick even during seasons of fasting.

[27] *Rule*, 42–43 (chap. 22), and *Documents*, ed. Pantin, 115. Harvey, *Living and Dying*, 131, mentions the wearing of special nightclothes at Westminster.

[28] *Documents*, ed. Pantin, 114: "Nullusque monachus retineat in sua custodia ... libros sine brevi et scriptura indentata, cuius una pars remaneat in manibus sui prelati." This article makes more detailed the prohibition of the *Rule*, 51 (chap. 33).

had begun with the war between Athens and Thebes.[29] Whereas Chaucer's Monk had been interrupted by the Knight, who wanted to hear no more tragic tales, the Monk of Bury returns to this forbidden subject by offering a tragic "prequel" to the Knight's own tale. By renewing this monastic claim that chivalric ambitions were inherently and inevitably liable to reversals of Fortune, Lydgate offers a pointed riposte to the Knight as an embodiment of aristocratic values and practices, which had come to include aggressive criticism of monastic values and practices after the lead taken by Henry V. Because this hefty literary effort can be estimated as part of Lydgate's continuing counsel to royalty, the reclamation of his standing as a pious monk was essential to validating his role as adviser to a king who had turned suddenly critical of the Benedictines generally.[30]

It is in terms of these persistent exculpations of personal conduct that I want to speculate about Lydgate's circumstances for poetic occupation, circumstances that themselves may have fallen within the purview of the king's 1421 criticisms. Article ten stated that no monk should have a private room or cell separate from the communal dormitory. Yet monastic officials such as the cellarer and sexton, administrative offices of the kind that Harry Bailey assumes the Monk fills (Prologue to the *Monk's Tale*, 1935–38), did invariably occupy private apartments, as did other distinguished monks – monks clearly less distinguished than John Lydgate.[31] It is impossible to imagine him producing such a massive amount of verse, reckoned to total nearly 140,000 lines, if this writer who enjoyed such successful relations with the royal court were obliged to participate fully in the communal life of the monastery. This regular lifestyle would have included repeated interruptions for long liturgical services, day and night, shoulder to shoulder with the lowly "novys" and "povre cloysterer" mentioned so disparagingly by Harry Bailey (Prologue to the *Monk's Tale*, 1939).

Article ten made one important exception to this prohibition against private quarters, as well as allowing dispensation from dietary restrictions and from the regular round of offices, by repeating the *Rule*'s provision for monks who were infirm, whether by illness or old age or both.[32] This is where I suspect Lydgate

[29] A. C. Spearing, "Lydgate's Canterbury Tale: *The Siege of Thebes* and Fifteenth-Century Chaucerianism," in *Fifteenth-Century Studies*, ed. Robert F. Yeager (Hamden, Conn.: Archon, 1984), 333–64; Bowers, "Alternative Ideas of *The Canterbury Tales*," 38–49; and Simpson, "Lydgate's *Destruction of Thebes* and Chaucer's *Knight's Tale*," 21–33.

[30] Patterson, "Making Identities," 73–77 and 93–97; Seth Lerer, *Chaucer and His Readers* (Princeton: Princeton Univ. Press, 1993), 22–56; Larry Scanlon, *Narrative, Authority, and Power: The Medieval Exemplum and the Chaucerian Tradition* (Cambridge: Cambridge Univ. Press, 1994), 332–50; and Judith Ferster, *Fictions of Advice: The Literature and Politics of Counsel in Late Medieval England* (Philadelphia: Univ. of Pennsylvania Press, 1996).

[31] *Documents*, ed. Pantin, 114. Harvey, *Living and Dying*, 77, notes that private apartments had become the norm for monastic officials and other prominent brothers.

[32] *Rule*, 54–55 (chaps. 36-37), and *Documents*, ed. Pantin, 114.

exploited a major loophole, seizing upon Chaucer's original rationale for the Canterbury journey to give thanks to the saint who had aided the pilgrims "whan that they were seeke" (*GP*, 18). Lydgate too claims that he traveled to Canterbury "aftere siknesse" in fulfillment of a vow to the saint. What is more, the monastic poet goes out of his way to disclose his advancing age when he gives his name: "I answerde my name was Lydgate / Monk of Bery, nygh fyfty yere of age" (92–93).[33] Thereafter his status as an aging invalid becomes almost an obsession with the Host, who uses the monk's lingering ill health as the pretext for relaxing all manner of religious strictures during his overnight stay in Canterbury. Focusing his concern on the intestinal ailment "collis passioun,"[34] the Host observes that Lydgate is so thin and pale that he must eat heartily and spice up his meal with medicinal herbs such as fennel, anise, cumin and coriander. He must also bundle up warmly in bed and refrain from rising at midnight (113–20). And it is the Host who stresses the hygienic value of their merry society: "A company, parde, shal do you good!" (125).

I suspect the poet uses the Host as a voice of secular opinion to ventriloquize permission for actions already taken, exemptions already exploited, and dispensations already transformed by Lydgate into a lifestyle of mobility, personal comfort and social-climbing ambition. The erasure of controversy becomes part of what Patterson describes as "a process of making identical ... overcoming division, correcting waywardness and suppressing dissent"[35] in the sense that the Host's prescriptions coincide exactly with Lydgate's own preferences without the slightest hint of social friction. Theirs becomes a contemporary enactment of social solidarity and affability that offers correction to the ancient tragedy of political destabilization so consistently represented in the *Thebes* that follows. The troubled binarism of patron and poet has been reinscribed as an exchange between the innkeeper and the monk which conceals within its humorous, bantering tone the poet's abiding anxiety over the divisiveness threatening the venerable alliance between the crown and the cloister in 1421. Thus the Host, with his solicitous concern for Lydgate's physical well-being, functions principally as a lay authority sanctioning the poet's own desires for special privileges founded quite legitimately upon claims of delicate health.[36]

[33] John Burrow, *The Ages of Man* (Oxford: Clarendon Press, 1988), 30–32, shows how Lydgate elsewhere endorsed the four-ages scheme of Avicenna, who wrote that old age or the "age of diminution" began at 40 and lasted till 60. Though he in fact lived until 1449, Lydgate in 1420 would have understood himself to be well into old age.

[34] *Colica passio* was a potentially fatal intestinal blockage; see *On the Properties of Things: John Trevisa's Translation of Bartholomaeus Anglicus De Proprietatibus Rerum*, gen. ed. M. C. Seymour, 3 vols. (Oxford: Clarendon Press, 1975-88), 1.252.

[35] Patterson, "Making Identities," 72.

[36] S. S. Hussey, "Chaucer's Host," in *Medieval Studies Presented to George Kane*, ed. Edward Donald Kennedy et al. (Woodbridge: D. S. Brewer, 1988), 153–65, proposes that Harry Bailey organizes the pilgrimage fiction in ways, as we see here, fully incorporated into Lyd-

In her study of the equally wealthy community of Westminster Abbey, Barbara Harvey observes that chambers in the infirmary became highly desirable because their occupants were automatically relieved of the obligation to participate in the monastic routine *and* because the rooms were comfortable and quiet. Since the infirmary was closed off from the foot-traffic that was almost constant elsewhere, it became the site favored by those absorbed in their studies.[37] One of the official responses to the king's articles stressed this same point, maintaining that private chambers were necessary for the careful concentration required by students, advanced scholars, and administrative officials.[38] But Lydgate eschews such argumentation by falling back on the allowance made by the king's own articles for the elderly and infirm. In this way he was able to justify exactly the exemptions that he needed to perform his work as a poet and advice-giver to royalty: personal privacy, healthy diet, undisturbed sleep, and plenty of peace and quiet. One stops just short of proposing a forerunner to Marcel Proust sequestered in his cork-lined bedroom and complaining constantly of ill health, real or fancied, while churning out a vast amount of writing. All of these self-representations and rhetorical maneuvers accord with what Derek Pearsall has recently confirmed as the one thing certain about the poet's character: "he enjoyed the comforts and privileges that fame and money procured, and he put himself to considerable effort to make sure that he had them."[39]

Finally, Lydgate's decision to represent himself as a pilgrim to the shrine of St. Thomas cannot have been taken casually in view of the saint's controversial status during this period. Left unstated in the poet's veneration of the martyr is the devotion shared by the father of his royal patron. Henry IV had broken with tradition by choosing not to be buried in Westminster Abbey. Perhaps uncomfortable with the prospect of being surrounded by the substantial monuments of the Plantagenets whom he had supplanted – including the still empty tomb of Richard II whose specter haunted him psychologically and politically[40] – he followed the example of his uncle the Black Prince by preferring entombment at Canterbury after his death in 1413. The burial there in 1410 of his half-brother John Beaufort, earl of Somerset, suggests that Canterbury was already being considered as the official mausoleum for the Lancastrian dynasty. Henry IV's connection with the cathedral was symbolically bolstered, if not primarily moti-

gate's continuation where the Host's voice is granted overriding authority.

[37] Harvey, *Living and Dying*, 87–88.

[38] *Documents*, ed. Pantin, 120: "quod doctores post emeritos in studio labores privatas cameras suas gradui congruentes non haberent, quod scolares eciam circa sermones occupati in cellis distinctis non existerent, et quod officiarii pro eorum neccessariis conservandis distinctis seu privatis cameris cellulisque carerent."

[39] Pearsall, *John Lydgate (1371–1449): A Bio-bibliography*, 17.

[40] Paul Strohm, "The Trouble with Richard: The Reburial of Richard II and Lancastrian Symbolic Strategy," *Speculum* 71 (1996): 87–111.

vated, by the fact that he had been anointed with the holy oil discovered there and believed to have been a gift from the Virgin to Thomas Becket.

In short, Henry V's father and royal predecessor had wagered heavily upon the sanctity of St. Thomas of Canterbury. As Christopher Wilson explains, "the claim to have received unction with the oil of St. Thomas put the Lancastrian succession under the patronage of Canterbury's and England's premier saint in the most public and unambiguous manner."[41] Royal endorsement on such a grand ceremonial scale paved the way for Henry V himself to grant a great deal of public ostentation to the cult of St. Thomas, even in the arena of international competition as a saint whose Englishness could rival the Frenchness of St. Denis and St. Clovis.[42] Thus Lydgate's literary enactment of the Canterbury pilgrimage with his grateful homage to the saint's restorative powers and his confidence in the rite's legitimacy – proclaimed with the bold exclamation "I ha therof no shame!" (95) – implied recognition of the political status of the martyr while offering tacit rebuttal to Becket's most vocal critics, described in the next section of this paper.

The Canterbury Interlude

Chaucer's authentic frame-narrative had proceeded fitfully after the dazzling achievement of the *General Prologue*. There was the expansiveness of the Wife of Bath's Prologue, but there were also the minimalist gestures for the Squire and Prioress, and no prologues at all for the Physician and Shipman. What completely disappears is something that hardly existed in the first place: the pilgrimage itself. It is seldom appreciated how unexpectedly the Canterbury pilgrimage is announced after the famous *reverdie* opening and how obliquely the destination at the shrine of St. Thomas Becket is described: "to Caunterbury they wende, / The hooly blisful martir for to seke" (*GP*, 16–17). The saint's name is never mentioned here, and it occurs only three times in the entire work, then only in oaths.[43] Never mentioned as such, his shrine's rituals and relics are almost exclusively encrypted in the poet's most deft and wickedly funny lampoons.[44] And the pilgrims never finally arrive at their destination in Canterbury,

[41] Christopher Wilson, "The Tomb of Henry IV and the Holy Oil of St. Thomas of Canterbury," in *Medieval Architecture and Its Intellectual Context*, ed. Eric Fernie and Paul Crossley (London: Hambledon, 1990), 181–90; at 186.

[42] Allmand, *Henry V*, 415–17.

[43] *Miller's Tale*, 3291, 3425, 3461. Even the specificity of these oaths is far from certain; see Ed Malone, "Doubting Thomas and John the Carpenter's Oaths in the *Miller's Tale*," *ELN* 29 (1991): 15–17. The Host's welcome also omits Becket's name (*GP*, 769–70).

[44] Daniel Knapp, "The Relyk of a Seint: A Gloss on Chaucer's Pilgrimage," *ELH* 39 (1972): 1–26; Melvin Storm, "The Pardoner's Invitation: Quaestor's Bag or Becket's Shrine," *PMLA* 97 (1982): 810–18; John V. Fleming, "Chaucer and Erasmus on the Pilgrimage to Canterbury: An Iconographical Speculation," in *The Popular Literature of Medieval England*, ed.

getting no closer than the "thropes ende" mentioned in the vaguest terms in the *Parson's Prologue* (12).

For the generations of Chaucer's academic readers in the wake of New Criticism, the incompleteness of the pilgrimage narrative presented an urgent challenge to reconstituting the author's final intentions in order to formulate a sense of the work's organic wholeness. To this end, Ralph Baldwin's *The Unity of the Canterbury Tales* (1955) exerted tremendous influence with its thesis that the Parson's metaphorical view of pilgrimage imposed a retroactive structure upon the entire collection and that the poet intended, and could only have intended, a one-way journey:

> Here the Canterbury Pilgrimage becomes by metaphorical "pressure" the pilgrimage to the Celestial City. Canterbury, the destination of the pilgrims, becomes the City of God; the *wey* to Canterbury becomes the way to the City of God; the pilgrims, wayfarers in time, become *potius mystice quam chronice*, wayfarers to eternity. Chaucer's Canterbury Pilgrimage becomes, and this is the *sovransenso*, the pilgrimage of the life of man.[45]

This view breathed new life into the consensus of the nineteenth-century Chaucer Society that Ellesmere's ordering of the fragments could be conveniently repaired by the "Bradshaw shift," which would align the geographical references for a unidirectional journey to Canterbury.[46] The authoritative pronouncement of D. W. Robertson's *Preface to Chaucer* (1962) imposed this preemptive construction upon the entire collection:

> Any pilgrimage during the Middle Ages, whether it was made on the knees in a labyrinth set in a cathedral floor, or, more strenuously, to the Holy Land, was ideally a figure for the pilgrimage of the Christian soul through the world's wilderness toward the celestial Jerusalem.[47]

Thomas J. Heffernan, Tennessee Studies in Literature, 28 (Knoxville: Univ. of Tennessee Press, 1985), 148–66; and Julia Bolton Holloway, *The Pilgrim and the Book: A Study of Dante, Langland and Chaucer* (New York and Frankfurt: Peter Lang, 1987), 93–135.

[45] Ralph Baldwin, *The Unity of the Canterbury Tales* (Copenhagen: Rosenkilde and Bagger, 1955), 92. E. Talbot Donaldson anticipated this view in "Chaucer the Pilgrim" (1954); reprinted in his *Speaking of Chaucer* (London: Athlone, 1970), 10: "the pilgrimage seems no longer to have Canterbury as its destination, but rather, I suspect, the Celestial City of which the Parson speaks."

[46] For a review of these issues of tale-order, see Bowers, "Alternative Ideas of *The Canterbury Tales*," 23–27.

[47] Robertson, *A Preface to Chaucer*, 373. Follow-up studies include Edmund Reiss, "The Pilgrimage Narrative and the *Canterbury Tales*," *Studies in Philology* 67 (1970): 295–305; Esther C. Quinn, "Religion in Chaucer's *Canterbury Tales*: A Study of Language and Structure," in *Geoffrey Chaucer: A Collection of Original Articles*, ed. George D. Economou (New York: McGraw Hill, 1976), 55–73; and Zacharias P. Thundy, "Significance of Pilgrimage in Chaucer's *Canterbury Tales*," *Literary Half-Yearly* 20 (1979): 64–77.

Donald Howard elaborated this view in the most impressive volume of Chaucer criticism published in the 1970s: "The pilgrimage, so conceived as a one-way journey, gave *The Canterbury Tales* an over-all unity, a 'frame.'"[48] V. A. Kolve's monumental *Chaucer and the Imagery of Narrative* reformulated the notion for the 1980s when he proposed a parabolic movement away from a literal journey at the poem's opening, upward to a spiritual *via* at its close.[49] Even Stephen Knight's concise politicizing of the argument, which viewed the *Canterbury Tales* as a canny response to the English Rising of 1381 whereby the poet transformed social revolt into pilgrimage, continues to see the frame-narrative's contests finally subsumed into a spiritual conclusion contingent upon the notion of a metaphorical journey.[50] In the most substantial and energizing volume of Chaucer criticism published so far in the 1990s, Lee Patterson deconstructs the literality of pilgrimage as a unidirectional pattern, but without really challenging the authority of the Ellesmere order which so strongly implies this sense of linear purposiveness.[51]

Although the Parson's concept of pilgrimage as a spiritual redirection to the celestial Jerusalem is based on theological authorities as venerable as St. Augustine and derives its literary currency from vernacular texts as well known to Chaucer as Guillaume de Deguilleville's *Le Pélèrinage de vie humaine*, far less attention has been paid to the heated controversies surrounding the actual practice of pilgrimage during the late fourteenth and early fifteenth centuries, especially pilgrimages to the shrine of St. Thomas Becket at Canterbury.[52] Far from

[48] Donald R. Howard, *The Idea of the Canterbury Tales* (Berkeley and Los Angeles: Univ. of California Press, 1976), 30; and the extended discussion at 159–73. See also his *Writers and Pilgrims: Medieval Pilgrimage Narratives and Their Posterity* (Berkeley and Los Angeles: Univ. of California Press, 1980), 77–103, and James Dean, "Chaucer's Repentance: A Likely Story," *Chaucer Review* 24 (1989): 64–76.

[49] V. A. Kolve, *Chaucer and the Imagery of Narrative: The First Five Canterbury Tales* (Stanford: Stanford Univ. Press, 1984), 231.

[50] Stephen Knight, *Geoffrey Chaucer* (Oxford: Blackwell, 1986), 66–70.

[51] Lee Patterson, *Chaucer and the Subject of History* (Madison: Univ. of Wisconsin Press, 1991), 20, and for his acceptance of Ellesmere's authority, 41–46. Patterson, "Making Identities," 76, accuses Lydgate of misrepresenting Chaucer's poem: "By positing a return trip Lydgate ignores Chaucer's final understanding of his pilgrimage as unidirectional and presided over by the Parson; Lydgate instead reinstates the Host's discredited festive model of circular movement centered upon the Tabard Inn." See also Paul Beekman Taylor, "Time in the *Canterbury Tales*," *Exemplaria* 7 (1995): 371–93.

[52] Long neglected, too, has been the literality of the Canterbury pilgrimage that so fascinated Victorian scholars such as Frederick J. Furnivall, who included in his *Temporary Preface to the Six-Text Edition of Chaucer's Canterbury Tales*, Chaucer Society, 2d. ser., 3 (London, 1868) two appendices, one on Queen Isabella's pilgrimage of 1358, the second on King Jean II of France's pilgrimage of 1360. For a recent bibliography, see Linda Kay Davidson and Maryjane Dunn-Wood, *Pilgrimage in the Middle Ages: A Research Guide* (New York: Garland, 1993), 176–78. For example, it is seldom noted that the "Pilgrim's Way" led to Canterbury from Winchester, not from the London starting-point of Chaucer's band; see Julia Mary Ady,

universally accepted, these practices were condemned as wastes of money as well as occasions for drunkenness and lechery, and these condemnations became fiercely voiced by the lay and clerical dissidents who were increasingly cordoned off as heterodox and dubbed Lollards by their opponents. Although John Wyclif seems to have concerned himself less with pilgrimage than with the veneration of images, at times even defending the saintly status of Becket, his followers soon harshened their rhetoric and made St. Thomas their principal target.[53]

The boundary between orthodoxy and heresy was not clearly drawn in every area of religious practice during the last two decades of the fourteenth century, with much common ground persisting between acceptable and condemned forms of devotion.[54] Rejection of the physical pilgrimage in favor of a metaphorical concept, already granted literary expression in *Piers Plowman* before the emergence of more radical forms of Wycliffism,[55] became a standard topos in the catalogue of Lollard tenets exactly during the period in which Chaucer was writing the *Canterbury Tales.* Most likely composed at the end of the fourteenth century, *Sixteen Points on which the Bishops Accuse Lollards* warned those who might be interrogated with the questions routinely posed by prosecutors and the responses sought as proof of heresy. The following would have been considered a typical "Lollard" position on pilgrimage:

> Also we graunten þat it is leueful and medeful to go on pilgrimage to heuenwarde, doing werkes of penance, werkis of riȝtfulnes and werkis of mercy, and to suche pilgrimage alle men ben boundoun after þer power wile þei lyuen here.[56]

The Pilgrims' Way from Winchester to Canterbury (1893; reprint: New York: AMS Press, 1974).

[53] J. F. Davis, "Lollards, Reformers and St. Thomas of Canterbury," *University of Birmingham Historical Journal* 9 (1963): 1–15; Jonathan Sumption, *Pilgrimage: An Image of Mediaeval Religion* (Totowa, N.J.: Rowman and Littlefield, 1975), 272–73; Margaret Aston, "Lollards and Images," in her *Lollards and Reformers* (London: Hambledon, 1984), 132–43; and Anne Hudson, *The Premature Reformation: Wycliffite Texts and Lollard History* (Oxford: Clarendon Press, 1988), 301–9.

[54] J. A. F. Thomson, "Orthodox Religion and the Origins of Lollardy," *History* 74 (1989): 39–55. Paul Strohm, "Chaucer's Lollard Joke: History and the Textual Unconscious," *Studies in the Age of Chaucer* 17 (1995): 23–42, agrees that the Lollardy of the period 1380–1400 was drastically mixed: "The social terrain of Lollardy was always less even than contemporary polemics supposed, and fourteenth-century Lollards seem from the beginning to crop up at all points on the social scale" (33).

[55] John Burrow, "The Action of Langland's Second Vision," *EIC* 15 (1965): 247–68.

[56] *Selections from English Wycliffite Writings*, ed. Anne Hudson (Cambridge: Cambridge Univ. Press, 1978), 23, with comments on the manuscript and dating of the text, 145.

The copy of the *Twelve Conclusions of the Lollards* affixed to Westminster Hall during the session of Parliament in 1395 was more precise in its rejection of pilgrimage as the occasion for idolatry, concluding with a swipe at Becket's status as an authentic martyr.[57] Since the publication of these *Conclusions* prompted Roger Dymmok to write his *Liber contra XII errores et hereses Lollardorum*, which addressed its introductory epistle directly to Richard II, it is clear that ideological work at the highest official levels was being undertaken during the mid-1390s.

The campaign for branding Wycliffites as heretics meant isolating and condemning as errors many widely held complaints, including complaints against the abuses of pilgrimage. Though Dymmok's reply to the eighth conclusion deals mostly with venerating saints and making offerings to sacred images, he cites various scriptural examples in support of the practice of pilgrimage by leaning heavily upon the same purpose put forward by Chaucer: the healing of the sick.[58] There is, however, one signal difference. Whereas Dymmok launches his argument by claiming that pilgrims could be miraculously cured by visiting the relics of a saint, Chaucer clearly implies (*GP*, 18) that the pilgrims travel to Canterbury to give thanks for recoveries already effected at home, without the benefit of actual contact with relics. It is noteworthy that Lydgate, too, in his Prologue to *Thebes*, did not seek his cure in Canterbury, and therefore avoided controversy by making explicit that he visited the shrine to give thanks for health already restored.[59]

Anne Hudson has surmised that William Thorpe, the notorious Lollard, was already dodging episcopal prosecution around 1386 and again around 1396, that is, during the same period in which Chaucer was working on the *Canterbury Tales*.[60] Because Thorpe's extended comments on the misconduct of pilgrims has often been cited as a commentary on the behavior of Chaucer's pilgrims, especially the raucous sociability of their mixed company,[61] some of his remarks are worth quoting in full:

> Also, sire, I knowe wel þat whanne dyuerse men and wymmen wolen goen þus aftir her owne willis and fyndingis out on pilgrimageyngis, þei wolen ordeyne biforehonde to haue wiþ hem boþe men and wymmen þat kunnen wel synge

[57] *Wycliffite Writings*, ed. Hudson, 27.

[58] Roger Dymmok, *Liber Contra XII Errores et Hereses Lollardorum*, ed. H. S. Cronin (London: Wyclif Society, 1922), 192 (viii.7).

[59] Sumption, *Pilgrimage*, 138–40, discusses the fulfillment of vows.

[60] *Two Wycliffite Texts: The Sermon of William Taylor 1406, The Testimony of William Thorpe 1407*, ed. Anne Hudson, EETS, o.s., 301 (1993), xlv–liii, considers the dating of the earlier interrogations by Bishop Braybrooke (betwen 1382 and 1386) as well as Arundel (ca. 1396).

[61] For example, Edith Rickert, *Chaucer's World*, ed. Clair C. Olson and Martin M. Crow (New York: Columbia Univ. Press, 1948), 264–65.

> rowtinge songis, and also summe of þese pilgrimes wolen haue wiþ hem baggepipis so þat in eche toun þat þei comen þoru3, what wiþ noyse of her syngynge, and wiþ þe soun of her pipinge, and wiþ þe gingelynge of her Cantirbirie bellis, and wiþ þe berkynge out of dogges aftir hem, þese maken more noyse þan if þe king came þere awey wiþ his clarioneris and manye oþer mynystrals. And if þese men and wymmen ben a moneþe oute in her pilgrymage, manye of hem an half 3eere aftir schulen be greete iangelers, tale tellers and lyeris.[62]

Here we find contemporary complaints against the Miller's bagpiping (*GP*, 565–66), the singing of the Summoner and the Pardoner (*GP*, 672–73), the jingling bells on the Monk's bridle (*GP*, 169–71), and particularly the reputation of pilgrims as great tellers of tales. What cannot be omitted from critical evaluation, however, is the fact that these complaints, which Chaucer seems to have assimilated from some broad stratum of popular disapproval, had become linked in the 1390s with the repertory of Lollard invectives. The satire had become freighted, in ways the poet himself came to understand all too well, with the topics of social dissidents who were in the process of being stigmatized as heretics by religious writers such as Dymmok with connections to the royal court as close as Chaucer's own.

It is therefore striking that Thorpe's distinction between "trewe pilgrimes and fals pilgrimes" could just as well have been spoken by Chaucer's Parson, even including his use of the imagery of branches to describe the seven deadly sins:

> I clepe hem trewe pilgrymes trauelynge toward þe blis of heuene whiche, in þe staat, degree or ordre þat God clepiþ hem to, bisien hem feiþfulli for to occupie alle her wittis, bodili and goostli, to knowe treweli and to kepe feiþfulli þe heestis of God, hatynge euere and fleynge alle þe seuene dedli synnes and euery braunche of hem.[63]

Exculpatory evidence such as the Parson's personal participation on the pilgrimage and his emphasis upon the need for confession may clear him of any charges of harboring true Wycliffite leanings,[64] but the allegation persists based upon his overall manner of living, which the poet himself seems to idealize. Concerning

[62] *Two Wycliffite Texts*, ed. Hudson, 64.

[63] *Two Wycliffite Texts*, ed. Hudson, 61–62.

[64] Douglas J. Wurtele, "The Anti-Lollardry of Chaucer's Parson," *Mediaevalia* 11 (1989 for 1985): 151–68. Michael Olmert, "The Parson's Ludic Formula for Winning on the Road," *Chaucer Review* 20 (1985): 158–68, finds less spiritual motive in a tale calculated by its narrator to win the storytelling game. See generally Glending Olson, "Chaucer's Idea of a Canterbury Game," in *The Idea of Medieval Literature: New Essays on Chaucer and Medieval Culture in Honor of Donald R. Howard*, ed. James M. Dean and Christian K. Zacher (Newark: Univ. of Delaware Press, 1992), 72–90.

Chaucer's own religious leanings, sixteenth-century readers were prejudiced by the Lollard tract adapted by Thomas Godfray as the *Plowman's Tale*, which William Thynne in turn placed in the privileged final position in his 1542 edition of the *Canterbury Tales*. Together with the puritanical sentiments of the Parson, this attribution meant that Reformation readers were certain to associate Chaucer with the teachings of Wyclif and the proto-Protestant doctrines of his followers.[65] Members of the nineteenth-century Chaucer Society found this view congenial to their own notion of a poet ahead of his time as a proponent of religious reform.[66] However, for anyone examining the decades immediately after the poet's death when evidence first became available for assessing the earliest reader-responses, the challenge becomes gauging the extent to which the poet's writings were implicated in a proliferating array of Lollard controversies. The most famous episode probably represents the least typical: a copy of the *Canterbury Tales* was produced as evidence for prosecuting a case of heresy against John Baron of Amersham in 1464.[67]

More productive is an examination of the strategies of containment legible in various attempts to mend and expand the pilgrimage narrative as such. Composition of the longest and most dramatically rich continuation of Chaucer's *Tales* – the 732-line *Canterbury Interlude* – is commonly thought to belong to the period around 1420, though it survives uniquely in Northumberland MS. 455 dated much later, ca. 1450–70.[68] Like Lydgate's Prologue to the *Siege of Thebes*, the *Canterbury Interlude* serves as evidence that the generations of readers following Chaucer's death did not instinctively view the *Canterbury Tales* as "unfinished but complete" (in Donald Howard's famous phrase),[69] nor did they assume that the pilgrimage narrative automatically generated a one-way design to which Chaucer's poem had already conformed.

The escalating controversy over pilgrimages constitutes an important component in the textual environment to be considered by anyone wishing to argue the Parson speaks only for himself, not for the author, when imposing this spiritual concept upon the journey. Charles Owen has long upheld the views of Root and

[65] See David Lyle Jeffrey, "Chaucer and Wyclif: Biblical Hermeneutic and Literary Theory in XIVth Century," in *Chaucer and Scriptural Tradition*, ed. Jeffrey, 109–40; Linda Georgianna, "The Protestant Chaucer," in *Chaucer's Religious Tales*, ed. C. David Benson and Elizabeth Robertson (Woodbridge: D. S. Brewer, 1990), 55–69; and John M. Bowers, "Piers Plowman and the Police: Notes Toward a History of the Wycliffite Langland," *Yearbook of Langland Studies* 6 (1992): 1–50; at 36–42.

[66] See, for example, Hugo Simon, "Chaucer a Wicliffite: An Essay on Chaucer's Parson and Parson's Tale," *Essays on Chaucer*, Chaucer Society, 2d. ser., 16 (London, 1876), 227–92.

[67] Anne Hudson, "Lollardy: The English Heresy?" in her *Lollards and Their Books* (London: Hambledon, 1985), 142: "the instance is isolated, and is usually dismissed as an instance of neurotic officiousness on the part of the bishop's minions." See also Margaret Aston, "Lollardy and Literacy," in her *Lollards and Reformers*, 208.

[68] *Continuations and Additions*, ed. Bowers, 55–79.

[69] Howard, *The Idea of the Canterbury Tales*, 1.

Manly that the poet intended certain tales for the homeward journey,[70] and the fact that no early manuscript of the *Canterbury Tales* correctly arranged the fragments in an order aligning the geographical references to create a one-way trip suggests that no near-contemporary readers enforced the sense of formalist determinism insisted upon by so many critics since Ralph Baldwin. My own article "Alternative Ideas of the *Canterbury Tales*" used the evidence of Lydgate's *Thebes* and the Northumberland manuscript's *Canterbury Interlude* to argue that these two early fifteenth-century "reader responses" embraced the concept of a round-trip for the collection as a whole.[71] Missing from my 1985 study was any consideration of how this literality, so often condemned as a failing among Chaucer's early imitators, served very specific ideological ends. The *Canterbury Interlude* confronts controversy directly by bringing Chaucer's pilgrims to their destination in the cathedral, allowing them the completion of the sacred rite *and* the continuation of their profane lives.

The *Canterbury Interlude* negotiates the delicate operation of reviving some of Chaucer's satirical themes while colorfully dramatizing exactly the most controversial elements of the literal pilgrimage which the original poet had scrupulously avoided. The pilgrims arrive in Canterbury, they visit the cathedral, they venerate the shrine of St. Thomas, and they make their donations to his relics.[72] The care that the anonymous fifteenth-century writer invested in describing these rituals is so expert in its knowledge of local practices that one recent scholar has argued that the *Beryn* poet may have been one of the Benedictine monks actually charged with custody of the shrine.[73] Whoever executed this "missing link" in the frame-narrative, he insisted upon maintaining the literality of the pilgrimage without allowing it to spiral upward into metaphor. The *Interlude* is more eventful, more alive with the comings and goings of the various

[70] Charles A. Owen, Jr., "The Alternative Reading of *The Canterbury Tales*: Chaucer's Text and the Early Manuscripts," *PMLA* 97 (1982): 237–50. Earlier proponents of the round-trip theory included Robert K. Root, "The Manciple's Prologue," *Modern Language Notes* 44 (1929): 493–96, and John M. Manly, "Tales of the Homeward Journey," *Studies in Philology* 28 (1931): 613–17.

[71] Peter W. Travis, "Affective Criticism, the Pilgrimage of Reading, and Medieval English Literature," in *Medieval Texts and Contemporary Readers*, ed. Laurie A. Finke and Martin B. Shichtman (Ithaca: Cornell Univ. Press, 1987), 201–15, uses reader-response theory to propose that medieval readers were accustomed to imagine themselves "rewriting" the story as an essential aspect of their reading experience.

[72] Stephen Medcalf, "Motives for Pilgrimage: *The Tale of Beryn*," in *England in the Fourteenth Century: Proceedings of the 1991 Harlaxton Symposium*, ed. Nicholas Rogers (Stamford, Lincolnshire: Paul Watkins, 1993), 97–108, proposes that the pilgrims are more genuinely spiritual than usually understood.

[73] Peter Brown, "Journey's End: The Prologue to *The Tale of Beryn*," *Chaucer and Fifteenth-Century Poetry*, ed. Boffey and Cowen, 143–74. For a different view of authorship, see Richard Firth Green, "Legal Satire in *The Tale of Beryn*," *Studies in the Age of Chaucer* 11 (1989): 43–62.

characters, than all of Chaucer's authentic prologues combined. So engaging are the pilgrims' voices and personalities in the original *Canterbury Tales* that we are not likely to notice how few events actually occur in the frame: the Pardoner and the Host kiss, the drunken Cook falls off his horse, the narrator calculates the hour by measuring his shadow. The *Interlude*'s scenes in which the Knight and Squire inspect the city's fortification and the Wife of Bath rests in the inn's herb-garden with the Prioress, for example, are cross-cut with episodes of the Pardoner's fabliau-like misadventure with the Kit the tapster.[74] Bustling activity becomes a cunning substitution for psychological depth and moral complexity.

In a closely related reading, Glending Olson has detected "a sort of literary and social conservatism" at work in the *Canterbury Interlude* "that mutes or at least dampens some of the most ebullient and anti-authoritarian Canterbury voices."[75] Olson focuses upon the Pardoner as the principal site for rewriting Chaucer's most disturbing and subversive characters, who as a group have been largely silenced as agents of challenge, contest and confrontation. The *Beryn* poet has recast the Pardoner to resemble Absolon from the *Miller's Tale*, rendering him ineffectual but sexually "normal" rather than impotent or homosexual. More to the point, nothing is said about the Pardoner's professional chicanery as a purveyor of pardons, and there is no mention of the sham relics that had provoked such nervous recognition of the unstable distinction between the authentic and the bogus.[76] The Pardoner is denied any psychological depth. He is reduced to manageable terms by the logic of fabliau debasement, and finally he is tricked, robbed, beaten, humiliated, and allowed to slink away as a comic butt, a triviality, a cliché.[77] In the process, he has entirely ceased to operate as a weapon of satire against Canterbury relics.

The *Canterbury Interlude* pursues a middle course by describing how the pilgrims reached their destination at the shrine of St. Thomas while also admitting that some of the individuals were less than pious in their behavior, both before and after. The Friar uses the occasion to sneak a peek at the Nun, the Miller stupidly guesses at the images in the stained-glass windows, and the Summoner squabbles over a cache of Canterbury souvenirs shoplifted by the

[74] See Bowers, "Alternative Ideas of *The Canterbury Tales*," 27–30, and Karen A. Winstead, "The *Beryn*-Writer as a Reader of Chaucer," *Chaucer Review* 22 (1988): 225–33.

[75] Glending Olson, "The Misreadings of the *Beryn* Prologue," *Mediaevalia* 17 (1994 for 1991): 201–19; at 204.

[76] William Komowski, "'Coillons,' Relics, Skepticism and Faith on Chaucer's Road to Canterbury: An Observation on the Pardoner's and the Host's Confrontation," *English Language Notes* 28 (1991): 1–8.

[77] This is also the view of Frederick B. Jonassen, "Cathedral, Inn, and Pardoner in the Prologue to the *Tale of Beryn*," *Fifteenth-Century Studies* 18 (1991): 109–32.

Miller and Pardoner.[78] Yet despite the commotion stirring around the fringes, hardly a hint of criticism impinges upon the central act of devotion:

> Then passed they forth boystly, goglyng with hir hedes,
> Kneled adown tofore the shryne, and hertlich hir bedes
> They preyd to Seynt Thomas, in such wise as they couth.
> And sith the holy relikes ech man with his mowth
> Kissed, as a goodly monke the names told and taught.
> And sith to other places of holynes they raughte
> And were in hir devocioun tyl service were al doon,
> And sith they drowgh to dynerward, as it drew to noon. (163–70)

Even more remote from these central devotions are the Pardoner's unhappy encounters with Kit, a conniving female whose double-dealings confirm Thorpe's caustic remarks on the seedy side of the pilgrimage trade:

> [S]iche madde peple wasten blamfulli Goddis goodis in her veyne pilgrymageyng, spendynge þese goodis vpon vicious hosteleris and vpon tapsters, whiche ben ofte vnclene wymmen of her bodies.[79]

The continuator does not blink at these abuses. Quite the contrary, he rejoices in the retribution visited upon the Pardoner whose misconduct so grossly profaned the sacred journey. What he leaves entirely intact is the validity of the pilgrimage itself, in theory and in practice, as a ritual which Chaucer had slighted in the *General Prologue* and then omitted altogether at the end, appearing instead to endorse the Parson's notion of a "parfit glorious pilgrymage / That highte Jerusalem celestial" (Prologue to the *Parsons Tale*, 50–51). Not that the lack of closure to the frame-narrative entirely cancels the ambivalence detected by Linda Georgianna: "Fully aware of the multiple motives impelling people to go on pilgrimages, Chaucer is drawn to the practice precisely because it provides Christians *both* an opportunity to heed a profound spiritual call to renewal and redemption *and* a way to defer and displace the full recognition of the need for mercy for as long as possible."[80] This finely registered sense of doubleness is literalized in the double drama of the *Canterbury Interlude* in which the pilgrims as a group successfully complete their spiritual rendezvous with Becket's relics,

[78] David Wallace, "Pilgrim Signs and the Ellesmere Chaucer," *Chaucer Newsletter* 11.2 (1989): 1–3, uses this text to discuss the practice of selling Canterbury "signs" to the visitors to Becket's shrine.

[79] *Two Wycliffite Texts*, ed. Hudson, 64.

[80] Linda Georgianna, "Love So Dearly Bought: The Terms of Redemption in *The Canterbury Tales*," *Studies in the Age of Chaucer* 12 (1990): 85–116; at 98. A complementary reading is offered by David Lawton, "Chaucer's Two Ways: The Pilgrimage Frame of *The Canterbury Tales*," *Studies in the Age of Chaucer* 9 (1987): 1–40.

while the Pardoner fails miserably in his sexual rendezvous with the scheming tapster.

As a highly individual attempt at editorial reorganization, the Northumberland manuscript itself refutes the concept of a unidirectional journey by deploying the fragments to provide tales for the homeward trip. After the turn-around episode of the *Interlude* itself come the Merchant's *Tale of Beryn* (his second tale), the conclusion to the *Summoner's Tale*, Chaucer's *Melibee* (his second tale), the *Monk's Tale*, the *Nun's Priest's Tale*, the *Manciple's Tale*, and the *Parson's Tale*.[81] Because the manuscript is deficient at the end, we do not know whether the same anonymous continuator provided a conclusion that would have brought the pilgrims back to the Tabard Inn for the announcement of the Host's verdict, followed by a costly, bibulous banquet. I think not. Probably the writer concentrated his modest talents upon the real ideological business of the continuation, and this meant fulfilling the intention for the pilgrims to visit Canterbury's shrine of St. Thomas. As a result, the poet's enterprise has done more than reshape the "roadside drama" so that it conforms with the design long advocated by Charles Owen.[82] The Northumberland manuscript has reinstated this round-trip pattern of pilgrimage, as actually practiced by orthodox but fallible Christians in fifteenth-century England, as the dominant narrative trope preempting the Lollard metaphor of a one-way spiritual progress.

Finally, the poet's concern for the literal enactment of pilgrimage helps to account for the stylistic register of the *Canterbury Interlude* as a whole, which Jean Jost has rightly characterized as "distinctly uncourtly."[83] By contrast, Lydgate directed his *Thebes* Prologue to a courtly audience, and the armorial insignia of the Duke of Suffolk on the superb British Library Arundel MS. 119 indicates that the work found such an audience even if the original patron, Henry V, had died prior to a formal dedication. The *Beryn* poet's lower social aim is reflected in the unmistakably bourgeois appearance of the Northumberland

[81] Bowers, "Alternative Ideas of *The Canterbury Tales*," 33–38, describes the idiosyncratic organization of Northumberland. See also M. C. Seymour, *A Catalogue of Chaucer Manuscripts*, 2 vols. (Aldershot: Scolar Press, 1995–97), 2.34–39.

[82] Charles A. Owen, Jr., *Pilgrimage and Storytelling in the Canterbury Tales* (Norman: Univ. of Oklahoma Press, 1977), 217: "The pilgrims will end up where they began, eating a meal at the Tabard." Perhaps the notion of "roadside drama" was most fully explored by Robert M. Lumiansky, *Of Sundry Folk: The Dramatic Principle in the Canterbury Tales* (Austin: Univ. of Texas Press, 1955). See also Frederick C. Jonassen, "The Inn, the Cathedral, and the Pilgrimage of the *Canterbury Tales*," in *Rebels and Rivals: The Contestive Spirit in the Canterbury Tales*, ed. Susanna Freer Fein, David Raybin and Peter C. Braeger (Kalamazoo: Medieval Institute Publications, 1991), 1–35, for a Bakhtinian reading of the pilgrimage as a duality combining carnival abandon and Lenten mortification.

[83] Jean E. Jost, "From Southwark's Tabard Inn to Canterbury's Cheker-of-the-Hope: The Un-Chaucerian *Tale of Beryn*," *Fifteenth-Century Studies* 21 (1994): 133–48: "Its ideas are not noble, its aspirations not courteous, its characters neither courtly nor exemplary, its poetry not edifying" (133–34).

manuscript. If I am correct in my sense that the *Interlude* partly engages in an ideological project, the writer felt no need to pursue this work on the courtly level of address. Whereas Wycliffism may have found some sympathizers in the household of Richard II, the movement lost all of its social cachet during the first decade of the fifteenth century, and the Wycliffite heresy was utterly extinct as an aristocratic phenomenon after Oldcastle's rebellion in 1414.[84] The Lollard controversies remained very much alive in the middle stratum of English society – the stratum occupied by the unfortunate John Baron whose copy of the *Canterbury Tales* was produced as evidence of heresy in 1464 – and it is to this sector of Chaucer's widening national audience that the *Beryn* poet directed his continuation with its soft-sell defense of the Canterbury pilgrimage as a legitimate religious practice.

Afterthoughts

If Chaucer allowed within the achieved text of the *Canterbury Tales* an array of gaps, interruptions, ruptures, ellipses, and discursive fragments, which have in turn invited a variety of responses from modern critics, the attempts made by two writers of the fifteenth century to supply those "missing parts" constitute a second category of evidence, offering a second occasion for interpretation. "What is methodologically interesting," Patterson noted in one of his earliest efforts at evaluating a fifteenth-century response to Chaucer's work, "is precisely the amount of interpretation that is required to recover the act of interpretation itself."[85] Chaucer's poetry drew its fiercest wit and its most disturbing truths from the social tensions that energized life in London during the 1390s, and the force of his textual engagements persisted after his death to aggravate those tensions or, as we have seen, to provoke responses calculated to dampen those energies. Some social antagonisms passed from the scene. Other social contests, such as the criticism of monks and the debate over pilgrimage, assumed greater urgency and involved the full technology of institutional self-protection.

The real subversiveness of Chaucer's provocations can be detected in his ability to lure later continuators into a sort of ambush, forcing them to focus critical attention on precisely these same controversial topics in their efforts to adjust, qualify and correct. Thus Lydgate was drawn back into the controversies surrounding the laxity of the Benedictines, and the author of the *Canterbury Interlude* confirmed the misbehavior of low-class pilgrims in the process of realizing a fulfillment of the ritual practice which Chaucer had omitted and –

[84] Hudson, *Premature Reformation*, 394.

[85] Lee Patterson, "Ambiguity and Interpretation: A Fifteenth-Century Reading of *Troilus and Criseyde*" (1979); reprinted in *Negotiating the Past: The Historical Understanding of Medieval Literature* (Madison: Univ. of Wisconsin Press, 1987), 116.

more perilously still – which his Parson had translated into a spiritual metaphor in the manner of Lollards such as William Thorpe.

What proved to be the most decisive installment to the fifteenth-century rewriting of the *Canterbury Tales* was the construction of the one pilgrim most notably absent from the *General Prologue*: Chaucer himself. Within a decade of the poet's death, the Ellesmere manuscript provided a painted portrait of Chaucer with precise, realistic details found nowhere in the text. An almost identical likeness, probably based on a common model, appears in the British Library Harley MS. 4866 of Hoccleve's *Regement of Princes*, a work written for Prince Henry in 1412–14.[86] The decorative portrait occasioned by Hoccleve's stanzas of respectful commemoration includes praise for Chaucer's devout service to the Virgin and is followed immediately by a defense of images against their opponents, not mentioned by name but certainly understood as Lollards. When Hoccleve writes that "somme holden oppynyoun and sey / Ðat none ymages schuld imaked be,"[87] he further demeans his enemies by refusing to grant them a name. What the later poet seems to be doing – and doing decisively – is dismantling Chaucer's ambiguous relationship with Wycliffism by rewriting it as antagonistic resistance. The explicitly named Chaucer, who is devoted to rosaries, pilgrimages and Marian piety, is invoked to stand in solid opposition to that nameless "somme" (like Stephen Greenblatt's "Other") who represent a destructive threat to these same orthodox practices.[88]

Pearsall has proposed that just as it was necessary for Henry V to refute prior suspicions that he was "soft" on Lollardy in order to fashion himself as a strong nationalist monarch, it was necessary as an ancillary component of this Lancastrian cultural policy for Chaucer's reputation to be rescued, revised, and drained

[86] For various assessments of the Chaucer portraits, see Michael Seymour, "Manuscript Portraits of Chaucer and Hoccleve," *Burlington Magazine* 124 (1982): 618–23; David R. Carlson, "Thomas Hoccleve and the Chaucer Portrait," *Huntington Library Quarterly* 54 (1991): 283–300; Leger Brosnahan, "The Pendant in the Chaucer Portraits," *Chaucer Review* 26 (1992): 424–31; Pearsall, *The Life of Geoffrey Chaucer*, 285–305; and Sylvia Wright, "The Author Portraits in the Bedford Psalter-Hours: Gower, Chaucer and Hoccleve," *British Library Journal* 18 (1992): 190–201.

[87] Hoccleve, *Works*, vol. 3, *The Regement of Princes, and Fourteen of Hoccleve's Minor Poems from the Egerton MS. 615*, ed. F. J. Furnivall, EETS, e.s., 72 (London: K. Paul, 1897), 179–81, lines 4985–5010.

[88] Accusations of heresy function here much as later charges of atheism. See Stephen Greenblatt, "Invisible Bullets" (1981); reprinted in *Shakespearean Negotiations* (Berkeley and Los Angeles: Univ. of California Press, 1988), 22: "I am arguing not that atheism was literally unthinkable in the late sixteenth century but rather that it was almost always thinkable only as the thought of another. This is one of its attractions as a smear; atheism is a characteristic mark of otherness."

of controversy in order for him to be installed as a strong National Poet.[89] It mattered more and more what sort of author he was, and less and less what sort of poetry he had actually written. Once this sanitation of the poet's identity had been completed, the fiction of the author's official status became the ideological precondition for scribes transmitting his writings, for poets such as Lydgate and the *Beryn* poet taking him as their model, and for an expanding national public receiving his work as "always already read" in ways that effectively preempted, effaced and rendered illegible the inflammatory topics that the poet had so skillfully embedded in his writings. It is remarkable how his most outrageous characters such as the Pardoner were rendered "psychologically opaque and socially quiescent"[90] in the minds of later readers for whom the *Canterbury Tales* became entirely decorous and decorative – in short, something of a coffee-table book.

In the long and syntactically cascading introduction to the *Thebes* Prologue, Lydgate does his part to distance Chaucer from controversy. He includes a twenty-line commendation to the "Floure of poetes thorghout al Breteyne" (40) and thus grants greater space to the "Chief registrer of this pilgrimage" (48) than the original poet-narrator had claimed for himself anywhere in the *Canterbury Tales*.[91] Yet the act of rendering Chaucer as a monumental figure has the paradoxical effect of rendering him as an absence, a memory, a dropout from the dramatic action of the frame-narrative, a voice silenced in the process of being transformed into a text. Somewhat like the saint venerated inside the cathedral itself, the original Canterbury poet has been translated by death into something more valuable for becoming inaccessible – a literary relic, so to speak – someone who can restore poetical vitality in the way St. Thomas restored physical health.

The *Beryn* poet more effectively empowered Chaucer by burying him. Instead of praising the dead master in the manner of Lydgate and Hoccleve, this continuator gives him no mention at all. This refusal to name Chaucer as the original author makes the *Interlude* into a proper forgery, a spurious installment

[89] Derek Pearsall, "Hoccleve's *Regement of Princes*: The Poetics of Royal Self-Representation," *Speculum* 69 (1994): 386–410; at 397–408. See also Bowers, "The House of Chaucer & Son," 135–43.

[90] I take this phrase from Patterson, *Chaucer and the Subject of History*, 31: "the psychologically opaque and socially quiescent Plowman, whose portrait assiduously effaces the very real economic struggles of Chaucer's contemporary world, struggles that were in other texts expressed precisely by means of the figure of the plowman."

[91] Chaucer does not include any self-portrait in the *General Prologue*; the Man of Law does not seem to know the poet is present when he remarks on the literary output of Chaucer (Prologue to the *Man of Law's Tale*, 46–89); and the Host does not know his identity when he asks Chaucer the pilgrim to tell a tale (Prologue to the *Tale of Sir Thopas*, 694–704). See Lee Patterson, "'What Man Artow?': Authorial Self-Definition in *The Tale of Sir Thopas* and *The Tale of Melibee*," *Studies in the Age of Chaucer* 11 (1989): 117–75.

designed to be accepted as an authentic part of the literary production. Assigned to the central position of the Northumberland manuscript where it was less likely to be detected as apocryphal, this continuation not only restructures and redefines the essential nature of the *Canterbury Tales* but also reforms the essential nature of Chaucer himself. He becomes an author for whom the literality of pilgrimage and the veneration of Becket's shrine posed no problem, stirred no controversy, and instead spelled "business as usual" for a group of pilgrims representing the robust and entirely orthodox middle stratum of English society.

Ordinatio and Rhetoric: Signs for Reading *Cleanness*

LAWRENCE M. CLOPPER, *Indiana University*

Scholars who have studied Cotton Nero MS. A.x seem to imagine that these elegant poems came to reside in this rather modest vellum manuscript through ill-fortune. Until recently, the illustrations as well were described as crude, another indication that the manuscript was of lowly status. As a consequence, we have come to distrust the *ordinatio* of the manuscript as both unauthorial and insignificant. Most recent editions of other manuscripts do not attempt to transmit the visual semiotics of manuscripts because they are difficult if not impossible to reproduce and because of scepticism that paragraph-markers or decorated capitals are authorial or rational. Nevertheless, visual semiotics are not arbitrary or randomly sprinkled through the text. Although it is impossible to show that authors directed their scribes where to place markers, the medieval scribe, without authorial direction, could deduce appropriate places for the signing of structure if he heeded the texts' rhetorical devices. At least in manuscripts prepared with care and attention, writers and scribes shared an understanding of the conventions for presenting a text; the scribe's job was to help the writer communicate with his audience. The languages of rhetoric and manuscript presentation can help read a problematic text like *Cleanness*.

Because the poem opens with a scriptural text, the Sixth Beatitude, and proceeds to illustrate its theme with biblical exempla, most readers understand the poem to be a sermon or homily.[1] However, as W. A. Davenport has shown most graphically, the narratives are utterly at odds with such a homiletic framework.[2] Indeed, several influential critics have complained that the narratives

[1] Studies that take a homiletic approach will be cited below. Few other models have been proposed, but see Edward Wilson, *The Gawain-Poet* (Leiden: Brill, 1976), 72–75 (*Cleanness* and cycle drama), and W. A. Davenport, *The Art of the Gawain-Poet* (London: Athlone Press, 1978), 55–102 (*Cleanness* and the catena of tales). T. D. Kelly and John T. Irwin, often with great insight, describe the way the poem functions as a parable, but they do not argue it has any formal similarity to the parable ("The Meaning of *Cleanness*: Parable as Effective Sign," *Mediaeval Studies* 35 [1973]: 232–60).

[2] Davenport, *Art of the Gawain-Poet*, 83–85, but also throughout the analysis.

escape the poet's control or that the poet elaborates the stories at inordinate length and thereby distorts the homiletic intent and structure of the poem.[3] The manuscript supports Davenport's contention, for the incipit of the poem has none of the scribal signs that mark the work to follow as a sermon, nor does the internal rhetoric identify the work with homilies. Further, sermons are not the only texts that incorporate biblical narrative. The poet was no doubt familiar with extended biblical narratives, such as the *Cursor Mundi* and the Pepysian *Gospel Harmony*, or instructional manuals such as *Handlyng Synne*, which insert narratives within a didactic frame. Indeed, there is a close structural parallel to *Cleanness* in *Handlyng Synne*, or rather in segments of works like it. All of these poems employ rhetorical devices like those in *Cleanness*. Our poet has "romanced" his narratives not only by medievalizing and reimagining them within an aristocratic cultural milieu, but also by importing rhetorical devices from historical narrative to create a high style as far from Robert Mannyng's as "fylþe" ought to be from the nostrils of the poet's God. The romance style is intended to entertain and attract the reader, but it is neither affectation nor simple adornment. It is not merely a way to establish access to ideas he wishes to promote, but a way to assert an authority for his exempla, insofar as the rhetoric of romance establishes that the narrative is historical and true. More important, formal rhetorical devices aid the reader in following the logic of the poet's demonstration: they divide the narrative, point the moral, and signal the distinctions crucial to the revelations that follow. Putting aside the question of whether the *ordinatio* of *Cleanness* is authorial, I wish to suggest that any competent scribe would know where to tell the rubricator – assuming he was not the scribe – to adorn these texts. We need not accept that manuscript capitals are authorial to argue that a scribe would know where to place them and other ornaments by reading the text and recognizing its rhetorical strategies. Modern readers in turn may use the medieval scribe's *ordinatio* as a guide to reading a difficult poem like *Cleanness*, a poem that seems to occupy its own unique genre. I wish to illustrate that the poet embedded a recognizable rhetoric in the poem signaled by a visual semiology, both of which guide the reader in interpreting *Cleanness*.

Ordinatio and Sermon Form

The presumption that *Cleanness* is a sermon or, at the least, homiletic, has proved an impediment to our appreciation of the poem. It is generally agreed that the "sermon" does not remain true to the theme posited at the beginning of the poem because of the miscellaneous nature of the elements within the intro-

[3] Dorothy Everett, *Essays on Middle English Literature*, ed. Patricia Kean (Oxford: Clarendon Press, 1955), 68–74; Pamela Gradon, *Form and Style in Early English Literature* (London: Methuen, 1971), 119–24; and A. C. Spearing, *The Gawain-Poet* (Cambridge: Cambridge Univ. Press, 1970), 41–73, who calls it a noble, yet unsuccessful experiment.

duction to the "sermon" body. The problem is compounded when subsequent narratives radically narrow the theme, as the first two large narratives appear to do, or when the narrator abandons the issue of "fylþe of þe flesche" for the sin of sacrilege.

Three elements in the "prologue" define the interests of the poem: the opening lines indicate that the discussion will center on "cleanness" and God's wrath at "fylþe" (1–6); the Sixth Beatitude states that the "pure of heart" shall reap the reward of "cleanness" and see God; and the parable fuses the first two in vivid story form.[4] The "clene," from all ranks of society, come to the feast – the Kingdom of Heaven – where they see the Lord. The filthy refuse or are cast out.

But various problems arise from other parts of the prologue and its relation to the main body of the poem. Immediately following the opening lines, the poem narrows to focus on clergy who are "clene" without but soiled within (7–16a). Thus begins a recurrent image reiterating the point of the opening lines: The Lord is so courteous and "clene" that he is "scoymus" of "fylþe," so appalled by it that when he comes upon it he is incited to anger (16b–22). The reference to the clergy questions the poem's audience. If *Cleanness* is addressed to the clergy, then why does the narrator later in the poem urge readers to confess their sins to their spiritual fathers? If the poem is concerned with clerical celibacy (one meaning of "cleanness"), why do the first extended narratives, which deal with sexual filth, go to such lengths to praise heterosexual relations? On the other hand, if the poem is addressed to the laity, as these sections suggest, why does the poet "mislead" his audience with the reference to the clergy at the beginning of the poem? Further, although sexual purity is a matter of concern to clergy and laity alike, it is difficult to see how, as the narrator asserts, immoral sexual relations among either are worse than the sins of Lucifer and Adam with their universal consequences.

Similarly, the work's theme is inadequately represented by the exempla that follow. The focus on "fylþe of þe flesche" in the first episodes distorts the Beatitude because while sexual purity may be a part of "purity of heart," it is not equivalent to it. This "distortion" is further compounded by the shift to "sacrilege" in the last exemplum. Although the Baltazar story might illustrate the Beatitude by negative example, it is unrelated to the terms defined in the opening lines and preceding exempla on "cleanness" and "fylþe of þe flesche."[5]

[4] All citations are from *The Poems of the Pearl Manuscript*, ed. Malcolm Andrew and Ronald Waldron, York Medieval Texts, 2d series (Berkeley and Los Angeles: Univ. of California Press, 1978).

[5] Most scholars point to the weakness of structure. Charlotte C. Morse has provided the most detailed defense and explanation of the unity of the poem and the relation of Baltazar's feast to the earlier part, "*Cleanness*," in her *The Pattern of Judgment in the Queste and Cleanness* (Columbia: Univ. of Missouri Press, 1978), 129–99; but see also Pamela Gradon, *Form and Style*, 119–24; Earl G. Schreiber, "The Structures of *Cleanness*," in *The Alliterative Tradition in the Fourteenth-Century*, ed. Bernard S. Levy and Paul E. Szarmach (Kent: Kent State Univ.

The shift in topic is generally acknowledged to be the major defect of the poem; thus, the passage on Christ's "cleanness" immediately preceding it (from about line 1049 to about line 1056) has come under greatest scrutiny as providing an "explanation." The passage, often called the "transition," is thought to mark or signal a significant change in the poet's interests, particularly since that is spelled out immediately prior to line 1056 where the poet refers to God's greater anger at sacrilege.[6]

I do not wish to argue that these problems do not exist for modern readers; the literature demonstrates that they do. Nor will I argue that the structure of the poem is simple. But I believe the problems have been aggravated and the poem distorted by two wrong assumptions: (1) that the poem is a sermon or homiletic, and (2) that the passage describing Christ's "cleanness" is a "transition."

First, *Cleanness* is not entered into the manuscript as a sermon.[7] Medieval Latin and Middle English prose sermons are preceded by the Latin scriptural text that is to be the theme, often rubricated or otherwise set off to operate as a finding device when sermons are grouped in a collection.[8] Sermons in verse are not common, but those in the Northern Homily Cycle conform to the pattern outlined here, as does the sermon on the feast of Corpus Christi in the Vernon manuscript.[9] *Cleanness* is *didactic* but not *homiletic* in any generic sense.

Press, 1981), 131–52; Theresa Tinkle, "'The Heart's Eye': Beatific Vision in *Purity*," *Studies in Philology* 85 (1988): 451–70; Monica Brzezinski, "Conscience and Covenant: The Sermon Structure of *Cleanness*," *JEGP* 89 (1990): 166–80; and Jane E. Lecklider *Cleanness: Structure and Meaning* (Cambridge: D. S. Brewer, 1997).

6 Morse, "*Cleanness*," 171–85, suggested the "transition" was the center point of history and the poem, and Tinkle, "'Heart's Eye,'" has shown how the passage fits within the progression of increasingly clearer visions of God. For another analysis of imagery of "clannes" in the passage, see Elizabeth Armstrong, "*Purity*," *Explicator* 36 (1977): 29–31.

7 Michael Means ("The Homiletic Structure of *Cleanness*," *Studies in Medieval Culture* 5 [1975]: 165–72) and Doris E. Kittendorf ("*Cleanness* and the Fourteenth Century *Artes Praedicandi*," *Michigan Academician* 11 (1979): 19–30) have attempted to fit the parts of the poem within the structures of fourteenth-century sermons, but most scholars are less rigid about the matter and are content to characterize the poem as "sermonic" or "homiletic." Although Means and Kittendorf use the same "traditional" sermon structure and cite the same authorities, they agree on only point: that the Sixth Beatitude is the theme. See also Brzezinski, "Conscience and Covenant," but we should note that she uses the term "sermon structure" loosely; her essay is actually a thematic study.

8 Printed examples from the period appear in *The Sermons of Thomas Brinton, Bishop of Rochester (1373–1389)*, ed. Sister Mary Aquinas Devlin, O.P., Camden Society, 3d ser. (London: Offices of the Royal Historical Society, 1954), 85–86; and *English Wycliffite Sermons*, ed. Anne Hudson and Pamela Gradon, 5 vols. (Oxford: Clarendon Press, 1983–1996). Hudson includes photostats of manuscripts as examples of layouts (see her frontispiece and the illustrations between pp. 134–35).

9 *The Northern Homily Cycle*, ed. Saara Nevanlinna, *Mémoires de la Société Néophilologique de Helsinki* 38 (1972) and 41 (1973); and *The Minor Poems of the Vernon MS*, ed. Carl Horstmann, 2 vols., EETS, o.s., 98, 117 (London: K. Paul, Trench, Trübner, 1892–1901), 1.168–97. Several poems call themselves sermons (Carleton Brown and Rossell Hope Robbins,

If we allow that the poet did not intend to write a sermon but to create lively biblical narratives linked by didactic purpose, we might first observe the way the elements noted above fit together. The opening image of the courteous and courtly lord (16b–22) is repeated throughout the poem: in the parable, in the characterization of God in the Noah passage, in the figure of the three angels who appear to Abraham and the angels who go to Sodom, in the figure of Christ, and in Nabugodenozar (a *figura de bono*) and Baltazar (*de malo*).[10] In the parable are two kinds of "unclene" people: those who refuse the invitation and the one who comes and is thrown out. These correspond to those who forget their "kynde" (the lord) and engage in "fylþe of the flesche," and Baltazar who comes filthy to the Lord's marriage feast with his concubines and who desecrates the holy vessels. The issue of sacrilege exists in the poem from the beginning in the priests at the altar who are "honest vtwyth and inwith alle fylþez."

Therefore, there are two kinds of "fylþe" in the poem from the beginning: physical – especially sexual – soiling and sacrilege. The first begins with the flesh but is also a spiritual soiling; the second may involve physical objects – the sacred vessels – but obviously is exemplified better as the soiling of something sacred, such as a priest or person who has sacramentally cleansed himself and returned to his vomit.[11] Both of these are distinguished from soiling occasioned by labor or dirt. The guests who refuse to come to the feast are not soiled by material dirt (from plowing) or sexual sin (from marrying) or from worldly lordship (from owning a "borȝ") but from being too concerned about those things (61–70).[12] They are like the antediluvians and the Sodomites, who sin against "kynde" by not recognizing their spiritual kinship to the lord. The unwelcome guest comes because he has been invited, but we are told that the Lord can see the smallest spot on a garment, so the guest's sins are magnified such that he seems clothed in filth, which is unrelated to his status or occupation in

Index of Middle English Verse [New York: Columbia Univ. Press, 1943], items 419, 1857, 2763), but use the term in the loose sense of "speaking" or "moral treatise" (*MED* sb[1], sb[3]); they do not use a scriptural text for an incipit or as the theme of their remarks. Similarly, the *Speculum Gy de Warewyke*, ed. Georgiana Lea Morrill, EETS, e.s., 75 (London: K. Paul, Trench, Trübner, 1898), calls itself a sermon but is a penitential manual.

[10] A number of scholars have remarked on the repetitions in the poem: see Elizabeth B. Keiser, "The Festive Decorum of *Cleanness*," in *Chivalric Literature*, ed. Larry D. Benson and John Leyerle, Studies in Medieval Culture, 14 (Kalamazoo, Mich.: Medieval Institute Publications, 1980), 63–74, 158–64; Jonathan Nicholls, "Feasts and Feasting in *Cleanness*," in his *The Matter of Courtesy: A Study of Medieval Courtesy Books and the Gawain-Poet* (Woodbridge: D. S. Brewer, 1985), 85–102; Ruth E. Hamilton, "Repeating Narrative and Anachrony in *Cleanness*," *Style* 20 (1986): 182–88; and Tinkle, "'Heart's Eye.'"

[11] Morse, "*Cleanness*," has characterized the vessel as the controlling image that binds all the narratives together.

[12] Stephen Wailes summarizes the commentary traditions in his *Medieval Allegories of Jesus' Parables*, Publications of the UCLA Center for Medieval and Renaissance Studies, 23 (Berkeley and Los Angeles: Univ. of California Press, 1987).

the world (beggars, plowmen and other laborers are welcomed) but is related to his moral condition. He is like the priests at the opening, presenting himself as "clene" but found to be filthy within, the moral equivalent of Baltazar, splendidly dressed but rotten at the center.

Analysis thus far suggests a way to read the poem as a unified sermon, but while the reading indicates thematic consistency, it does not address the problem of form. The poem is still open to the charge that the narratives overwhelm the sermon structure and thus defeat the didactic point. We need, therefore, to turn to the question of form.

Cleanness and the Penitential Manual

Cleanness bears a superficial resemblance to a penitential manual like *Handlyng Synne*: An article, here "cleanness," is divided into its "contraries," "cleanness" and "fylþe," and then in successive "chapters" the sin is refined into *genera*. Occasionally, an exemplum is inserted to illustrate the particular nature of the subspecies. To be sure, there are significant differences. The much larger *Handlyng Synne* has an externally imposed superstructure – commentary on the ten commandments, seven deadly sins, articles of the creed, and so forth – into which exempla are inserted. It contains an analysis of a sin under a general heading and then the manual turns to each of the branches, with exempla along the way, to illustrate the forms of the sins and possibly the *remedia*. *Handlyng Synne* is an internally rambling work. Below the superstructure, the discourse goes where it will, without concern for proportion (some stories are long, others short). It is not organized syllogistically; it does not move through a series of premises to a conclusion. Rather, it is conceptual; the elements within a section belong to the same category, often bewilderingly so.

Cleanness is neither a duplicate of *Handlyng Synne* nor a simple extract from such a manual. First, it is much more orderly and economical; indeed, the germinal idea and the sequence of the first episodes derive from a single scriptural source, 2 Peter 2.[13] A chronology determines the Old Testament exempla in *Cleanness*, whereas in the manual the exempla come from many, usually nonbiblical sources – the fathers, history, contemporary events – and may be in any order. The list of forms the sins take could be cut or extended because there is no pattern or logical limit. Mannyng might begin speaking of arrogance in men, move to the clergy's pride in dress, and then on to the pride women take in their hair. In fact, Mannyng justifies the formlessness of *Handlyng Synne* as part of the strategy for the reader's "handling" of his own sins:

[13] First noted by Carleton Brown in "The Author of *The Pearl*, Considered in Light of His Theological Opinions," *PMLA* 19 (1904): 121.

On þys manere handyl þy dedys
And lestene & lerne wan any hem redys.
Þou darst neuere recche whar þou begynne,
For euery whare ys begynnyng of synne.
Whedyr outys þou wylt opone þe boke,
Þou shalt fynde begynnyng on to loke.
Oueral ys begynnyng – overal ys ende,
Hou þat þou wylt turne hyt or wende. (117–24)[14]

The reader need not begin at the beginning of the book but may start and end anywhere. He is encouraged to create his own text and to begin groping his soul wherever the book falls open.

Cleanness differs from *Handlyng Synne*, therefore, because it has one didactic point that it wishes to pursue in an orderly fashion. Nevertheless, comparison of the two works in greater detail can suggest the way that *Handlyng Synne* might have influenced the construction of *Cleanness*. I have chosen to focus on the sections devoted to the sins of Pride and Lechery because I believe they can both provide illuminating parallels to and show stark differences between the two works.

The description of a sin usually begins with its number and some placement in the scheme of things; thus Pride is not only the first sin in the list but the eldest (2993). She has walked everywhere and done many wrongs, yet she prefers to reside with great "lordyngys." The first division of Pride is "vnbuxumnesse aȝens þy kynde" – a theme developed in *Cleanness* – except that in the manual, the idea is more restricted. It is glossed as "aȝens fadyr or modyr," and the poet extends this "vnkyndenesse" to "vnbuxumnesse" to one's spiritual father. It is disobedience to one's superiors, especially disobedience inciting them to anger, that is admonished. The similarity of the language and issues with those in *Cleanness*, however, reveal the gap between the two writers. Mannyng takes a practical view of things; his concern is the relations that men in this world have with one another and the way they comport themselves. His focus is more on kinships than "kynde." The issues in *Cleanness* are far more basic: The sinners who are "unkynde" are not just arrogant or proud but violators of their spiritual *essentia*.[15]

To encourage his readers to abandon pride, Mannyng reminds them that they all descended from Adam (3036 ff.), who, as first man, had no rank or degree and who, through his sin, brought the common leveler, Death, into the world. The preacher elaborates his point in a list of various forms of pride: those arising from status, wealth, wisdom, or hypocrisy. And then at this arbitrary point, he

[14] Citations are from *Handlyng Synne*, ed. Idelle Sullens, Medieval and Renaissance Texts & Studies, 14 (Binghamton, N.Y.: Center for Medieval and Renaissance Studies, 1983).

[15] This is Jonathan A. Glenn's point in "Dislocation of *Kynde* in the Middle English *Cleanness*," *Chaucer Review* 18 (1983): 77–91.

segues into a tale: "And here y shal telle astyt / Of a cursed ypocryt" (3153–54). At the end of the tale, he draws the moral:

> Þys was shewed hem for to warne
> And þat god shulde no man scarne.
> Ypocrysye, þys ys þe synne,
> Feyr wyþ oute & wykked wyþ ynne. (3194–98)

He advises the proud of heart to "telle hyt to þy prest" (3206) and then continues analyzing the forms of the sin of Pride.

The pattern, if it can be called that, is repeated until Mannyng has exhausted the forms of Pride he chooses to include. Although exhortations are strewn throughout to seek shrift, Mannyng usually ends a section with a pointed encouragement to partake of the sacrament of penance. The section is then rounded off with a prayer or, in this instance, a formal rhetorical device, the *transitio*:

> Now of pryde shul we leue & dwelle
> And furþer of ouþer synnys telle. (3697–98)

The section devoted to Lechery exhibits the same associative organization yet has some thematic points of contact with *Cleanness* as well. The beginning of the article notes that Lechery is the last of the sins and furthest from heaven (7342), suggesting a reason for the poet's emphasis on "fylþe of þe flesche" as worse than those of Satan and Adam (193–248); however, Mannyng undercuts his point with the rationale that Lechery is worst because it damns two people. He cites seven kinds of lechery, all involving heterosexual relations in his thesis that one ought to avoid Lechery by taking one woman and marrying her. He acknowledges that God calls everyone to chastity of heart, but that some, "byshoppes and persones ... prestes & ouþre relygyones," are called "more specyaly"; therefore, he says,

> he byddeþ wyþ wrdes smerte
> Þat þey be alle chaste of herte.
> What ys hyt wrth to be wyþ outen clene
> Whan fylþe ys wyþ ynne þe sene? (7561–64)

Although none of his stories are biblical, he refers to Sodom and Gomorrah. Unlike the penitential manual *Virtues and Vices*, which will not name the sin because it is too offensive, *Handlyng Synne* acknowledges that the sin "stank"; however, Mannyng emphasizes that the Sodomites boasted about it everywhere.[16] It is better, Mannyng says, to heal the sin, or even to be quiet about it, than to revel in it.

I have sketched this section on Lechery not just to adumbrate my comments on the article on Pride but because Lechery is the last of the sins, the furthest from heaven, and the one immediately before the discussion of sacrilege:

> Of þese dedly synnes seuene
> Þat we wraþþe wyþ god of heuene,
> Of hem haue we touched nede
> As holy men haue wryte and seyd.
> ȝyt mowe we weyl nat werche
> ȝyf we forgete holy cherche.
> Holy cherche oure modyr dere,
> Of here shul we telle ȝow here,
> How men synne & on what wyse
> Aȝens þat falþ to here fraunchyse.
> Þat aȝens here fraunchyse falles,
> Sacrylege, men hyt calles. (8587–98)

As in *Cleanness*, sacrilege occurs when men break into the sanctuary and steal or misuse those things that are "halowede" (8603 ff.). This section of the manual comprises entertaining tales stressing the dire consequences of smiting priests, pasturing animals in the churchyard, doing "vnkynd vylany" there, and, particularly, attending or participating in carols, wrestling, summer games or dancing on sanctified ground.

The last exemplum is Baltazar's feast, a warning against using the church's goods for one's profit:

> ȝyf þou turnedest for wrldes wynnyng,
> Halewed place or holy þyng, ...
> Þat falþ to holy cherches seruyse,
> ... þou synnest dedly
> Yn sacrylege certeynly.
> Þar to shal y preue my sawe,
> By a tale of þe old lawe,
> And þys tale yn þat tyme fel
> Þat was of þe prophete Danyel. (9341–54)

[16] *The Book of Vices and Virtues: A Fourteenth Century English Translation of the Somme le Roi of Lorens D'Orléans*, ed. W. Nelson Francis, EETS, o.s., 217 (London, 1942), 228–29. For the unusual explicitness of the poet's treatment of sodomy, see Allen J. Frantzen, "Disclosure of Sodomy in the Middle English *Cleanness*," *PMLA* 111 (1996): 451–65; Michael Calabrese and Eric Eliason, "The Rhetorics of Sexual Pleasure and Intolerance in the Middle English *Cleanness*," *Modern Language Quarterly* 56 (1995): 247–75; and Elizabeth B. Keiser, *Courtly Desire and Medieval Homophobia: The Legitimation of Sexual Pleasure in Cleanness and Its Contexts* (New Haven: Yale Univ. Press, 1997).

Mannyng's somewhat garbled version of the story is similar in conclusion to the *Gawain*-poet's: no good ending results from things won through evil. Indeed, things pass quickly. From this moral loftiness, though, Mannyng passes quickly to the mundane: what one man earns, he says, his heirs will destroy. By the third heir, all will be gone. He draws the general moral:

> For sacrylege al þys ys tolde,
> Þat vesselment of cherche wyþholde.
> Chalyce, cloth, boke or lome,
> For sacrylege cumþ ofte hard dome. (9487–90)

Perhaps the *Gawain*-poet saw that a more profound conclusion could be drawn from the destruction of the mighty Babylon.

Possibly the general similarities in some of these themes and the juxtaposition of Lechery and sacrilege in both *Cleanness* and *Handlyng Synne* are without causal relation; nevertheless, the penitential manual offers us an instructive alternative to the sermon model proposed for our poem. Further, there is enough likeness in content and form to suggest the possibility that the *Gawain*-poet saw in *Handlyng Synne* or some similar work a model to write a didactic poem on the theme of "cleanness." I feel confident, in any event, that the *Gawain*-poet thought he could more effectively burnish the hearts of his readers by putting his uncompromising analysis of "cleanness" and "fylþe" into another recognizable and perhaps more appealing form: the romance chronicle.

The Rhetoric of Chronicle and Romance

The *Gawain*-poet "romanced" his tales and characters by transmuting a worldly language of love and courtesy into a spiritual tongue. He transformed and enlivened the penitential manual by envisioning moral categories within aristocratic terms. To dignify and elevate his discourse, he borrowed the rhetoric of historical narrative. However, I do not think he merely wanted to give his poem an air of history and authority – one purpose of historical rhetoric – but to use rhetorical devices to aid the reader in deciphering the poem. Further, whoever is responsible for the system of capitals created a second semiotic system, a visual one to work in conjunction with the rhetorical formulae, to mark meaningful sections of the poem. For purposes of my argument, it is not essential to prove that the capitals are authorial because it can be demonstrated that someone, perhaps the scribe, recognized the rhetorical strategies of the poem and so marked the capitals in appropriate places. My point is that the rhetorical strategies and the capitals work in harmony as aids to the reader.

As A. C. Spearing and others have observed, the three large and ten small capitals in the manuscript do not appear to have thematic import because they do not divide the poem according to the major narratives. A capital may appear in the middle of a narrative (e.g., that at line 125, about half way through the parable) or it may be absent from where we would expect it (e.g., "Daniel," 1157, rather than the apparent first word of the section at 1149, is capitalized).[17] Nevertheless, the three large capitals (1, 557, and 1157) do mark the poem into segments, each of which contains one of the primary narratives (the Flood, Abraham and Sodom, and Baltazar's Feast). The smaller capitals mark subdivisions of the material. Although the capitals rarely coincide with the beginnings of narratives, they occur at rhetorically defensible positions and suggest a structure different from those proposed for the poem to date in two significant respects: (1) they do not conform to the rigid sermon structure proposed by Doris Kittendorf and Michael Means or to the more general homiletic structure assumed to be there by nearly all commentators, and (2) they do not mark off the passage concerning Christ's cleanness as expected if it were a "transition" of the type Charlotte Morse and others have argued it to be.

For our purposes, we need only a brief introduction to the devices used in romance and chronicle and their effect.[18] Latin chronicles produced in England begin the annal of a year with a date. Subsequent entries within the entry might include festal dates (e.g., *circa festum Purificationis*), abbreviated references (e.g., *eodem anno*) or simple temporal words (e.g., *Tunc*) to indicate subdivisions of the annal. Not only is the initial date often rubricated but the first word or two of subentries are as well; consequently, markers are both dating devices as well as formal indicators of where a narrative begins and, consequently, where the preceding one ends.

As we move from Latin to English chronicle, especially verse ones, and from chronicle to romance, temporal referents are less tied to a given year, so they gain formal properties unrelated to specific dates. For example, many episodes in romance begin with references to festal days: *Sir Launfal* begins at Arthur's court at Pentecost; *Sir Gawain* begins at New Year's. The actual year of the supposed occurrence is not recorded because it is unimportant. Instead, a temporal reference marks the beginning of a narrative or indicates a turn in the narrative and so divides the narrative into episodes. To indicate a narrative shift within a larger narrative, the poet might use a very simple time word: "Now,"

[17] Spearing, *The Gawain-Poet*, 43. R. J. Spendal ("The Manuscript Capitals in 'Cleanness,'" *Notes and Queries* 221 [1976]: 340–41) argues they are thematic; he points to ways that the passages before each capital recall themes in other passages, a point which I elaborate in the discussion below. See also Donna Crawford, "The Architectonics of *Cleanness*," *Studies in Philology* 90 (1993): 29–45, who provides a mathematical analysis of the placement of the capitals to argue that the poet devised the archi-structure of the poem before filling in the content.

[18] I have described the rhetorical devices used in historical documents and romances of the late English Middle Ages in "The Form of Romance and the Resolution of Theological Issues," *Medievalia et Humanistica*, n.s., 15 (1987): 119–46.

"Then," or "When." Scribes may underscore the structural indicators with paragraph-markers or decorated capitals.

In some cases, these formal devices take on thematic significance. In the stanzaic *Morte Arthur*, for example, the most common rhetorical device for beginning episodes is "On a day" or "It befel upon a day." The device implies that events occur by happenstance, by "chaunce," that they are "aventures." This rhetoric is appropriate to tales that stress the fortuitous quality of life in this world where things do *seem* to happen in an arbitrary manner.

The most ornate romance devices are the *transitio* and the seasonal head-piece. *Transitio* mentions a past action before it proceeds to the next:

> Now wol I stynte of Palamon a lite,
> And lete hym in his prisoun stille dwelle,
> And of Arcita forth I wol yow telle. (*Knight's Tale*, 1334–36)[19]

This device, primarily narrative and without thematic import, is needed only in romances that have double or multiple plots, where the poet signals the cessation of one action and the commencement of a second. *Transitio* may clarify a narrative, point to another part of the story, or give a sense of high style.

There are few Middle English seasonal headpieces beyond those that appear in two verse romances, *Kyng Alisaunder* and *Of Arthour and Merlin*.[20] Perhaps best known, however, are the elaborated headpieces that Malory uses to begin chapter 4 (in Vinaver's edition) of the *Book of Sir Launcelot and Queen Guinevere* (on May, love, and the change of seasons) and the one that opens the last book, containing a contrast between the gladness of May and the tragic growth that destroyed the flower of all chivalry. In the two English poems, the seasonal headpieces have very restricted uses: In *Arthur and Merlin* they preface battle scenes and so are built on images of transience or court life when one was high on Fortune's wheel. Similar images are used in *Kyng Alisaunder*, but the headpieces may occur before battle scenes, lists or descriptions of warring parties, or council scenes.

Seasonal headpieces – and other important episode markers – begin with a large capital for the first word of the device. The device, however, may follow a coda to the preceding episode; consequently, a complex of formal indicators marks the conclusion of one episode and the beginning of the next:

[19] *The Riverside Chaucer*, ed. Larry D. Benson, 3d ed. (Boston: Houghton Mifflin Company, 1987).

[20] *Of Arthour and of Merlin*, ed. O. D. Macrae-Gibson, EETS, 268, 279 (London: Oxford Univ. Press, 1973–1979); *Kyng Alisaunder*, ed. G. V. Smithers, EETS, 227, 237 (London: Oxford Univ. Press, 1952–1957). My discussion of the epic style and rhetorical devices in these texts is based on my own analysis and the commentaries of Macrae-Gibson (*AM*, 2.68–75) and Smithers (*KA*, 2.29–40).

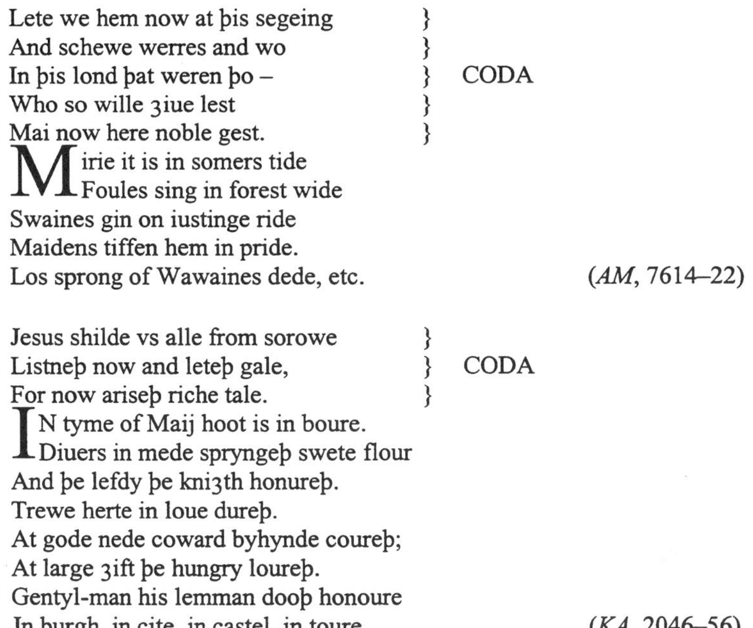

Lete we hem now at þis segeing }
And schewe werres and wo }
In þis lond þat weren þo – } CODA
Who so wille ȝiue lest }
Mai now here noble gest. }
Mirie it is in somers tide
Foules sing in forest wide
Swaines gin on iustinge ride
Maidens tiffen hem in pride.
Los sprong of Wawaines dede, etc. (*AM*, 7614–22)

Jesus shilde vs alle from sorowe }
Listneþ now and leteþ gale, } CODA
For now ariseþ riche tale. }
IN tyme of Maij hoot is in boure.
Diuers in mede sprynegeþ swete flour
And þe lefdy þe kniȝth honureþ.
Trewe herte in loue dureþ.
At gode nede coward byhynde coureþ;
At large ȝift þe hungry loureþ.
Gentyl-man his lemman dooþ honoure
Jn burgh, in cite, in castel, in toure. (*KA*, 2046–56)

Most codas are simple. They might state an aphorism (*KA*, 751–52) or be a moral expressed in a few lines (*KA*, 2888–96); they might invite the audience to hear more (*KA*, 656); they might specify the next episode or point a contrast (*KA*, 1743–46). The seasonal headpiece itself usually opens with a romance formula or temporal reference, then piles up images drawn from court life or the seasons or any evocative yet common experience. The images need not be related to one another nor express the mood of the episode that follows. Sometimes they establish the mood, sometimes they provide a contrast. The headpiece may conclude with a synopsis of or reference to the plot that follows (*KA*, 455–56, 1848). Sometimes toward the end of the device, other formulae suggest that the device is coming to its end and the narrative is about to be resumed (*KA*, 153, 1572).

In adapting romance rhetoric, the *Gawain*-poet elaborates the codas into moral disquisitions on the subject of "fylþe" and "cleanness" and, at major divisions, recalls the Sixth Beatitude. These codas are followed by sections initiated with manuscript capitals.

All capitals in *Cleanness* occur at rhetorically defensible points in the evolution of the poem. The first and largest capital introduces the subject of the poem and its first section (down to line 557). Smaller capitals within the first section occur at crucial narrative moments, but do not necessarily initiate them. Thus, the second capital, the first letter of a time word, occurs within the parable at the decisive moment when the Lord leaves his private room to come into the feast:

"NOW inmyddez þe mete þe mayster hym biþoȝt / Þat he wolde se þe semblé" (125–26).[21] The next capital appears at the first narration, that of Lucifer. The moral of the parable has been drawn (161–88) and the section concluded with a reference to the Sixth Beatitude (189–92). Then the narrator makes his first distinction: "BOT I haue herkned and herde of mony hyȝe clerkez" (193). The conjunction marks the distinction *and* the turn of the narrative; in addition, the poet has cued the turn with a variation on romance formulae ("Harkenez and herez"; "Listeneþ and lereþ"). The lines leading up to the third capital constitute a summary sweep of providential history (245–48) followed by the poet's primary distinction, the difference between the way God treats disobedience and "vntrawþe" as opposed to "fylþe of þe flesche." No capital is used when Noah is first introduced. Instead, we are told of God's decision to destroy the creatures of the earth and hear his instructions to Noah. Only after Noah has completed the work and God reappears to him do we have a capital: "NOW Noe ... art þou al redy?" (345). The "NOW" indicates a decisive turn in the narrative. The last marker in this section of the poem occurs at another dramatic moment in the story. The dove has been sent out twice and faithfully returns. The third attempt is announced with a variant on the device, "On a day":

> ON ark on an euentyde houez þe dowue;
> On stamyn ho stod and stylle hym abydez.
> What! ho broȝt in hir beke a bronch of olyue,
> Gracyously vmbegrouen al with grene leuez. (485–88)

The romance phrase usually suggests happenstance or "chaunce"; the *Gawain*-poet's reshaping of it here suggests providence.

The coda to this section iterates the moral. The audience is warned to beware of the "fylþe of þe flesche" because it arouses God's anger more than any other sin and are told not to come to God's court "sulped in sin," for no matter how small the spot, God's sight is such that He will see it. Therefore, it is essential that one be burnished as bright as beryl, sound on every side, without seam, and without "maskle oþer mote, as margerye-perle" (545–56).

The capital at line 557, larger than those in the section marked by the first capital (1), initiates a second movement in the poem and provides a transition to the Abraham narrative: "SYÞEN þe Souerayn in sete so sore forþoȝt / Þat euer He man vpon molde merked to lyuy" (557–58), and destroyed them for "fylþe" (559), he rues that he destroyed them all. Nevertheless, the narrator adds, men should not assume that God will not avenge "fylþe of þe flesche." Concluding this restatement of theme, the narrator gives an overview of the two stories that will follow:

[21] I have capitalized the whole first word here and throughout the discussion in order to suggest the effect of the decorated manuscript capitals.

And þere He fyndez al fayre a freke wythinne,
With hert honest and hol, þat haþel He honourez,
Sendez hym a sad sy3t: to se His auen face. (593–95)

God quite literally fulfills the promise of the Sixth Beatitude: He shows himself to Abraham, who is pure of heart.

The transition concludes with a reference to the second exemplum that also underscores the larger theme of the work:

Bot of þe dome of þe douþe for dedez of schame –
He is so skoymos of þat skaþe, He scarrez bylyue;
He may not dry3e to draw allyt, bot drepez in hast:
And þat watz schewed schortly by a schaþe onez. (597–600)

Like many lines that appear just before a seasonal headpiece or some other device, the last line points ominously to an episode yet to come. In this instance, however, the immediate episode is that of the visit of the angels to Abraham at Mamre. It begins boldly, "OLDE Abraham in erde onez he syttez" (601).

Like the capital that marks God's speech to Noah, that at line 689 emphasizes God's decision to reveal His intentions to Abraham. The lines that precede the capital describe God's inward thoughts as he struggles to decide whether he ought to tell Abraham what he is about to do. Having decided to speak, he says: "THE grete soun of Sodamas synkkez in Myn erez, / And þe gult of Gomorre garez Me to wrath" (689–90). The section ends with a formal *transitio*: Abraham goes his way, weeping for care, "Whyl þe Souerayn to Sodamas sende to spye" (780). As sometimes happens in romance, the last line of an episode is repeated or recalled in the first line of the next: "HIS sonde into Sodamas watz sende in þat tyme" (781).[22] The noun "sonde" echoes the verb "sende" in the preceding line; otherwise, the sentence is reversed so that the last words, "in þat tyme," recall the first word of the preceding sentence, "Whyl." Not only has the narrative turned, but the formal *transitio* and the reversal of line 780 in line 781 foreshadows the change of fortune about to befall Sodom.

The great destruction is prefaced with a condensed seasonal headpiece that is also a premonition:

RUDDON of þe day-rawe rose vpon v3ten,
When merk of þe mydny3t mo3t no more last. (893–94)

The device is naturalistic, noting that day has arrived and that the sun, as it sometimes does, comes up red. But it also recalls the emphasis on chance and

[22] E.g., lines 697–99 repeat lines 694–96 at a decisive turn in the narrative in *Amis and Amiloun*, ed. MacEdward Leach, EETS, o.s., 203 (London: Oxford Univ. Press, 1937).

change of fortune inherent in headpieces that precede battles. In addition, the redness of the dawn's rays, so vivid in the image, foreshadows, and will be paled by, the fires that destroy Sodom and Gomorrah.

This seasonal headpiece marks the beginning of the long description of the flight of Lot and his family, the turning of Lot's wife into a pillar of salt, and the destruction of the cities of the plain. The passage ends on the vivid account of the Dead Sea's "unkynde" qualities. The narrator points the moral:

> Alle þyse ar teches and tokenes to trow vpon ȝet,
> And wittnesse of þat wykked werk, and þe wrake after
> Þat oure Fader forþrede for fylþe of þose ledes.
> Þenne vch wyȝe may wel wyt þat He þe wlonk louies. (1049–52)

No capital marks the beginning of these lines, nor those immediately following when the narrator introduces the other half of his moral: that one must be "clene" if he wishes to come to God's court. Furthermore, no capital or formal rhetorical device occurs in the section that refers to Clopyngel and the *Roman de la Rose* and then goes on to develop the exquisitely "kyryous" (1109) qualities of Christ's "cleanness."

The omission of capitals may be significant because it allows that the poet and scribe did not regard the material between about line 1049 and 1148 or 1156 as a section separate from the two narratives that have just been recited, the visit to Abraham and the destruction of Sodom. If we look at this passage as a rhetorical strategy, the section on Christ's "cleanness" might better be described as a conclusion than a transition. There are, in fact, several movements in it.[23] First, lines 1049–52, cited above, summarize the moral of the Sodom exemplum, the basis of the comparison for the "cleanness" of Christ which follows; however, before he comments on that, the narrator repeats the second part of his theme: that those who wish to see God's court must cleanse themselves. He reorients Clopyngel's *Rose* to make the analogy that a man must pursue Christ just as a worldly lover pursues his beloved, with the same intensity and with the same desire to imitate that which he would be possessed by. If he would "dele drwrye wyth Dryȝtyn," then he must conform himself to Christ and make himself as clean as the polished pearl itself, for Christ, throughout his life, would have nothing to do with filth.

At the conclusion of the description of Christ's life, the narrator returns to the question of how one might come to see "þat Syre vpon throne" (1112). He replies that though all men are mired and soiled, the "Mayster" (1113) is merci-

[23] I know of only one other rhetorical strategy that is this complex and lengthy, that between the first and second parts of *Kyng Alisaunder* (4739–4840), when the poet says he will turn from Alexander's martial exploits to his adventures in his quest of knowledge.

ful. A person may shine through shrift and become, through penance, as pure as a pearl.

The last line of the first section of the poem also admonished the listener to be burnished until he became like a pearl "Withouten maskle oþer mote" (556). Here the narrator elaborates upon the image. Pearls are not the most valuable gems, yet they are highly esteemed for their clear hues, their perfect roundness, and their purity. Further, they increase in luster with wearing; yet if the gem is forgotten and grows dull, it can be polished by washing it in wine and, "by kynde" (1128), it will become clear again. Similarly, folk befouled by ill chance and soiled by sin may go to shrift, receive penance, and be polished by the priest "Wel bryȝter þen þe beryl oþer browden perles" (1132). The passage thus has analogues in Mannyng's encouragement to seek shrift.

Yet beware, the poet adds, for the cleansed pearl that slips back into sin displeases Dryȝtyn (1136) and entices him to take a great vengeance, because when a soul is reconciled to Dryȝtyn (1139), He holds it His. If it tastes evil (that is, either tastes evil to Dryȝtyn or touches evil itself), then He loses it, as if it had been stolen by thieves, and so God's wrath is kindled. Clearly this statement is modeled on previous ones regarding "fylþe," but now the "fylþe" specified is not sexual immorality or sinning in general but returning to a way of living one knows is wrong. Some scholars have noted this "flaw" in the development of the sermon's "theme." In comparing the parallel with *Handlyng Synne*, however, we see that the poet has moved from one kind of sin, Lechery, to another, sacrilege. The first is a fleshly sin. The second is analogous to it, as Mannyng implies: having considered bodily sins that are spiritually soiling, we may now turn to analogous spiritual sins, the adulterous relations involving those things "halewed" to God.

The narrator of *Cleanness* makes an abrupt transition – that God's wrath is kindled even if the abuse involves not the body but a basin, bowl or dish that once served Dryȝtyn (1146), but in the context of the manual, the transition from Lechery to sacrilegious use of chalices, cloths, plate, and "vesselment" seems not so bizarre. The narrator says that God forbids any of these things be fouled because he is so "scoymus" (1148) in his righteousness, as was shown once in Babylon.[24] The poet creates a brief pointer to the tale to follow (1149–52), concluding with a variation of a traditional romance device:

> ȝif ȝe wolde tyȝt me a tom telle hit I wolde,
> Hov charged more watz his chaunce þat hem cherych nolde
> Þen his fader forloyne þat feched hem wyth strenþe,
> And robbed þe relygioun of relykes alle. (1153–56)

[24] The reference makes two associations: with the feasting God made with Abraham, and with the "renkez of relygioun" at the beginning. It also recalls the feast image in Christ's breaking of the bread.

The description of Christ's "cleanness" provides the moral of and conclusion to the second set of exempla, Abraham and Sodom, the last twelve or sixteen lines being transitional. Furthermore, they are incremental. The first sections of the poem, both the Noah and Abraham/Lot portions, indicate the punishment for "vnkyndenesse"; now the poet will consider what happens when someone has been cleansed (figured in Nabugodenozar) and returns to "fylþe" (figured in Baltazar), which is sacrilege.

The authority with which the last major segment of the poem begins is unmistakable:

> DANYEL in his dialokez devysed sumtyme,
> As ȝet is proued expresse in his profecies,
> Hov þe gentryse of Juise and Jherusalem þe ryche
> Watz disstryed wyth distres, and drawen to þe erþe. (1157–60)

The new element in the theme is reasserted in the lines that follow. Because the people who had promised high God to "halde of Hym euer" (1162) were found untrue in their faith, God's wrath was awakened, and He aided the faithful of the false law to destroy the false in the true faith.

Before the final capital, the coda points ominously to Baltazar's coming ill-fortune: "Al watz þe mynde of þat man on misschapen þinges, / Til þe Lorde of þe lyfte liste hit abate" (1355–56). The capital marks not the introduction of Baltazar (1333) but the moment of his fateful decision to call the people to his feast of filth:

> THENNE þis bolde Baltazar biþenkkes hym ones
> To vouche on avayment of his vayneglorie;
> Hit is not innoghe to þe nice al noȝty þink vse
> Bot if alle þe worlde wyt his wykked dedes. (1357–60)

The last two lines echo Mannyng's statement about the Sodomites. It is not the "stynking" deed itself that is so offensive but the desire that everyone know it.

Although the exemplum focuses on the sacrilege, the "fylþe of þe flesche" is vividly present. The poet tells us that Baltazar sits alone on the dais with his concubines – whom he calls "ladies" – an affront compounded by the fact that the king holds his empire in "lust and in lecherye and loþelych werkkes" even though he has a wife (1349–52). Indeed, his wife is not at this infamous feast. She appears to be the only "clene" person in the palace. Her language suggests that she believes in God, and it is she who enters the hall to counsel Baltazar to summon Daniel (1586–1618).

Daniel reads the fearful prophecy scraped into the wall by the hand of God. Night comes quickly and no other dawn breaks before the prophesied judgment is carried out (1753–56). The swiftness of the vengeance recalls that when Nabugodenozar blasphemed against God:

> Watz not þis ilke worde wonnen of his mowþe
> Er þenne þe Souerayn saȝe souned in his eres:
> "Now Nabugodenozar innoȝe hatz spoken,
> Now is alle þy pryncipalté past at ones,
> And þou, remued fro monnes sunes, on mor most abide." (1669–73)

Darius's entry into Babylon contrasts with the protracted siege of Jerusalem, implying that Baltazar's sin is greater than that of the unfaithful Jews, so retribution is swifter. Baltazar's fall imitates Nabugodenozar's but his is beyond amendment because he had been more arrogant by never acknowledging God and then by his sacrilege:

> And þus watz þat londe lost for þe lordes synne,
> And þe fylþe of þe freke þat defowled hade
> Þe ornementes of Goddez hous þat holy were maked.
> He watz corsed for his vnclannes, and cached þerinne,
> Done doun of his dyngneté for dedez vnfayre,
> And of þyse worldes worchyp wrast out for euer,
> And ȝet of lykynges on lofte letted, I trowe:
> To loke on oure lofly Lorde late bitydes. (1797–1804)

The poet's moral returns us to the parable, the Sixth Beatitude, and the thematic statement initiating the poem. Then he repeats the link to the beginning in words recalling the aristocratic milieu of his demonstration. He has shown in "thrynne wyses" that "uncleanness" cleaves the Lord's heart, entices him to anger, and builds up his wrath. "Clannes" is his comfort. He loves "coyntyse." Those who "seme arn and swete" shall see his face (1805–10).

The poet has not distorted the Sixth Beatitude by narrowing "purity of heart" to "fylþe of þe flesche," nor has he made it peculiar by reading it as sacrilege. Rather, he has implied that there are only two kinds of "fylþe": sins against "kynde" and sins against God, although ultimately both are sins against God, as is all sin. They differ, therefore, not in essence but in kind and degree. Sins against "kynde" can be against self or anyone or anything created by God (Kynde), because the sinner by his actions refuses to acknowledge the sanctity of God's creation and of human "kyndeness." Sins of sacrilege are also sins against "kynde," as suggested by the perverse element in Baltazar's feast, but in addition are committed after one has acknowledged divine "kynde" and kinship. To know that one has sinned, one must first realize he has fallen away from the divine precept and archetype. Once the penitent knows he is of the "kynde" of Christ, through the kinship of His flesh, he confirms his knowledge through the sacrament of penance and rededicates himself through taking of the eucharist.

Having been cleansed, having handled the body of Christ, to turn back to his sins would be like a dog returning to his vomit (2 Peter 2:22). It is as much a sin of sacrilege as that of priests who are "honest vtwyth and inwith alle fylþez." These two images are brought together in a grotesque parody of the taking of the sacrament when Baltazar orders the vessels to be brought out and filled with wine so that his "ladyes" may "lape" from them (1434) and when he and others are said to "[likke] vp" the sweet "lykores" (1521).

Ordinatio, Rhetoric and Meaning

My argument has been that the poet marked the major divisions of his poem with conventional rhetorical indicators and that these are scribally enhanced by the use of capitals. We can never be sure that the capitals in the manuscript are all that the poet might have wished, for some rhetorical devices are left uncapitalized (e.g., the series of "Nows" in the Jerusalem passage, 1225–1308). But even a deluxe, professionally prepared manuscript does not rubricate every device; rather, capitals are reserved for use in conjunction with elaborate devices such as seasonal headpieces or for major turns in the narrative. Even if our author did not indicate capitals in his copy, some scribe recognized the rhetorical strategies (or many of them) and so knew where to place capitals.

Some negative evidence may support the idea that the capitals observe authorial intent. The *Gawain*-poet provides a formal rounding off of sections, putting material appropriate to a coda just before a word written in capitals. Material of this sort does not appear anywhere else in the poem (except, it might be argued, in the disputed passage traditionally called the "transition"). For example, we might expect to find the Sara episode rounded off with a moral or a pointer toward the next episode, but we do not. Instead, the narrative continues without comment. The angels rise up and go toward Sodom, God considers whether he should reveal his intentions to Abraham, and then, when God speaks, the manuscript uses the capital. Although the poet may elaborate his theme at the beginning of a marked section, usually the theme is restated or the imagery recalls the Beatitudes and the parable in the codas.

I think *Cleanness* is a well crafted poem. The vividness of its narration is undisputed. The care with which the poet recalls the parable and the Beatitude in the exempla is acknowledged. My discussion resolves two issues that still trouble readers: that the narration overwhelms the homiletic intent of the poem, and that the poet changes course when he moves to his last exemplum. But the assumption that the section on Christ's "cleanness" is a "transition" to some wholly new topic, sacrilege, or that it is a New Testament interlude between the Old Testament and a figural representation of the last days has misled us. I read this remarkable passage as the grand finale to the poet's first point, that God acts wrathfully against "fylþe of þe flesche," both sexual immorality and sins that soil the holy vessel of the body (an image developed by Morse). The following lines pointing to the final exemplum are a rhetorical device to mark the conclusion of a narrative and lead into a new episode or narrative. The poet makes two moves at this point: he turns from filthiness against "kynde" to the filth of sacrilege and simultaneously asserts that, horrible as God's vengeance was with regard to "fylþe of þe flesche," it is swifter and, ironically, more decisive and immediate when the sin is sacrilege.

My reading also asks that we alter our understanding of the poem's tone. The poem is didactic, but not homiletic. The narrator does not exhort. I think he asks his readers to "handle" their sins, to meditate on them, and then, if they find them, to go to shrift, tell their priest, accept his penance, and beware lest they sink back into that sin. I do not find that the poem's "realism" works against the effectiveness of its narratives as parables or moral exempla, as some scholars have complained. I do not think the attention to worldly detail and character draws the reader away from ethical consideration of the exempla; rather, it enhances it, much as Mannyng's turning to the mundane, his translation of moral categories into the most innocuous activities of daily life, strengthens his purpose.

The *Gawain*-poet, to be sure, is no Robert Mannyng. He has no intention of providing a random and necessarily incomplete list of the varieties of "fylþe." He pierces to the essence. He does not ask that one grope his conscience to determine if he is literally and only a sodomite; rather, he asks the handler of his sins to consider whether he has soiled himself in action or intent "aȝens kynde." The "romancing" of the narrative creates a familiar – not an actual – universe so that the reader can meditate on essences that are not easily defined or that, if they were summarized, might seem too simple and too mundane to occasion concern. Instead, the poet's strategy is to ask:

> Can you imagine how the lord of the manor would react if you showed up at a feast wearing soiled garments? The affront would evoke an immediate and intense reaction. The lord would sweep the *vilain* from his house. Do you imagine, then, that the Lord who created the heavens and the earth would be less fastidious with regard to those who are "sulped in synne"?

If a person wishes to come to Christ's court and "se that Syre in sete," then he must be "clene." To know what "cleanness" is, he must be able to recognize "fylþe" – not according to rote, not by memorizing a list of the varieties of "fylþe," which might encourage legalistic quibbling over what is or is not sin in any given instance, but by understanding what "fylþe" *is*. If "fylþe" is anything "aȝens kynde," then he needs to know what "kynde" is, and to know *that* is to know himself. Further, if he knows his "kynde" is also that of Christ and *then* returns to his vomit, he has committed sacrilege, an irrevocable staining of the soul. The medium does not detract from the message. It circles back to it just as does the moral to the Baltazar episode and just as the narrator's last words circle back to the poem's opening:

> clannes is His comfort, and coyntyse He louyes,
> And þose þat seme arn and swete schyn se His face.
> Þat we gon gay in oure gere þat grace He vus sende,
> Þat we may serue in His syȝt, þer solace neuer blynnez.

“Lo, here lyflode ynow, yf oure beleue be trewe”: Poverty and the Transfiguration of History in the Central Visions of *Piers Plowman*

KATHLEEN M. HEWETT-SMITH, *University of Richmond*

Unlike the concrete, historically based representations of indigence in the plowing of the half-acre episode, the images of poverty at the center of William Langland’s *Piers Plowman* are overtly ideal, forcefully allegorical.[1] From the end of Hunger’s speech in Passus 8 to the appearance of Need at the poem’s end there are no representations of poverty as a personal indignity or social evil; instead, need is intellectualized, presented as a means of moral strengthening and spiritual renewal.[2] This essay will argue that Langland’s attempt to objectify poverty, to disentangle it from the web of historical circumstance that so endangers the proper spiritual understanding of need, is a means of reinforcing the mode of allegory itself, of containing and finally recuperating the palpable and physical within an intellectual or spiritual design. In these central visions, I will suggest, Langland moves deliberately from a concrete, immediate, and topical

[1] Because it presents the most extensive discussions of the poor and the problem of poverty I refer specifically to the C-version of *Piers Plowman* and cite William Langland, *Piers Plowman: An Edition of the C-Text*, ed. Derek Pearsall (Berkeley: Univ. of California Press, 1978). Any reference to the B-version will be explicit and follow the text found in *Piers Plowman: The B Version*, ed. George Kane and E. Talbot Donaldson, rev. ed. (London: Athlone, 1988). Some recent studies that emphasize the half-acre episode’s connection to historical actuality include Kathleen M. Hewett-Smith, “Allegory on the Half-Acre: The Demands of Faith,” *Yearbook of Langland Studies* 10 (1996): 1–20; Robert Frank, “The ‘Hungry Gap,’ Crop Failure and Famine: The Fourteenth-Century Agricultural Crisis and *Piers Plowman*,” *Yearbook of Langland Studies* 4 (1990): 87–107; and David Aers, “*Piers Plowman*: Poverty, Work, and Community,” in his *Community, Gender, and Individual Identity: English Writing 1360–1430* (London: Routledge, 1988), 20–72.

[2] Derek Pearsall explores briefly this shift in focus in the central visions in his “Poverty and Poor People in *Piers Plowman*,” in *Medieval Studies Presented to George Kane*, ed. Edward Donald Kennedy, Ronald Waldron, and Joseph S. Wittig (Cambridge: D. S. Brewer, 1988), 167–85.

representation of the suffering of the poor, seductive in its insistence of the importance of the literal level of signification, to a powerful, authoritative, and totalizing idealization of poverty in which all conflict is resolved through faith. This shift is achieved not suddenly, but through a series of ruminative discussions of the problem of the poor: the pardon's categorizing of worthy and unworthy poor, Rechelesnesse's presentation of the doctrine of patient poverty, and Patience's encounter with Haukyn. Before discussing these particular scenes, however, I will explore briefly the conflicting strains of thought concerning need available to Langland.[3] This will be a schematized account; my intent is to suggest only the general currents of ideology, as it is against these broad patterns of understanding that we construct our own versions of "reality."

I

Medieval attitudes toward the poor were deeply ambivalent. On the one hand, and doubtless in part in response to the classical praise of poverty as a form of moral and philosophical exercise, the Middle Ages encouraged the idealization of poverty as a religious virtue. Based in the teachings of the Gospels, the belief that the pauper was created in the image of Christ was extremely influential. Because they are representatives of Christ on earth, symbols of the incarnation itself, the poor are accorded special consideration. Furthermore, because Christ chose to be poor, poverty itself takes on a special status.[4] To be poor is to be one of God's chosen. "Blessed are ye poor" *(Beati pauperes)*, says Luke in the first Beatitude, "for yours is the kingdom of God" (*quia vestrum est regnum Dei*).[5] Matthew, in a spiritualizing of Luke's social word, reconfigures the Beatitude: "Blessed are the poor in spirit, for theirs is the kingdom of heaven" (Matt. 5:3; *Beati pauperes spiritu, quoniam ipsorum est regnum caelorum*), and most

[3] There are now several general studies of poverty in the Middle Ages. Those most relevant to my thesis are Janet Coleman, "Property and Poverty," in *The Cambridge History of Medieval Political Thought, c. 350–c. 1450*, ed. J. H. Burns (Cambridge: Cambridge Univ. Press, 1989); Lester K. Little, *Religious Poverty and the Profit Economy in Medieval Europe* (Ithaca: Cornell Univ. Press, 1978); Michel Mollat, *The Poor in the Middle Ages: An Essay in Social History*, trans. Arthur Goldhammer (New Haven: Yale Univ. Press, 1986); *Etudes sur l'histoire de la pauvreté*, ed. Michel Mollat, 2 vols. (Paris: Sorbonne, 1974); Miri Rubin, *Charity and Community in Medieval Cambridge* (Cambridge: Cambridge Univ. Press, 1987); and Brian Tierney, *Medieval Poor Law: A Sketch of Canonical Theory and its Application in England* (Berkeley: Univ. of California Press, 1959).

[4] The homilies of the Church Fathers, preached in such cities as Antioch and Constantinople, were often forceful commentaries on those passages of the Bible that dealt specifically with the special status of the poor. See the discussion of poverty in the homilies of Clement of Alexandria, John Chrysostom, Basil, Gregory of Nyssa, and Ambrose in Mollat, *Poor in the Middle Ages*, 18–24.

[5] Luke 6:20. Citations of the Vulgate are from *Biblia Sacra* (Paris: Desclée, 1927). Translations are from *The Holy Bible*, Douai-Rheims version (New York: P. J. Kenedy, 1914).

medieval commentators follow Matthew in emphasizing not the actualities of material distress but the less tangible spiritual qualities nurtured by indigence.[6] As we shall see, this contradiction in the Gospels between actual and spiritual poverty strikes at the heart of the medieval ambivalence toward need.

While throughout the Middle Ages the poor were most often considered the ideal earthly representatives of Christ, their poverty was at the same time viewed as a mark of permanent disgrace. The Old Testament repeatedly represents need as a certain mark of God's disfavor, an unambiguous sign of shame:[7]

> My son, in thy lifetime be not indigent:
> for it is better to die than to want.
> The life of him that looketh toward another
> man's table is not to be counted a life:
> For he feedeth his soul with another man's meat.
> But a man, well instructed and taught, will look to himself.[8]

The act of begging shatters the ideal image of spiritual poverty and substitutes for it an image of shame, self-loathing, laziness, and ignorance. The realities of indigence not only disallow complete idealization of the poor but also seem to provoke a sense of horror and disgust. Because of the condemnation of wealth and ease implicit in their very existence, the poor, despite their special status, were often treated with abuse and contempt. In his striking commentary on Matthew, for example, John Chrysostom rails against the actual, and perhaps all too common, injustices inflicted upon the poor:

> Who then are they? They that are possessed of lands, and reap the wealth that springs from the earth. And what can be more unjust than these? For if anyone were to examine how they treat their wretched and toilworn laborers, he will see them to be more cruel than savages. For upon them that are pining with hunger, and toiling throughout all their life, they both impose constant and intolerable payments, and lay on them laborious burdens, and like asses or mules, or rather like stones, do they treat their bodies, allowing them not so much as to draw breath a little, and when the earth yields, and when it doth not yield, they alike wear them out, and grant them no indulgence. And what can

[6] Jean Leclercq, "Aux origines bibliques du vocabulaire de la pauvreté," in *Etudes sur l'histoire*, ed. Mollat, 1.35–43.

[7] Old Testament passages that condemn poverty and related ills include Deut. 28:15–24, Lev. 26:14–26, Isa. 3:24, and Prov. 6:6–11 and 23:21.

[8] Fili, in tempore vitae tuae ne indigeas;
melius est enim mori quam indigere.
Vir respiciens in mensam alienam,
non est vita ejus in cogitatione victus;
alit enim animam suam cibis alienis:
Vir autem disciplinas et eruditus custodiet se. (Eccl. 40:29–31)

> be more pitiable than this, when after having labored throughout the whole winter, and being consumed with frost and rain, and watchings, they go away with their hands empty, yea moreover in debt, and fearing and dreading more than this famine and shipwreck, the torments of the overlookers, and their dragging them about, and their demands, and their imprisonments, and the services from which no treaty can deliver them![9]

For Chrysostom, the poor are subjected not only to the cruelties of nature but to the oppression of those who in economic self-interest treat the indigent as though they were less than human, as "asses" or "stones." The force of his invective suggests that the idealization of poverty as a religious virtue, though doubtless the most deeply powerful intellectual response to the question of need, was but one method of conceptualizing the poor during the Middle Ages. What is most apparent in the medieval response to poverty is its deep sense of ambivalence. As Mollat observes, to the medieval mind

> [m]aterial distress can degenerate into total collapse, sanctifying humility can turn into humiliation, instead of being an honourable distinction, poverty can become disgrace. Poverty is acquainted with patience, is familiar with envy. It stirs charitable comparison and philanthropic sympathy or else provokes revulsion, contempt, fear and condemnation. Poverty is bound to charity, but also to hatred. It always produces shock and alarm. As a stumbling-block of paradox the presence of a poor man is embarrassing, for it troubles men's consciences, upsets the ordinary assurances of life and flouts the sense of self-esteem.[10]

Though the number of poor was large throughout the Middle Ages, their presence was accepted, even expected, and it was the duty of every Christian to respond charitably, with compassion if not with urgent concern.[11] Though almsgiving did relieve some of the suffering of the poor, it by no means solved the problem of indigence.[12] In fact, charitable giving acted more importantly to preserve the established social order by confirming the inevitability of poverty

[9] John Chrysostom, *Homily on Matthew 18:21*, quoted in Wolfgang Stegemann, *The Gospel and the Poor*, trans. Dietlinde Elliott (Philadelphia: Fortress, 1984), 20.

[10] Quoted in Geoffrey Shepherd, "Poverty in *Piers Plowman*," in *Social Relations and Ideas: Essays in Honour of R. H. Hilton*, ed. T. H. Aston et al. (Cambridge: Cambridge Univ. Press, 1983), 176.

[11] See Mollat, *Poor in the Middle Ages*, 38–53.

[12] Seminal studies on medieval charity include Rubin, *Community and Charity*; Dyer, *Standards of Living*, 234–57; and Tierney, *Poor Law*, 45–67, and his "The Decretists and the 'Deserving Poor,'" *Comparative Studies in Society and History* 1 (1958–59): 360–73.

and by defining the needy primarily as the means by which the rich, through embracing the poor with alms, might achieve heavenly grace.[13]

The notion that the rich are saved by the poor is continuous throughout the Middle Ages but, as we shall see, is particularly prominent (and problematic) in the late fourteenth century. "It is for the rich to pay, the poor to pray" (*Diuitis est erogare, pauperis est orare*) preaches Thomas Brinton, and in the early fifteenth-century *Dives and Pauper*, Pauper warns the rich man: "þouȝ at þe dredful dom whan þey schul stondyn at þe barre aforn þe souereyn iuge, Crist Ihesus, þan elmesse dede schal ben þe beste frend þat þey schul han, for þat schal spekyn for hem & preyyn for / hem and sauyn hem ȝif þey schul ben sauyd."[14] In *Standards of Living in the Later Middle Ages* Christopher Dyer notes that in the view of the clergy "the rich and poor could be bound together in a complementary relationship, in which the rich exhibited mercy and pity by their gifts, and the poor reciprocated with gratitude and prayers. A social contract was thus advocated; the rich were morally improved, and the poor, by accepting their lot with patience and resignation, would also gain salvation."[15] While Dyer's view might at first seem more temperate than Mollat's, it nonetheless depends upon the poor "accepting" or idealizing their poverty, suppressing the realities of need by turning their attention away from this world and toward the next. This spiritualizing of need not only guarantees their own salvation, but makes them vital instruments in the salvation of the rich.

Often cited in the Middle Ages as the paradigm for the social, political, and moral relations between rich and poor was the biblical parable of Dives and Lazarus, in which a rich man feasts while a beggar lies starving at his door (Luke 16:19–31).[16] After both men have died, Lazarus is taken into heaven and, sitting next to God, judges Dives unworthy of grace. This story emphasizes not only the obligation of the rich to give to the poor on earth, but also the eschatological reversal of the social hierarchy in which the poor will sit in judgment over the rich. In his commentary on the parable, Bruno of Segni begins by noting these general moral lessons: "These words are most necessary both for the rich and for the poor, because they bring fear to the former and consolation to the latter."[17] For Bruno the poor are to be content with present material discom-

[13] Mollat notes that it was a commonplace assumption during the Middle Ages that the "pauper would seem to have been created and placed in the world for the sake of the rich man's salvation" (*Poor in the Middle Ages*, 106).

[14] *The Sermons of Thomas Brinton, Bishop of Rochester (1373–1389)*, ed. Sister Mary Aquinas Devlin (London: Royal Historical Society, 1954), Sermon 44, 1.194; *Dives and Pauper*, ed. Priscilla Heath Barnum, 1 vol. in 2 parts, EETS, 275, 280 (London: Oxford Univ. Press, 1976), 2.283.

[15] Dyer, *Standards of Living*, 236.

[16] One helpful study of medieval interpretations of the parables is Stephen Wailes, *Medieval Allegories of Jesus' Parables* (Berkeley: Univ. of California Press, 1987).

[17] Quoted in Wailes, *Medieval Allegories*, 255.

fort for, as we have seen, it is their path to salvation, while the rich are to fear the power and influence the poor will attain in the heavenly kingdom.

The inversion of sociopolitical status depicted in the parable of Dives and Lazarus is one of the oldest traditions in the Gospels.[18] As Wolfgang Stegemann observes, "the 'messianic' claim of Jesus and his followers was primarily socially oriented; ... it aimed for the reversal of the contemporary social order with a focus on eradicating the misery of the poor."[19] While Bruno of Segni advises that the rich "fear" the power the needy will wield in the life hereafter, Stegemann observes that the Gospels suggest that their "fear" might extend to a mistrust of the poor in the "contemporary social order" as well. For early medieval Christians, although poverty was inevitable and charity essential, the very presence of the poor might contain the seeds of social subversion.

Contributing to this perception of poverty as a condition potentially disruptive of the social order were the fierce thirteenth- and fourteenth-century conflicts between the friars and the Parisian secular masters over poverty and religious mendicancy.[20] In its earliest phases the debate centered around the conflicts between the Spiritual wing of the Franciscans and its more conservative element, the Conventuals.[21] In an effort to remain true to St. Francis's teachings the Spirituals claimed that to emulate the life of Christ was to live in actual poverty, without possession or ownership. This claim to "absolute" poverty opposed directly the established church's acceptance of and practical need for property. The Conventuals, on the other hand, in attempting to recognize the material demands of a growing order, submitted to Papal authority and acknowledged the necessity of the use of material goods. As a result of this schism within the Franciscan movement the question of the degree and quality of poverty itself came to be seen as disruptive of social and religious order. According to Gordon Leff, "Poverty became transformed from an adjunct to the life of the church into a challenge against it: from an end in itself into a signal for the end of the existing dispensation."[22]

Later phases of the controversy, beginning in 1321, focused upon the theological implications of the doctrine of Christ's absolute poverty. These were intellectual debates that sought to discredit altogether the notion of complete

[18] Walter Pilgrim, *Good News to the Poor: Wealth and Poverty in Luke – Acts* (Minneapolis: Augsburg, 1981), 57–63.

[19] Stegemann, *Gospel and the Poor*, 30.

[20] The antimendicant controversy has been addressed in M. D. Lambert, *Franciscan Poverty: The Doctrine of the Absolute Poverty of Christ and the Apostles in the Franciscan Order 1210–1323* (London: S. P. C. K., 1961); Gordon Leff, *Heresy in the Later Middle Ages: The Relation of Heterodoxy to Dissent, c. 1250–1450*, 2 vols. (Manchester: Manchester Univ. Press, 1967), 2.51–255; and David Burr, *Olivi and Franciscan Poverty: The Origins of the 'Usus Pauper' Controversy* (Philadelphia: Univ. of Pennsylvania Press, 1989).

[21] See Leff, *Heresy in the Middle Ages*, 2.51–66, and Lambert, *Franciscan Poverty*.

[22] Leff, *Heresy in the Middle Ages*, 2.58.

indigence. The rejection of the Franciscan principle of the absolute poverty of Christ in John XXII's bull *Cum inter nonnullos* (1323) signaled the defeat of the radical fraternal notion of need. By denying that Christ and the Apostles had always lived without possessions and that what they had used had been of necessity and not of right, John, in assuming dominion and ownership of property, in effect repudiated both propertylessness and poverty. The bull "made a myth of evangelical poverty, and it made [the Franciscan] claim to emulate it hollow."[23] Ultimately the antimendicant debate over poverty functioned to deflect concern from the social realities of the problem of indigence and to "divert attention to more intellectually manageable issues."[24]

By the late fourteenth century significant increases in the numbers of urban as well as rural poor – primarily the result of successive attacks of plague and famine – forced new attention to the disparity between the religious ideal of poverty and the overwhelming actualities of distress. Rather than initiating a movement of charitable concern, however, the growth in the number of needy caused widespread anxiety, particularly among wealthy landowners.[25] The indigent were mistrusted, even feared, as agents of social change and disruption. Vagrancy was on the rise as workers left their tenancies in search of better wages and living conditions.[26] The response was repressive labor legislation which sought not only to curtail the independence of the needy laborer, but also to preserve the social hierarchy, to make clear the moral distinction between rich and poor.[27]

II

Langland's *Piers Plowman* is in part a response to the social crisis of late fourteenth-century poverty, a response that, like the traditions of poverty themselves, is deeply ambivalent about the place and function of the poor in a Christian society. How does one reconcile an immediate and oppressive social reality with the conflicting demands of traditional moral and spiritual ideals? *Should* these be reconciled? The images of the poor at the center of *Piers Plowman* at once acknowledge the reality of human suffering and at the same time transfigure that reality in such a way that material distress becomes spiritual concern. Allegory recuperates history.

After Hunger has been appeased with the best fruits of the harvest at the end of the plowing of the half-acre episode, the narrator of *Piers Plowman* interrupts the discourse of dearth with a prophetic warning that every worker must "wyn-

[23] Leff, *Heresy in the Middle Ages*, 2.166.
[24] Pearsall, "Poverty and Poor People," 173.
[25] See Mollat, *Poor in the Middle Ages*, 191–293.
[26] See Mollat, *Poor in the Middle Ages*, 191–293, and Aers, *Community*, 20–35.
[27] See Mollat, *Poor in the Middle Ages*, 115-93.

neth whiles ȝe mowe," for relief from famine is only temporary as "Hunger hiderwardes hasteth hym faste" (C.8.343–44).[28] In these early passus, as I have argued elsewhere, neither the workers in the field nor the reader of the plowing scene has been able completely to ignore the immediate demands of the material reality of famine, even when those demands interfere with the soul's efforts to understand spiritual truths.[29] As we move into the poem's central visions, however, we find an apparent resolution to the problem of reconciling the demands of life in the world with the requirements of a more abstract spiritual practice:

> Treuthe herde telle her-of and to Peres sente
> To taken his teme and tilion þe erthe,
> And purchasede hym a pardoun *a pena et a culpa*,
> For hym and his ayres for euere to ben assoiled,
> And bad hym holden hym at hoem and eryen his leyes
> And alle þat holpe hym to erye, to sette or to sowe
> Or eny manere mester þat myhte Peres auayle,
> Pardoun with Peres þe plouhman perpetuelly he graunteth. (C.9.1–8)

Truth – the elusive, abstract, original goal of the pilgrimage – has apparently observed the muddle on the half-acre and offers a fittingly abstract solution: a pardon for all who help Piers "to erye, to sette or to sowe." Truth seems to have forgotten the difficulty Piers encountered in getting the rebellious workers on the half-acre to complete these very tasks. In its effort to overlook the complex demands of economic necessity, Truth's Pardon initiates the central visions' movement beyond concern for the mundane problems of need, beyond history itself, toward an idealized representation of poverty.

Truth's Pardon is perhaps the most widely discussed image in *Piers Plowman*. Critical studies of the pardon episode have focused primarily, and rather insistently, upon the nature of the pardon itself, its validity, and the significance of its destruction at the end of Passus 7 of the B-text.[30] Little scholarly attention has been directed, however, to the nearly three hundred verses that constitute a

[28] Morton W. Bloomfield emphasizes the apocalyptic nature of this and other prophecies in the poem in *Piers Plowman as a Fourteenth-Century Apocalypse* (New Brunswick: Rutgers Univ. Press, 1962), 112, 211–12. For a fuller analysis of Langland's prophetic voice, see Theodore L. Steinberg, *Piers Plowman and Prophecy: An Approach to the C-Text* (New York: Garland, 1991).

[29] See my "Allegory on the Half-Acre: The Demands of History."

[30] Influential studies of the Pardon scene in *Piers Plowman* include Nevill Coghill, "The Pardon of Piers Plowman," *Proceedings of the British Academy* 30 (1944): 303–57; Robert Frank, "The Pardon Scene in *Piers Plowman*," *Speculum* 26 (1951): 317–31; John Lawlor, "*Piers Plowman*: The Pardon Reconsidered," *Modern Language Review* 45 (1950): 449–58; Rosemary Woolf, "The Tearing of the Pardon," in *Piers Plowman: Critical Approaches*, ed. S. S. Hussey (London: Methuen, 1969), 50–75. See also David A. Lawton, "*Piers Plowman*: On Tearing and Not Tearing the Pardon," *Philological Quarterly* 60 (1981): 414–22.

detailed gloss on the actual text of that document.[31] These lines bring before us once again the model of the good society, first articulated in the dreamer's description in the Prologue of the various folk on the field, and revisited in Passus 8 in Piers's attempts to institute an estate-based social system on the half-acre.[32] In the world of Truth's Pardon, kings and knights must defend the church and "ryhtfulliche in reumes ruylen þe comune" (C.9.10) if they are to be eligible for grace. Bishops will be "yblessed" if they act "as they sholde" and "liue as þei lereth men" (C.9.13, 19). Merchants and lawyers must practice their trades with "clene consience," putting aside "couetyse of wynnynge" and considering first the welfare of the less advantaged (C.9.26). Laborers must work "lellyche and lauhfollyche" (C.9.59), and all must give to the poor, with careful discrimination. Truth presents in these three hundred lines a kind of contractual agreement in which the participants will receive heavenly mercy "yf they ben as they sholde," that is, if they live in accordance with the social as well as moral requirements of their estates. "Alle þe peple hadde pardon ynow þat parfitliche lyuede" (C.9.43). To live "parfitliche," it would seem, is to live in one's place. According to Morton Bloomfield, "Until man's relations with man and to God are set on a just foundation and each *status* performs its proper functions, no true reformation of society is possible. Until we get such a reformation, love or grace cannot manifest itself."[33] In an effort to reform the community, Truth's Pardon prescribes not specific, mundane behaviors that might respond to actual circumstance, but a manner of living that corresponds to the general precepts of an established code of conduct. In contrast, the social order Piers establishes on the half-acre is designed to encourage individual support of a specific mundane actuality, the plowing of the field. One worker must "sowe þe sak for shedynge of the whete" (C.8.8), while other women with "longe fyngres" (C.8.9) will spin wool and flax. The knight will "hunte hardelyche" (C.8.28) hares and foxes, and Piers will oversee production on the field. These unique individuals are assigned specific tasks in exchange not for some elusive spiritual reward but for their very "lyflode" (C.8.15). Truth's Pardon, however, outlines general modes of conduct for the collective groups of medieval estates. It is prescriptive rather than descriptive. In addition, we do not see its figures enact any of the gloss's prescribed "ryhtful" behavior, but are left to imagine its successful completion. The pardon is static rather than active, is not a representation of reality but an interpretation of it. It is, after all, a gloss, a text generated by the interpretation of another text, a model of society generated by a preconceived notion of ideal

[31] Critics who do discuss in any detail the text of the gloss on Truth's Pardon address in particular the C-reviser's insertions. See especially E. Talbot Donaldson, *The C-Text and its Poet* (New Haven: Yale Univ. Press, 1949), 121–55, and Shepherd, "Poverty in *Piers Plowman*," 171–75.

[32] See C.Prol.19–94; C.8.7–34.

[33] Bloomfield, *Piers Plowman as a Fourteenth-century Apocalypse*, 132.

conduct. Indeed, although we discover at the end of the passus that the actual text of the Pardon consists of only "two lynes" from the Athanasian Creed, "and nat a lettre more" (C.9.286), its gloss too has achieved the status of text. Its advice to merchants, for example, is apparently written "in þe margine" of the document and, furthermore, the narrator (perhaps Langland himself) suggests that it is painful to "rede" the gloss's description of the poor (C.9.22, 82).[34] In a sense, Truth's Pardon has transformed the society of the half-acre into a text to be read and interpreted, a text which might support abstract, allegorical significance. Truth's new social system, with its prescriptive demands for ideal behavior, begins the movement in the central visions of *Piers Plowman* from outer to inner, from a literal to a figural understanding of life in the world.

While the gloss of the pardon works generally to idealize human behavior, to take away its active, individual connection with social actuality, it also works specifically to contain the social group most dangerous to the proper spiritual understanding of need, the poor themselves. The B- and C-versions of *Piers Plowman* differ most significantly in their discussions of the problem of the needy. In the pardon section, however, both texts agree that the poor are not in any way to be perceived as victims of social injustice. The question raised in the pardon concerning the indigent is not what to do about poverty – charitable giving is the obvious answer – but who is worthy of that charity:

> Beggares and biddares beth nat in þat bulle
> Bote the sugestioun be soth þat shapeth hym to begge.
> For he þat begeth or biddeth, but yf he haue nede,
> He is fals and faytour and defraudeth the nedy
> And also gileth hym þat gyueth and taketh agayne his wille.
> For he þat gyueth for goddes loue wolde nat gyue, his thankes,
> Bote ther he wiste were wel grete nede
> And most merytorie to men þat he ȝeueth fore. (C.9.61–68)[35]

Having spoken of the need for discriminatory charity in the Hunger episode, Langland makes clear in this passage that charity must seek out the truly needy. Those beggars who are fraudulent, who have no need, are "fals" and "faytour." They "beth nat in þat bulle" and will not receive the benefits of the pardon, for they disrupt the act of proper discriminatory giving by deceiving ("gileth") the giver. In a sense, however, the deserving poor, too, are excluded from the terms of the pardon. Except in their capacity as recipients of alms they have no place in the social order Truth depicts. They have no vocation or estate but are marginalized, useful only as an outlet for charitable giving. While knights and

[34] Certainly, too, the narrator summarizes and reports the contents of the gloss as though he had an actual text before him.

[35] Cf. B.7.65–71.

bishops, merchants and lawyers are given instructions as to how they should conduct themselves, the needy poor are described in terms of how they might enable the just ("merytorie") conduct of members of the other estates. This passage moves from admonitions for "he þat begeth" to concern for "he þat gyueth," as the intellectual problem of discerning "guile" supersedes the injunction to active giving.

Although both the B- and C-versions of *Piers Plowman* move toward the spiritualization of poverty in the gloss on Truth's Pardon, they do so in different ways. The B-text is unequivocal in its condemnation of beggars who ask for more than their daily bread: "He haþ ynouȝ þat haþ breed ynouȝ, þouȝ he haue noȝt ellis" (B.7.86):

> For þei lyue in no loue ne no lawe holde.
> Thei wedde no womman þat þei wiþ deele
> But as wilde bestes with wehee worþen vppe and werchen,
> And bryngen forþ barnes þat bastardes men calleþ. (B.7.90–93)

These rapacious suppliants are perceived literally as animals, "wilde bestes" whose inarticulate "wehees" reveal at once their willing abandonment to physical desire and their essential difference from other human beings. They are antisocial in their contempt of the law, and disruptive of the bonds of proper moral as well as social organization as they refuse to marry and produce legitimate offspring. David Aers suggests that Langland's particular unease with the destruction of the nuclear family is at least in part a response to the newly developing family formation of mobile workers in the late fourteenth century:

> [T]he landless family was not a unit of production bound to a family holding. In so far as it was an economic unit, it depended on each individual selling her or his labour-power on the market as an autonomous worker. Under these circumstances traditional parental controls and sanctions were loosened, for the means of subsistence was attained by individual access to the labour-market, not to a family holding. Such changed conditions would lead to changed and more mobile patterns of household formation, among which marriage might become at least possible at earlier ages and undertaken more independently of parental wishes than had been customary.[36]

Though Langland may well have been responding to actual historical conditions in this description of beggars, the dehumanization of those who were considered undeserving poor was, as we have seen, at the same time a well-used device of disparagement, one which Langland seems content here to embrace.

Langland's negative characterization of beggars in the gloss on Truth's Pardon recalls Piers's initial angry response to those workers on the half-acre who

[36] Aers, *Community*, 52–53.

turned toward drink rather than toil.[37] Many canonists believed that those poor who were able to work but chose to devote their time to illicit or wasteful pleasures were the only group to whom alms should be denied as a matter of principle.[38] According to the twelfth-century decretist Huguccio we must judge as undeserving of alms he who "is able to work and to get food for himself by his labor, but chooses not to, and instead plays all day long with dies and cubes" (*potest laborare et suo labore sibi victum querere et non vult, set tota die ludit in alea vel taxillis*).[39] In the plowing episode, Piers's initial denunciatory response to the willfully disruptive shirkers was later tempered by his acknowledgment of and sympathy for the harsh realities of need they experience in the "duntes" of Hunger (C.8.205–300). The Pardon's first depiction of indolent beggars, on the other hand, avoids any such sympathetic response to the constraints of material actuality. These figures are presented as more than willfully idle. Laziness seems only one small weakness in the midst of much larger moral failings. The Pardon's beggars are by their very natures apt to all forms of social as well as moral disruption. They are apt to sin. Therefore, Langland suggests in the gloss, one must ask first not how to help them, but which of them to help.

The B-version of *Piers* offers a straightforward guideline for determining which needy persons are deserving of both pardon and charity:

> Ac olde men and hore þat helplees ben of strengþe,
> And wommen wiþ childe þat werche ne mowe,
> Blynde and bedreden and broken hire membres
> That taken þis myschief mekeliche as Mesels and oþere,
> Han as pleyn pardon as þe Plowman hymselue;
> For loue of hire lowe herte oure lord haþ hem graunted
> Hir penaunce and hir Purgatorie vpon þis pure erþe. (B.7.100–106)

In a specific allusion to the Beatitudes, old men, women, children, the sick – all those who cannot help themselves – are worthy of "pleyn pardon" if they accept their lot ("mischief") with "lowe herte." They do not disturb the social order, but instead contribute to its stability by providing an acceptable outlet for charitable giving on the part of the other estates. As Geoffrey Shepherd observes, "A well-ordered society needs justice and the fruits of labour: for its full health it also needs to exercise charity. The rich need the poor as much as the poor need the rich."[40] Passive victims of mischance, these poor are the "appropriate" recipients of alms. Furthermore, voiceless and unindividuated, they are convenient vehicles for successful allegorical representation.

[37] Cf. C.8.123–48.

[38] Brian Tierney, "The Decretists," 368–71.

[39] Quoted in Tierney, "The Decretists," 370.

[40] Shepherd, "Poverty in *Piers Plowman*," 174.

In the C-text, however, Langland complicates the B-version's simplistic view of need by thrusting the actualities of distress before us. Before he gives us the guidelines for proper discrimination so eagerly presented in B, Langland inserts an extended description of the plight of the poor into the C-text gloss on the Pardon:[41]

> Woet no man, as y wene, who is worthy to haue;
> Ac þat most neden aren oure neyhebores, and we nyme gode hede,
> As prisones in puttes and pore folk in cotes,
> Charged with childrene and chief lordes rente;
> Þat they with spynnyng may spare, spenen hit on hous-huyre,
> Bothe in mylke and in mele, to make with papelotes
> To aglotye with here gurles that greden aftur fode.
> And hemsulue also soffre muche hunger,
> And wo in wynter-tymes, and wakynge on nyhtes
> To rise to þe reule to rokke þe cradel,
> Bothe to carde and to kembe, to cloute and to wasche,
> And to rybbe and to rele, rusches to pylie,
> That reuthe is to rede or in ryme shewe
> The wo of this wommen þat wonyeth in cotes;
> And of monye oþer men þat moche wo soffren,
> Bothe afyngred and afurste, to turne þe fayre outward,
> And ben abasched for to begge and wollen nat be aknowe
> What hem nedeth at here neyhebores at noon and at eue. (C.9.70–87)

Upon first consideration, this passage is both shocking in its apparent realism and, perhaps, surprising in its sympathetic view of the indigent. "No man" knows how to discover the truly needy. As Shepherd has observed, the C-insertion forcefully conveys the "felt and inner bitterness of poverty."[42] The presentation works in an almost cinematic fashion, drawing us in, moving from the general, panoramic image of "oure neyhebores" to "prisones in puttes," then to "pore folk in cotes," and finally to the intimate scene of a darkened cottage inhabited by a poor woman and her children. More importantly, however, it works gradually to engage our emotions, to provoke an almost empathetic response to the plight of the needy.

The passage begins with language that echoes a sermonlike, New Testament discourse, "[W]ho is worthy to haue; / Ac þat most neden aren oure neyhebores, and we nyme gode hede" (cf. "Thow shalt love thy neighbor as thyself" [*Diliges proximum tuum tamquam te ipsum*] of Mark 12:31). The statement is general.

[41] The complete insertion in the C-text of *Piers Plowman* runs from lines 70–161. With the addition of these 92 lines in C, the poor are the social group most extensively discussed in the gloss on the Pardon. Another insertion into the gloss, lines 187–281, deals with the question of the place of hermits in the system of estates.

[42] Shepherd, "Poverty in *Piers Plowman*," 172.

"Oure neyhebores" refers not to actual, immediate human beings, but to the collective, almost allegorical group of "neyhebores," common to religious discourse, that comprise the earthly community of Christians. A medieval audience would most certainly recognize the statement and would expect it to be followed by either a discussion of the corporal works of mercy due one's "neighbor" (cf. Matt. 25:34–40)[43] or, and perhaps more commonly, a reading and explication of the parable of the Good Samaritan (Luke 10:30–37). The central moral *quaestio* presented in this parable, "*quis horum trium videtur tibi proximus fuisse illi qui incidit in latrones*?" ("which of these three, in thy opinion, proved himself neighbor to him who fell among the robbers?"), strongly echoes the opening statement of the passage.

As the passage continues, however, we find not a generalized discussion of acts of mercy, but an increasingly intimate portrait of an individual human being. The language of the passage, too, becomes increasingly more concrete and mundane. Solid, common nouns and verbs of common labor proliferate: "mylke," "mele," "papelotes," "gurles," "fode," "cradel," "rusches," "rokke," "carde," "kembe," "cloute," "wasche," "rybbe," "rele," "pylie." These words thrust before us with a kind of immediate tangibility the precarious material existence of an individual poor woman.[44] We are exposed to the actual, physical conditions she must endure: "wo in wynter-tymes" and "wakynge on nyhtes." The allusion to "wynter-tymes" and "nyhtes" further suggests that this pauper's "wo" is as inevitable as the seasons and the days, as the course of time itself. Instead of the more usual positive view of the cyclicity of time, which suggests that "spring" will always come, that day will follow even the darkest of nights, this woman's life seems only an eternity of winters and nights. As a result, we cannot transform our image of this woman and her children into some kind of idealized or objectified representation of poverty. Instead, we are absorbed and shocked by the plight of a "neyhebore" who must "soffre muche hunger." Furthermore, the poetic line itself adds to our sense of intensifying emotional in-

[43] The passage certainly recalls the corporal works of mercy proposed in Matt. 25:34–40: "Come, ye blessed of my Father, possess you the kingdom prepared for you from the foundation of the world. For I was hungry and you gave me to eat, I was thirsty and you gave me to drink; I was a stranger, and you took me in: Naked, and you covered me: sick, and you visited me: I was in prison, and you came to me. Then shall the just answer him, saying: Lord, when did we see thee hungry, and feed thee; thirsty, and gave thee drink? And when did we see thee a stranger, and took thee in? or naked, and covered thee? And when did we see thee sick, or in prison, and came to thee? And the king answering, shall say to them: Amen I say to you, as long as you did it to one of these my least brethren, you did it to me."

[44] While I find that the personal intimacy of this passage draws us closer to the horrifying actualities of distress, Jill Mann draws the same conclusion from a different point of observation: "The poverty of the poor is most clearly shown in the simple fact that they are 'not there' in the[se] lines describing their lives; they are, as it were, only the emptiness which is filled up with the daily round of wearing tasks and pitiful items of food and drink" ("Eating and Drinking in 'Piers Plowman,'" *Essays and Studies* 32 [1979], 32).

volvement in this part of the insertion. Embraced by two lines whose first alliterative stave is the word "wo" (78, 83), lines 79, 81, and 82 seem to surge in their shared, forceful "r" alliteration as they culminate in the poet's own self-conscious expression of pity: "That reuthe is to rede or in ryme shewe" (82).[45] The ineffability topos, though common to Chaucer, is rare in Langland, and would seem rather florid in the midst of his relentlessly plain style. Indeed, one of the poem's only admissions of verbal inadequacy occurs in Passus 5 of the B-text – it is cut from the C-version – as the narrator reveals that he "kan noȝt faire shewe" what "bifel" Robert the Robber after his sorrowful confession to Repentance (B.5.471).[46] That Langland should use this topos here suggests just how powerfully overwhelming this portrait of poverty is.

Langland's authorial intrusion would seem to confirm (and to ensure) the intensely sympathetic response that these lines have evoked in the reader. That feeling is so forceful that we risk losing our aloof moral perspective and indulging in indignation and outrage at this social injustice, those "chief lordes rente[s]." Furthermore, the mundane intimacy of the scene with its insistence on the literal, material actualities of distress threatens our ability to read the passage allegorically. I have been suggesting, however, that Langland's intent in his discussion of the poor in the gloss on Truth's Pardon is to objectify poverty, to disentangle it from the web of historical circumstance that so endangers the proper moral as well as allegorical understanding of need. The final three lines of the C-text insertion serve to restore that moral perspective as they transform our sympathy for the distress of the poor into admiration for their ability to endure discomforts nobly:[47]

> Bothe afyngred and afurste, to turne þe fayre outward,
> And ben abasched for to begge and wollen nat be aknowe
> What hem nedeth at here neyhebores at noon and at eue. (C.9.85–87)

Langland uses the intensive adverbial prefix "af" (from "of" – "ofhyngred" and "ofþurste") to emphasize that these poor are not merely hungry and thirsty, but are exceedingly famished.[48] Even so, they do not complain or ask for pity and

[45] Cf. C.16.16.

[46] Another is placed in the mouth of the naive dreamer who, after he has experienced his first vision, challenges, "What þis meteles bymeneth, ȝe men þat ben merye, / Deuyne ȝe, for y ne dar, by dere god almyhten" (C.Prol.217–18).

[47] The association of patient endurance and spiritual poverty may be traced to fifth- to seventh-century attempts to expand the virtue's application to daily life while dissociating it from its common connection to martyrdom. A summary of late medieval notions of patience is Ralph Hanna's "Some Commonplaces of Late Medieval Patience Discussions: An Introduction," in *The Triumph of Patience: Medieval and Renaissance Studies*, ed. Gerald R. Schiffhorst (Orlando: University Press of Florida, 1978), 65–87.

[48] Cf. C.16.15.

alms, but "turne þe fayre outward" and are "abasched for to begge." They present a "fayre," an appearance or outward image, that masks the inner, physical reality of their plight. More materially, the image may suggest that in order to keep up an acceptable appearance, the poor "turne" their clothes "outward" so that the threadbare faces the inside. In a sense, they have transformed themselves into idealized allegories of the literal actuality of need. Our sympathy and indignation for the poor aroused by the earlier lines of the passage, though not rejected, have been replaced by a kind of general admiration for the pauper's ability to endure such utter distress humbly and patiently.

These last three lines have brought us back to the question that opens the passage, "Who is worthy to have?" Our concern has been directed away from social inequity and toward consideration for the proper moral behavior of the poor. I do not mean to suggest that Langland discounts the suffering of the needy. Certainly we may see the depths of his social compassion in Piers's horror at Hunger's brutality in the plowing of the half-acre (cf. C.8.171–78) and we cannot deny the power of the Pardon's portrait of need. Still, even in the plowing scene, we see Piers realize that "fere of famyen" was not enough to engender "filial loue" (C.8.215–16). For Langland, the spiritual ideal of poverty must take precedence. Unlike the B-text's simplistic, ahistorical images of the poor in the gloss on Truth's Pardon, the C-insertion, through its "realistic" representation of poverty, arouses the most basic motive for charity, our sense of "filial loue." Ultimately, however, it turns that love in the proper moral direction, in a direction that can at once support allegory and embrace a transfigured vision of history, that might allow us to accept the traditional ideology of need presented in the central visions of *Piers Plowman* even in the face of material actuality.

At this point in the Pardon's gloss, the C-text returns to the matter of B as it now easily invokes the spiritual ideal of poverty:

> Ac olde and hore, þat helples ben and nedy,
> And wymmen with childe þat worche ne mowe,
> Blynde and bedredne and broken in here membres,
> And alle pore pacient, apayed of goddes sonde,
> As mesels and mendenantes, men yfalle in meschief,
> As prisones and pilgrimes and paraunter men yrobbed
> Or bylowe thorw luther men and lost here catel after,
> Or thorw fuyr or thorw floed yfalle into pouerte,
> That taketh thise meschiefes mekeliche and myldeliche at herte,
> For loue of here lowe hertes oure lord hath hem ygraunted
> Here penaunce and here purgatorye vppon this puyre erthe
> And pardon with the plouhman *a pena et a culpa*. (C.9.175–86)

This passage is very similar to its counterpart in the B-version. Both categorize the deserving poor as old men, women, children, and the sick, all of whom are "helples." Both stress the meekness with which these victims of mischance bear the burden of indigence. As Pearsall observes, "the essential point of emphasis is now that it is the patience and humility with which the distresses of poverty are endured that make it a form of spiritual purgation."[49] C, however, adds to this traditional group those poor who are victims of social evils, "men yrobbed / Or bylowe thorw luther men and lost here catel after," and natural disaster, "thorw fuyr or thorw floed yfalle into pouerte."[50] As in its earlier insertion, the C-text here refuses to reject the inevitable hazards of life in the world. Again, however, it transforms those actual difficulties into an idealized image of noble suffering, "purgatorye." Langland offers, instead of remedies for physical distress, a strategy of interpretation of that distress – as a present "purgatorye" – which offers no change in the material condition but slides it into a scheme of spiritual salvation. Earthly experience must now be understood allegorically.

The images of poverty in the gloss on Truth's Pardon thrust the reality of need before us only to revise or reinterpret that reality in abstract spiritual terms. Through them we move gradually, even painlessly, in a kind of spiritual metamorphosis from material to spiritual concern. Piers himself learns that he must refigure his understanding of the plowing of the half-acre and in the B-text decides that he shall "cessen of [his] sowyng ... & swynke noȝt so harde" (B.7.122).[51]

> Ne aboute my bilyue so bisy be na moore;
> Of preieres and of penaunce my plouȝ shal ben herafter,
> And wepen whan I sholde werche þouȝ whete breed me faille.
> The prophete his payn eet in penaunce and in sorwe
> By þat þe Sauter vs seith, and so dide othere manye.
> That loueth god lelly his liflode is ful esy:
> *Fuerunt michi lacrime mee panes die ac nocte.*
> And but if luc lye he lereþ vs anoþer
> By foweles þat are noȝt bisy aboute þe bely ioye;
> *Ne soliciti sitis* he seiþ in þe gospel,
> And sheweþ vs by ensample vs selue to wisse.
> The foweles in þe firmament, who fynt hem at wynter?

[49] Pearsall, "Poverty and Poor People," 181. In his edition of the B-text of *Piers Plowman*, Schmidt likewise remarks on these lines: "It is not the suffering of the handicapped but the patience and humility they bear it with that wins God's favour" (*The Vision of Piers Plowman: A Critical Edition of the B-Text Based on Trinity College Cambridge MS B.15.17*, ed. A. V. C. Schmidt, 2d ed. [London: Everyman, 1995], 436, note to B.7.101–4).

[50] The allusion to disaster "thorw fuyr or thorw floed" may recall the prophetic warning at the end of Passus 8 that those who do not work well will be harmed "Thorw flodes and thorw foule wederes" (8.348).

[51] In his most infamous revision of the B-text Langland removes not only this speech but the entire tearing of the Pardon scene from the C-version of *Piers Plowman*.

Whan þe frost freseþ fode hem bihoueþ;
Haue þei no gerner to go to but god fynt hem alle. (B.7.123–35)

In a reversal of his earlier substitution of the "plouh pote" for the "pyk-staff" (C.8.64), "preieres and ... penaunce" will now do the work of the "plouȝ." In fact, Piers counsels a complete rejection of material concern in the faith that God will "fynt hem alle."

As if to emphasize the distance we have come from the rebellion on the half-acre Langland closes Passus 9 with urgent cautionary advice that echoes the prophetic warning that concludes the plowing scene (cf. C.8.343–54):[52]

Forthy y rede ȝow renkes þat riche ben on this erthe,
Vp truste of ȝoure tresor trionales to haue,
Be ȝe neuere þe baldere to breke þe ten hestes;
And nameliche ȝe maistres, mayres and iuges,
That haen the welthe of this world and wise men ben holde
To purchace ȝow pardoun and the popes bulles.
At þe dredful dome when dede shullen ryse
And comen alle bifore Crist acountes to ȝelde,
How we ladde oure lyf here and his lawes kepte
And how we dede day be day the doem wol reherce ....
Forthy y consayle alle cristene to crye god mercy,
And Marie his moder be oure mene to hym
That god gyue vs grace here ar we go hennes
Suche werkes to worche the while we ben here
That aftur oure deth-day Dowel reherce
At þe day of dome we dede as he tauhte. Amen. (C.9.334–43,348–53)

The prophetic message at the end of Passus 8 warns all "werkmen" to "wynneth whiles ȝe mowe" lest "famyne" and "pestilences" arise and "derthe be iustice." People must work now, in this world, with an eye toward staving off inevitable natural disasters. In the plowing of the half-acre, dearth is justice as the law of Hunger ultimately prevails. By the end of Passus 9, however, the dreamer ad-

[52] Ac y warne ȝow werkmen, wynneth whiles ȝe mowe,
For Hunger hiderwardes hasteth hym faste.
He shal awake thorw water, wastors to chaste,
And ar fewe ȝeres be fulfeld famyne shal aryse,
And so sayth Saturne and sente vs to warne.
Thorw flodes and thorw foule wederes fruyttes shollen fayle;
Pruyde and pestilences shal moche peple feche.
Thre shypes and a schaef with an viii folwynge
Shal brynge bane and batayle on bothe half þe mone.
And thenne shal deth withdrawe and derthe be iustice
And Dawe þe deluare dey for defaute
But yf god of his goodnesse graunte vs a trewe. (C.8.343–54)

vises us to not to "wyn," not to consider our position in the natural world, but to work according to "his lawes," the "ten hestes," so that we might by the "day of dome" earn heavenly grace. The demands of history have been superseded by the demands of justice, both physical and eschatological. Prophecy has been replaced by prayer as the dreamer concludes his message with "Amen."

The spiritualized interpretation of poverty established in the gloss on Truth's Pardon is strengthened and recurrently exemplified as we move into the central visions of *Piers Plowman*. After the introduction of the Pardon, the dreamer sets out on his search for Dowel and, in the manner of a traditional dream vision, encounters such abstract personifications as Thought, Wit, Study, Clergy, and Scripture.[53] These figures expound in turn upon the necessity of learning in achieving salvation, but are interrupted by an extended discussion of the virtues of indigence put forth by a figure labeled Rechelesnesse.[54] As his name suggests, Rechelesnesse seems to embody the very notion of "care-less-ness," *ne soliciti sitis*, the ultimate act of faith expressed through complete renunciation of the material world.[55] Because of his disinterest in mundane necessity, Rechelesnesse is aptly suited to the presentation of spiritualized need.[56]

While the gloss on Truth's Pardon idealizes the poor by disembodying their actual experiences, by transforming our understanding of their position in society, Rechelesnesse's discourse enriches and establishes the ideal of spiritual poverty by exploring it within the context of Biblical representations of need. He begins by invoking the orthodox notion that the poor person is a representative of Christ on earth, "For god, as þe gospel saith, goth ay as þe pore" (C.12.99). Rechelesnesse then continues his discussion of the ideal poor by referring to New Testament representations of indigence. No other passage in

[53] See Passus 10–11. Studies of the middle of the poem include Britton J. Harwood, "'Clergye' and the Action of the Third Vision in 'Piers Plowman,'" *Modern Philology* 70 (1973): 279–90, and Mary Carruthers, *The Search for St. Truth: A Study of Meaning in Piers Plowman* (Evanston: Northwestern Univ. Press, 1973), 81–148. Representative studies on the three lives in the central visions include Robert W. Frank, Jr., *Piers Plowman and the Scheme of Salvation: An Interpretation of Dowel, Dobet, and Dobest* (1957; reprint: New Haven: Yale Univ. Press, 1969), and John F. Adams, "*Piers Plowman* and the Three Ages of Man," *JEGP* 61 (1962): 23–41.

[54] Donaldson's discussion of Rechelesnesse in *Piers Plowman: The C-Text and Its Poet*, 169–75, is still the most useful study of the figure. See also Harwood, "'Clergye' and the Action of the Third Vision," 289–90.

[55] Though some have understood Rechelesnesse to represent carelessness or frivolity, critics generally agree that he signifies most persuasively the positive quality of "throwing oneself upon God" (Shepherd, "Poverty in *Piers Plowman*," 182). Wendy Scase claims "there is no evidence that, say, attribution of the praise of poverty to Rechelesnesse was felt by early readers to undermine the authority of the poverty polemic" (*Piers Plowman and the New Anticlericalism* [Cambridge: Cambridge Univ. Press, 1989], 77–78).

[56] A figure like Rechelesnesse would certainly have no place on the half-acre.

Piers Plowman contains more New Testament quotations on apostolic poverty.[57] The effect is to add yet another layer of textual authority to the already spiritualized image of the poor. Finally, in a movement reminiscent of that presented in the gloss to Truth's Pardon, Rechelesnesse transforms and abstracts the notion of poverty itself by yoking it to the virtue of patience:

> And alle þe wyse þat euere were, by auhte y can aspye,
> Preisede pouerte for beste, if pacience hit folowe,
> And bothe bettere and blessedere by manyfold then richesse.
> Althouh he be sour to soffre, þer cometh a swete aftur.
> As on a walnote withoute is a bittere barke
> And aftur þat bittere barke, be þe scale aweye,
> Is a cornel of confort, kynde to restore;
> So aftur, penaunce and pouerte, pacientliche ytake,
> Maketh man to haue mynde in god and his mercy to craue,
> The which is þe cornel of confort for alle cristene soules. (C.12.139–48)

Like the narrator of the fourteenth-century alliterative *Patience*, who sadly observes that "pouerte and pacyence are nedes playferes," Rechelesnesse links the two virtues inextricably in this guide to heavenly grace.[58] Patience must follow poverty, and it does so even literally in this account. The threefold repetition of the word "aftur" in the passage suggests that as proper Christians our attentions ought not to be directed toward present material discomfort but to what should follow thereafter, God's "mercy." In a sense, patience is the virtue one must finally seek, for God's "cornel of confort" is attained not through the experiencing of need but through steadfast endurance of distress. Poverty, patiently endured, has become a source of moral strengthening and spiritual focusing.[59]

With its agricultural imagery, Rechelesnesse's description of patient poverty also echoes a common medieval figure for allegorical reading. Though based in the gospels of Matthew and Luke, the figure is perhaps best expressed by Chaucer, "For Seint Paul seith that al that writen is, / To oure doctrine it is ywrite, ywis; / Taketh the fruyt, and lat the chaf be stille."[60] In this formulation, what we seek is the deeper meaning, the moral or philosophical Truth, the "fruyt" that is hidden in fable or writing beneath the less important "chaff." For Rechelesnesse, one discovers the value of poverty by allegorizing need, by breaking

[57] Donaldson, *The C-Text and Its Poet*, 171.

[58] *Patience*, in *The Poems of the Pearl Manuscript*, ed. Malcolm Andrew and Ronald Waldron (Berkeley: Univ. of California Press, 1978), 187, line 45. On the medieval tradition of linking patience and poverty see Frank, *Piers Plowman and the Scheme of Salvation*, 73–75.

[59] Pearsall, "Poverty and Poor People," 183.

[60] Chaucer, *The Nun's Priest's Tale*, 3441–43, in *The Riverside Chaucer*, ed. Larry D. Benson, 3d ed. (Boston: Houghton Mifflin, 1987). Cf. Matt. 3:12, "Whose fan is in his hand, and he will thoroughly cleanse his floor and gather his wheat into the barn; but the chaff he will burn with unquenchable fire." See also Luke 3:17.

through the tough literal shell of actual physical distress and recognizing its spiritually restorative properties: "As on a walnote withoute is a bittere barke / And aftur þat bittere barke, be þe scale aweye, / Is a cornel of conforte, kynde to restore." Rechelesnesse continues his discourse with a flurry of agricultural images, all designed to express figurally the rewards of patient poverty.[61] By linking patience and poverty, and by allegorizing these themes, these images achieve the sublimation of need.

From this point in the poem until the end of the central visions little more is said concerning simple poverty. Patient endurance of distress has become the dominant theme. The dreamer in *Piers Plowman* never does encounter a figure labeled Poverty.[62] Instead, after leaving Rechelesnesse and another guide, Imaginatif, he meets the middle section's central figure of authority, Patience.[63] Like the gloss on Truth's Pardon, Patience's discourse on poverty begins with what might at first seem a vivid recognition of the mundane actualities of need:

> Muche murthe is in May amonge wilde bestes
> And so forth whiles somur laste here solace duyreth,
> And moche murthe among ryche men is þat han meble ynow and hele.
> Ac beggares aboute myssomur bredles they soupe,
> And ȝut is wynter for hem worse, for weet-shoed þey gone,
> Afurste and afyngered and foule rebuked
> Of this world-ryche men, þat reuthe is to here.
> Now lord, sende hem somur somtyme to solace and to ioye
> That al here lyf leden in lownesse and in pouerte! (C.16.10–18)

The poor are hungry in summer, cold in winter, and lack comforts that even "wilde bestes" possess. Although the actual description of the needy in this passage is merely four lines long, it moves immediately to a level of intimate physical detail and arrests our sympathies. The poor are "bredles," "weet-shoed," and, in language that echoes the gloss on Truth's Pardon, "afurste" and "afyngered." The passage is a compassionate portrait of the realities of need. Robert Frank observes that the passage points toward extratextual historical experience as it vividly portrays the effects of the actual fourteenth-century agricultural crisis – the "hungry gap," that summer period in an agrarian society when the stores of winter are depleted and the bounty of fall is still to come.[64]

[61] See C.12.176–205, 218–33.

[62] Unlike the dreamer in Guillaume de Deguilleville's *Le Pélerinage de la vie humaine*, for example, who encounters both Poverty and Unwilling Poverty in his vision.

[63] An important study of Patience in *Piers Plowman* is Elizabeth D. Kirk, "'Who Suffreth More Than God?': Narrative Redefinition of Patience in *Patience* and *Piers Plowman*," in *The Triumph of Patience*, ed. Gerald Schiffhorst, 88–104. For a more general study of the virtue, see Hanna, "Some Commonplaces," 65–87.

[64] Frank, "'Hungry Gap,'" 89–90.

Why then would Patience ask that the Lord "sende [the poor] somur somtyme to solace and to ioye"? Certainly he uses the term "somur" in its figurative sense – heaven – the time of "ioye" after a life of "lownesse" and "pouerte" in this world. Furthermore, although the passage hints at social injustice through its emphasis on the division between rich and poor, it conveys no sense of poverty as a social evil. "Mitigation [for the sufferings of poor people] is offered exclusively in terms of the hereafter."[65] Ultimately Patience's argument, like the Pardon's, works to find a spiritual purpose, and finally a figural substitution, for the reality of need. Our sympathies are transformed once again by the easy orthodox notion that the poor will be rewarded in the next life for the hardships of this one.

After he has achieved this more subtle analysis of the spiritual consequences of poor people's experiences, Patience reverts to a traditional analysis of the spiritual advantage afforded the indigent in their confrontation with the seven deadly sins (C.16.43–113). He then continues his discourse by adding to the already highly intellectualized image of patient poverty the support of proverbial wisdom:

> *"Paupertas,"* quod Pacience, *"est odibile bonum, remocio curarum, possessio sine calumpnia, donum dei, sanitatis mater, absque solicitudine semita, sapiencie temperatrix, negocium sine dampno, incerta fortuna, absque solicitudine felicitas."* (C.16.116)
>
> ("Poverty," said Patience, "is a hateful good, freedom from cares, possession without calumny, a gift of God, mother of health, a path free from care, a mediator of wisdom, bargain without fraud, uncertain fortune, happiness free from anxiety.")[66]

Attributed to Secundus Philosophus, and commonly found in medieval collections of aphorisms, these schoolroom commonplaces embrace the oxymoronic quality of the image of poverty presented in the central visions of *Piers Plowman.*[67] Need is pitiful, undeniable, and inevitable; yet it contains the promise of salvation. This passage focuses not on the *odibile* physical aspects of poverty, but on its many moral and psychological benefits. It asks us to reread, to reinterpret the actualities of distress. Indeed, indigence is presented almost as something to be desired, a "freeing" from "solicitudine," the burden of material neces-

[65] Pearsall, "Poverty and Poor People," 183.

[66] Patience himself translates into English and expands this speech on poverty for the benefit of the unlearned Haukyn at C.16.120–56.

[67] *Piers Plowman*, ed. Derek Pearsall, note to C.16.116. Chaucer also observes, "Poverte is hateful good and, as I gesse, / A ful greet bryngere out of bisynesse," in the *Wife of Bath's Tale*, 1195–96.

sity. For Patience, and for Langland, though "hateful," poverty is finally a "good."

Patience's discourse on poverty in the B-text of *Piers Plowman* is delivered to one of the poem's most colorful representations of life in the world: Haukyn, the active man. As many critics have observed, Haukyn is perhaps "the most completely mundane creature in the poem."[68] Busy with such earthly activities as singing and selling, baking and bargaining, he appears the active counterpart of those folk on the field who "swonken ful harde" for their material needs.[69] In fact, he seems to recall the whole practical world of *Piers*'s opening visions:

> And þat am I, Actif, þat ydelnesse hatie,
> For alle trewe trauaillours and tiliers of þe erþe
> Fro Mighelmesse to Mighelmesse I fynde hem wiþ wafres.
> Beggeris and bidderes of my breed crauen,
> Faitours and freres and folk wiþ brode crounes.
> I fynde payn for þe pope and prouendre for his palfrey,
> And I hadde neuere of hym, haue god my trouþe,
> Neiþer prouendre ne personage yet of þe popes ȝifte. (B.13.238–45)

Like those earlier pilgrims and fieldhands, Haukyn recognizes fully the legitimate demands of material necessity and directs his energies toward fulfilling those needs. He is an attractive figure, one with whom we are at least partly sympathetic. When Patience and the dreamer meet Haukyn, however, they notice first that his cloak is stained with the seven deadly sins, the result of his worldly interest and activity. Patience then presents his discourse on poverty as a kind of solution to Haukyn's dilemma – if he were to have less interest in earthly comfort, heavenly grace would be his reward. Haukyn is so moved by Patience's speech that he weeps the tears of repentance:

> "Allas," quod Haukyn þe Actif man þo, "þat after my cristendom
> I ne hadde be deed and doluen for dowelis sake!
> So hard it is," quod haukyn, "to lyue and to do synne.
> Synne seweþ vs euere," quod he and sory gan wexe,
> And wepte water wiþ hise eighen and weyled þe tyme
> That euere he dide dede þat deere god displesed." (B.14.323–28)

Haukyn's tears, like those of Meed (B.2.239), might at first seem a deliberately excessive display of emotion – a show but not a conviction of contrition – and yet his plea has a ring of truth. He does not vow to make superficial amends –

[68] Carruthers, *The Search for St. Truth*, 118. The best study of Haukyn is still Stella Maguire's "The Significance of Haukyn, *Activa Vita*, in *Piers Plowman*," reprinted in *Style and Symbolism in Piers Plowman: A Modern Critical Anthology*, ed. Robert J. Blanch (Knoxville: Univ. of Tennessee Press, 1969), 194–208. See also John A. Alford, "Haukyn's Coat: Some Observations on *Piers Plowman* B. XIV. 22–7," *Medium Aevum* 43 (1974): 133–38.

[69] Maguire, "The Significance of Haukyn," 196–99.

unlike, say, Gluttony, who after confessing to the most excessive and disgusting dietary habits, vows to "faste for hunger or þurste: / 'Shal neuere fyssh on þe Fryday defyen in my wombe / Til Abstinence myn Aunte haue ȝyue me leeue'" (B.5.381–83) – but instead seems to admit that any penance he might choose would be inadequate. Unless he is truly "sory" he might as well be "deed". Haukyn confronts an undeniable human truth: "Synne seweþ us euere." The immortal soul will always be housed in the corruptible flesh. His tears shatter our objectivity and prevent the complete sublimation of physical needs espoused by Patience. Suddenly, this wave of emotion forcefully reminds us of our fallen nature, of the weaknesses of the human body and heart. A sinless life is an impossibility for a being who must live very much in the world. For Haukyn, the only alternative Patience seems to offer is no life at all. We see in Haukyn's despair the inescapable demands of the corruptible body and recall not the abstract lessons of these central visions of *Piers*, but the concrete images of material necessity presented in the plowing of the half-acre. As a result, Patience's teachings seem merely an unrealistic attempt to sublimate actual human experience.

In an effort, it seems, to overcome the interpretive fissure posed by the powerfully human figure of Haukyn, the C-version of *Piers Plowman* reduces Haukyn to a rather flat personification of life in the world, Activa Vita. He has no individual name, he has no cloak, and he does not repent. Whereas Haukyn made problematic the spiritual demands of patience upon the Christian who has to work and suffer in the world to survive, Activa Vita in the C-text provides merely a convenient straw man for Patience's traditional view of poverty as a virtue.

After the encounter with Haukyn, the central visions of *Piers Plowman* retreat from the material world into a fully spiritualized scheme of salvation. The episodes of the Tree of Charity, the Crucifixion and Harrowing of Hell, and the founding of Holy Church offer no vision of poverty. Even the deserving poor have receded from view. The vast middle of the poem has successfully transfigured history and moved our hearts from outer to inner, from material to spiritual concern.

The "Romance" of the *Castle of Love*

JANE ZATTA, *Southern Illinois University – Edwardsville*

Some time during the first half of the thirteenth century Robert Grosseteste, Bishop of Lincoln, wrote what was to become a very popular sermon, known as the *Chasteau d'Amour* (*Castle of Love*).[1] It is a brief salvation history written in "romanz," the vernacular French, to give doctrinal instruction to the non-Latin literate. Beginning with the loss of Paradise, it narrates man's redemption through two elaborate allegories in which man is compared to a landholding vassal who lost his rights as well as his freedom by a violation of his feudal obligations but was then restored to his inheritance by his lord's son who agreed to accept his judgment for him. One of the five translations of this work into English,[2] a work known as the *Myrour of Lewed Men*, was made in the fourteenth century by a monk of Sawley who freely adapted the *Chasteau d'Amour*, condensing the original and adding much doctrinal material. In the course of this work, the Monk of Sawley four times uses the term "romance" to refer to Grosseteste's work as well as his English translation, and it is clear that he is using the word to refer to a literary genre, not a language. As Paul Strohm and others have shown, by the late twelfth century the term "romanz," initially used to indicate the vernacular French (and thus the audience a work targeted) begins to be used to specify a particular type of story, though the heterogeneity of the works described by this term has puzzled modern critics.[3] Because the Monk of

[1] The work survives in sixteen manuscripts; see *The Middle English Translations of Robert Grosseteste's Chateau D'Amour*, ed. Kari Sajavaara (Helsinki: Société Néophilologique de Helsinki, 1967), 36, for a list. All quotations from the *Chasteau D'Amour* and its derivatives are from this edition.

[2] The English translations are the following: *The Castle of Love*, *The Myrour of Lewed Men*, *King and Four Daughters*, *Four Daughters*, and parts of the *Cursor Mundi*. See *Middle English Translations*, ed. Sajavaara, 101, for a description of the manuscripts.

[3] See Paul Strohm, "The Origin and Meaning of Middle English *Romaunce*," *Genre* 10 (1977): 1–28. He notes that the term "romans" in French came to refer to a type of literature in the thirteenth century whereas the use of the term "romaunce" occurs in English only in the fourteenth century, at first to refer to the language of a work and only gradually to refer to a type of literature.

Sawley uses the term to refer to two significantly different versions of the same work, he offers a particularly interesting perspective from which to examine the generic significance of the word "romance" in fourteenth-century England.

No genre has been more intractable to definition than medieval romance. Dieter Mehl, in his 1968 discussion, remarked that he would have abandoned the term "romance" altogether, were it not for the fact that scholars on the whole know what they mean by the term.[4] The interpenetration of romance and hagiography in particular has proved troublesome, and gave rise in the 1960s to the concept of a third genre somewhere in the middle, a genre of "secular hagiography" in the terminology of Ojars Kratins.[5] Other critics, such as John Finlayson and Susan Crane, have seen a fundamental contradiction between the values expressed by romance and those of religious literature. According to Finlayson, author of perhaps the most ambitious recent attempt to define medieval romance and to reconsider the canon that traditionally has been assigned to that genre, a story that is told primarily for its moral significance violates the nature of romance.[6] Crane agrees with Finlayson that romance and hagiography express antithetical values. In a study of the political, social, and religious conditions in England that influenced the development of insular romance, she argues that medieval insular romance as a genre underwrites an ideology of individual self-determination and secular success that is in no way compatible with the self-abnegation and denial of worldly interests that animate hagiography.[7] More

[4] Dieter Mehl, *The Middle English Romances of the Thirteenth and Fourteenth Centuries* (London: Routledge and Kegan Paul, 1968), vii.

[5] Ojars Kratins, "The Middle English *Amis and Amiloun*: Chivalric Romance or Secular Hagiography?" *PMLA* 81 (1966): 347–54.

[6] See John Finlayson, "Definitions of Middle English Romance, Pt. I," *Chaucer Review* 15 (1980): 44–60, and "Definitions of Middle English Romance, Pt. II," *Chaucer Review* 15 (1981): 168–81. "The basic definition of romance therefore, is that it is a tale in which a knight achieves great feats of arms, almost solely for his own *los et pris* in a series of adventures which have no social, political, or religious motivation and little or no connection with medieval actuality" (55). Finlayson's concern is to establish a norm against which to judge literary achievement and thus to question the romance status of works that, in his words, "speciously employ romance elements in a way that has got nothing to do with the essence of romance" (174). Finlayson maintains that of the religious romances in English, only Malory's Grail romance does not alter the specific meaning and basic nature of romance genre. The other religious romances, according to Finlayson, "violate, rather than adapt the romance .... That is, certain characteristic elements of romance are added to a story which is told primarily for its moral significance" (175).

[7] Susan Crane, *Insular Romance: Politics, Faith, and Culture in Anglo-Norman and Middle English Literature* (Berkeley and Los Angeles: Univ. of California Press, 1986). Crane argues that "hagiography models religious life on the rejection of worldly identity and family ties, and the surrender of personal will to God" (115), while romances, even the so-called pious romances, celebrate secular values of family, personal achievement, and success. Where romance and hagiography intersect, the explanation is that romance employs piety to enhance the attractiveness of the hero and to justify his political and material success. Hagiography, Crane

recent authors who articulate new concerns, such as the social and psychological selves that romances formulate and define, have changed the way genre is viewed, sometimes sharpening the distinctions, and sometimes erasing genre as a useful category. Andrea Hopkins revives the idea of an intermediate genre of religious romances. In flat disagreement with Finlayson, she defends the place of religious poems within the romance canon. "Those who have stated that religious subjects cannot be appropriately treated in romance are mistaken."[8] Hopkins argues that religious poems displaying characteristics of romance constitute a particular subset of the romance genre, not a variety of homiletic literature such as saint's life, homily, sermon, exemplum, etc. Hopkins concludes the introduction to her study by stating that she "proceeds on the premiss that the concept of romance was known and had meaning in the thirteenth and fourteenth centuries, whether the writers and readers of the poems concerned consistently called them by that name or not."[9] Jocelyn Wogan-Browne agrees with Hopkins that attempting rigid distinctions between romance and hagiography has led to a misunderstanding of both romance and religious literature. She notes that hagiography, no less than romance, is a vehicle for the economic socialization of young men in noble families who required it for both secular as well as ecclesiastical careers, since the Church provided a major career path for younger sons of the nobility and the gentry. Far from expressing values antithetical to romance, Wogan-Browne argues that hagiography "reinscribes a single patriarchal and feudal social structure, common to romance and hagiography, secular and sacred alike."[10]

While no critic today would refer to either version of the *Chasteau d'Amour* as a romance, the statements by its fourteenth-century translator and reworker offer a useful insight into the medieval understanding of the relationship between romance and religious literature. The *Myrour* poet employs the term dialogically and contrastively in a way that clearly shows that the values of romance and hagiography, far from being diametrically opposed, are extensively

argues, "freely appropriates fabulous, affective, and dramatic elements from romance when they can make images of holy life more compelling" (102). Thus, like Finlayson, while she rejects an intermediate genre of pious romances or secular hagiography, she rehabilitates some of the very romances that Finlayson discarded because she sees their primary purpose as a subtle manipulation and appropriation of religious piety in the interests of promoting an ethos that is distinctly secular.

[8] Andrea Hopkins, *The Sinful Knights: A Study of Middle English Penitential Romance* (Oxford: Clarendon Press, 1990), 31. Hopkins distinguishes between romance and other forms of homiletic literature on the basis of the method of presenting the lesson, which in the case of homiletic literature is done by stating a case and then adding examples by way of illustration, whereas romance involves the reader in vicarious identification with the character.

[9] Hopkins, *Sinful Knights*, 30–31.

[10] Jocelyn Wogan-Browne, "Romance and Hagiography ... Again," in *Readings in Medieval English Romance*, ed. Carol M. Meale (Cambridge: D. S. Brewer, 1994).

identical. The Monk of Sawley gives us much valuable information in his preface:

> Here begynnes a romance of Englishe of the begynnyng of the world and of al that a lewed man has nede for to knawe for hele of soule. This romance turned a munk of Sallay out of a Frenche romance that sir Robert, Bischop a Lyncoln made; and eked mikel therto, as him thought spedeful to edificacion and swettenes of devocioun, and lering of lewed men. And here is no thing sayd bot as haly writ says and grete doctours, and therfor thou that redys this and any comfort has therinne, pray God be way of charite to haue mercy on him that turned it in this maner. And if thou couayt to love God and to plese him, take mirrour and loke oft therinne. (320)

Directed at a lay audience, the *Myrour* is a primer of essential religious instruction, which the Monk does not consider incompatible with romance. Neither does he consider that his substantial additions of doctrinal instruction change the romance status of this work, although the additions he made are sufficiently extensive so that he distinguishes between his translation and the romance that Bishop Robert made: they are two, different romances. The Monk of Sawley freely adapted the *Chasteau d'Amour*, adding 473 lines (42% of the lines in the *Myrour*) and omitting 548 lines (32% of the *Chasteau*).[11] Whereas the reductions the Monk made were aimed at either condensing the narrative or removing references to abstruse theological doctrine and did not affect the content or frame of the original, the significant changes were lengthy additions to the poem's didactic apparatus. He adds a long description of the ten commandments, a description of the articles of faith, a lengthy explanation of the doctrine of transubstantiation as well as a description of the remaining sacraments, a list of the seven gifts of the Holy Ghost, the seven works of mercy, and a description of the coming of the Antichrist. The great emphasis the Monk places on the doctrine of the Trinity, the importance he gives to holy teachers (who, together with martyrs and virgins enjoy special privileges in Paradise), the lengthy explanation of the doctrine of transubstantiation, his insistence on the bodily resurrection of the dead, and the pronounced didactic orientation of his work all suggest issues raised by the Fourth Lateran Council. In response to the need for popular instruction after the Fourth Lateran Council, from the thirteenth century on, a number of popular works of religious instruction began to be written, such as *Handlyng Synne*, *The Pricke of Conscience*, *Cursor Mundi* and many others. Since most of these ultimately derive from one work, the *Summa virtutum ac vitiorum* (ca. 1260), they tend to be very similar in content, usually including the ten commandments, the seven deadly sins, the seven virtues, the seven sacraments, the seven gifts of the Holy Ghost, the seven works of mercy, and the fourteen (or so) articles of faith. It is clear then that the *Myrour* belongs to this

[11] *Middle English Translations*, ed. Sajavaara, 226.

didactic tradition of giving instruction in the religious obligations of the faithful.[12] These thirteenth-century manuals, which all make the point that contrition and penance are insufficient without confession, stress the dependence of the individual Christian on the institutional mediation of the Church. The Monk's purpose is to teach patience and obedient submission to the Church, of which the submission and obedience the individual owes to secular authority are an analogue. In his explanation of the fifth commandment, the Monk tells his reader that just as he owes "buxumnes and hounour" to his father and mother, so too does he to his spiritual mother, Holy Church, and to his lord and king.

Much about the work suggests that the Monk's concern is finding a method of teaching abstract and complex theological concepts such as the doctrine of the Trinity, or the doctrine of transubstantiation, and it seems that he considers romance an effective instrument for the communication of difficult and hard-to-believe subject matter. After introducing his work as a romance, he begins with a declaration of God's Trinity, which he implies is something that we must believe even if it eludes man's reason:

> Our mede is to trowe this with stable thoght,
> Al be hit that mannes skil proues it noght,
> But when we sal se god clerly,
> Than sal we knawe this witerly. (11–14)

That he considers romance a vehicle for making religious instruction not just pleasant but above all comprehensible is indicated in a passage in which the author in his own voice glosses the meaning of the Four Daughters of God. Here the function of romance as a means of communicating a mystery is clear. Romance is a form of literature suitable for the revelation of hidden meaning:

> Whoso redes this romance,
> Trowe in God with on substance,
> Bot on is God and persons thre,
> Non othir thing in God may be.
> Four sisters that we before rede
> Are four vertues in the godhede;
> To four doghters thai haue lyknyng,
> For thai procure all gode doyng;
> Bot all thai are on god of myȝtes mast,
> He is Fader and Sone and Haly Gast.

[12] See Hopkins, *Sinful Knights*, 59–60. In 1281 Archbishop Peckham stated that people were to be instructed four times per year in six points: the articles of faith, the ten commandments, the works of mercy, the seven deadly sins, the seven virtues, and the seven sacraments, with particular emphasis on penance.

If thou trowe this wele and stedfastly,
Thou may haue mede ay-lastandly. (301–12)

In order to understand the relationship that the Monk of Sawley saw between romance and his own purpose of instructing his audience in the duties of the faithful to the Church, we now turn to the *Chasteau d'Amour*. Grosseteste chose to present his doctrinal instruction in the form of a feudal allegory because the comparison between the situation of a disgraced vassal in the feudal political system and the sinful Christian's relationship to God allowed him to emphasize man's inability to help himself, his dependence on God, and thus the gratitude man owed God for his benevolence, infinitely superior to that of a secular king. God operates under exactly the same code of laws as contemporary English kings, and it is by comparison to feudal reality and its values of descent, inheritance, and land, that Grosseteste explains the generosity of God and presents the rewards of salvation. The Monk of Sawley saw Grosseteste's work not only as a romance, but as a romance that could serve to communicate the Christian's institutional obligations to the Church because it allowed the Monk to teach that the obedience and submission required by the Church ultimately serve to liberate and empower. The Monk of Sawley saw in Grosseteste's work the possibility of apotheosis and fulfillment not by rejecting feudal, hierarchical society based on roles of dominance and submission but by an imaginative transformation of earthly authority into a superior type of feudal relationship, the feudal kingdom of heaven.

Grosseteste, who opposed the performance of miracle plays and ordered his archdeacons to "utterly exterminate them" would no doubt have been shocked to know that his "little treatise," as he described his work, would ever have been considered a romance.[13] It is a poem of about 1,800 lines of French octosyllabic couplets, written with an aristocratic audience in mind, probably one of knightly retainers. The date of its composition is disputed: R. W. Southern places the date around 1230, while M. Domenica Legge and Kari Sajavaara, the most recent editor of the Middle English translations, argue for a date around 1250, not long before Grosseteste's death. If the date is as late as 1250, it might have been written for the sons of Simon de Montfort, who were living in the Grosseteste household at that time.[14] Although intended as a work of lay instruction, the work is a succinct expression of Grosseteste's theology and contains some passages of considerable difficulty. The central feature of Grosseteste' s theology is the Incarnation, which represents the fusion of God with the created universe through the unifying principle of a god-man that endows all created nature with

[13] M. Dominica Legge, *Anglo-Norman in the Cloisters* (Edinburgh: Edinburgh Univ. Press, 1950), 100–101.

[14] R. W. Southern, *Robert Grosseteste: The Growth of an English Mind in Medieval Europe* (Oxford: Clarendon Press, 1986), 229.

the divinity of the Creator. The deification of man through union with God was, according to Grosseteste, God's plan for man from the Creation, not merely an accident of the Fall.[15] The poem's most memorable feature is its use of elaborate allegories, none of which are original with Grosseteste: the king with a son and four daughters who debate man's punishment, and the Virgin Mary as a castle into which Christ enters to prepare for his battle with Satan.

The poem begins with an account of the Creation and Fall and an explanation of Old Testament law. Adam is presented as a feudal vassal who has violated his oath, thus losing his land and his freedom. The exposition of Old Testament law introduces an explanation of God's justice presented through the allegory of the king with four daughters and a son. Man here (rather than Adam) is the serf who has offended his king and fallen slave to his king's enemy, thus losing heritage, rights and freedom. The daughters of the king, representing Truth, Righteousness, Mercy and Peace, disagree over the fate of the vassal, and finally the king's son offers to take the serf's judgment for him so that man can be restored to his heritage in accord with the requirements of Righteousness and Truth as well as Peace and Mercy. This passage ends with a verse from Isaiah prophesying the coming of Christ and describing his attributes – Wonderful, Counselor, the mighty God, Father of the Age to Come, Prince of Peace – and it is the explication of these attributes which furnishes the structure for the rest of the poem. The meaning of the word "Wonderful" refers to the mystery of Christ's birth. The womb of the Virgin Mary is described as an extremely elaborate castle, heavily fortified with defensive outworks into which the Son enters in order to prepare to do battle with the devil. Christ is "Counselor" because of the help he gave man for the recovery of his heritage. He is "mighty God" not only because he defeats the devil but also by virtue of the many miracles he performed, "Father of the Age to Come" because he has given man a second engendering to replace what was lost with Adam, and "Prince of Peace" because he reunites God and man in Paradise. The story that emerges, punctuated by passages of theological doctrine, is that of a feudal vassal who betrayed his king and, having lost his inheritance and his freedom, was saved and restored to all his former rights and status by his king's son who went to battle for him against the enemy.

The *Chasteau d'Amour* is remarkable for the extensive feudalization of its presentation of salvation. The analogies Grosseteste uses to describe the rela-

[15] See Southern, *Robert Grosseteste*, 219–25, who describes Grosseteste's theology as one based on the Creation rather than one based on the Redemption. It is a man-centered theology, one that sees man at the center of the created universe, for whom everything was created. God's plan for the beginning was for the ultimate deification of man through union with God; the question therefore is why this took such a long time to achieve. Grosseteste thought that man's full potential was not realized at the moment of Creation and necessitated a period of growth and development. This view of the Redemption was not current in the thirteenth century, however, when St. Anselm's view prevailed, that the sole cause of God's Incarnation was Man's sin.

tionship between God and man assume the knowledge, experience, and aspirations of the baronial class, and in particular the great value attached to land tenure and the genealogical ideals of heredity and lineage that depend on the role of woman as chaste, inviolate spouse and mother, and thus the identification of marriage with lineage. The models, goals, and value systems of feudal society are used as an epistemological model to explain the nature of Christ's sacrifice and the benefits of salvation. Grosseteste presents the rewards of eternal life as a perfection of the objects of earthly desire: honor, high estate, land tenure, and lineage. Grosseteste's portrayal of Christ's redemption of mankind as if God were a secular king and mankind a rebellious vassal emphasizes man's complete inability to help himself, and thus the liberating and empowering nature of God's governance in contrast to secular governments. Grosseteste foregrounds man's debt of gratitude for God's compassionate justice by making the values and ideals of earthly and heavenly society absolutely parallel. The normative status given to feudal society allows Grosseteste to exalt the benevolence of God's government, whose ultimate aim is the glorification and deification of mankind through union with God.

Grosseteste presents God and Adam as a feudal lord and his vassal, described in remarkable legalistic detail. The advantages with which Adam in Paradise was endowed by God are described in terms of lineage, status, and land tenure:

> Se lui dona e saveir
> Beaute, poer, et franc voler.
> De tut le mund la seignurie
> E tuz jurs sanz murir la vie.
> Et parais en heritage. (90–94)

(He gave him knowledge, beauty, power, and free will. He had lordship over all the world and lasting life without death and Paradise as his heritage.)

Adam's honor and high status are repeatedly stressed:

> Avoit adam la seisine
> Allas come tost se decline
> Sa bunte e sa valur.
> Sa seignurie et son honor. (134–37)

(Adam had the seisin but alas how quickly decline his goodness and valor, his lordship and honor.)

Adam's seisin of Paradise is specified as an hereditary holding, terminology that had precise legal significance. Language specifying free heritage as a type of landholding came to be used more and more frequently after 1100 in royal charters describing grants to lay persons, and although it does not constitute a rigorously defined class of landholding, this language was significant in resolving disputes over succession and preventing land from reverting to a lord's demesne on the death of a tenant.[16] Free tenement meant moreover that the holder was entitled to possessory rights in the king's court whereas villein tenure was not protected by the king's court.[17] In feudal terms, then, Adam holds his seisin in one of the most privileged of tenurial relationships:

> Donqes ni out ci grant leesce
> Grant seignurie grant hautesce.
> Pur avoir cel heritage
> A li e trestut son lignage. (110–13)

(Never was there such great happiness, such great lordship, such nobility, to have that heritage for himself and for all his lineage.)

But Adam loses his seisin by violating the specific terms of his tenure, that is, by failure to keep the two laws set to him, natural law (by allowing his wife to rule his choices) and positive law (by disobeying God's commandment).[18] Adam obeys his wife, and thus the devil, rather than God who created them:

> Kant il la pome manga
> Ambdous le leys trespassa.
> E naturele e positive
> Par sa femme, la cheitive.
> Ka obeier plus desirout
> An diable qui dieu qui ly fesout. (138–43)

(When he ate the apple, he broke both laws, natural and positive, because of his wife, the wicked, who desired to obey the devil more than God who made them.)

[16] John Hudson, *Land, Law, and Lordship in Anglo-Norman England* (Oxford: Clarendon Press, 1994), 97, 97–106 passim.

[17] See Sir Frederick Pollock and William Maitland, *The History of English Law Before the Time of Edward I*, 2d ed., 2 vols. (Cambridge: Cambridge Univ. Press, 1968), 1.357.

[18] Breaches of homage constituted felonies, and these could bring the tenurial relationship to an end. The *Leges Henrici* states that "anyone who commits theft, is a traitor to his lord, flees from him in an encounter with the enemy or on the battlefield, or is convicted of having committed felony, is to forfeit his land." For example, in the time of King Stephen, when Robert of Meppershall stayed at Meppershall and left Biddlesden, for which he failed to render service to the earl of Leicester, or send anyone else in his stead, the land escheated to the earl who gave it to his steward, Ernald de Bosco, for his service (Hudson, *Land, Law, and Lordship*, 20).

In the case of a tenant who defaulted on the terms of his holding, one recourse was to the king's court in order to obtain a judgment returning the forfeited land to the lord's demesne, the sort of judgment pronounced against Adam:[19]

> Ou querra il mes aie.
> Kant perdu a per jugement
> Trustut son heritement. (151–53)

> (Where will he ever ask for help, when he has lost all his inheritance by judgment?)

Adam's loss of Paradise is explained in the terms of contemporary legal principles.

> Defaute apres, defaute fine
> Fet par droit perdre seisine.
> Encore a la cort lu rois
> U se lem icele lois. (170–73)

> (Default afterwards, default in the end causes by right the loss of inheritance even now in the court of the king where this law is respected.)

Although becoming a serf by any means other than birth was rare, disobeying or betraying one's lord was one way this could happen. Bracton speaks of a freedman reduced to slavery on account of ingratitude, and in 1204, King John threatened that knights who defaulted on their obligation to take up arms for him would be declared serfs forever together with their heirs. In addition to betrayal of one's lord or king, one undisputed way for a man to lose his freedom was to confess himself the serf of another in a court of record, another implication of Adam's submission to the devil:[20]

> Ore sunt de mal entechez
> Ke serfs devienent per pechez.
> Ki plus franc furent avant
> Ke rien qui soit en mend vivant.
> Nest il son serf apertement
> Au ki service il entent? (174–79)

[19] If a lord had a tenant who disavowed his tenure, one recourse was to the king's court in order to have a judgment brought that would return the property to the demesne (Pollock and Maitland, *History of English Law*, 1.352).

[20] See Pollock and Maitland, *History of English Law*, 1.424–26, on the legal status of serfs and the loss of freedom. "It is a principle of law that if a person has once confessed himself the serf of another in a court of record, he can never thereafter be heard to contradict this confession" (1.425).

(Now they are in a sad plight who have become serfs by sin, who before were freer than anything on earth. Isn't he clearly the serf of him whose service he obeys?)

Since serfs had no legal rights, Adam is ineligible to plead his case in court. Again, this corresponds to actual legal practice. A man who had declined into servitude could only recover his former freedom, and thus his right to protection in the king's court, by producing kin of free estate to press his claim for him. As a serf without lands, Adam was not entitled to protection of the law.[21]

Mes serf ne peut clamer mie
Heritez, ne seignurie.
Puis ke serfs est devenu
Son heritage est retenu.
Ne il ne ert james entendu
En nule cert respondu
Donques le covient autere quere
Si veut son dreit conquere
Ki soit de franche nacion
E pur lui mustre sa reison
Et pur clamer son heritage
Et kil soit de son lignage. (182–93)

(But a serf may by no means claim inheritance or lordship. Since he has become a serf and his inheritance is retained, he will never be heard or responded to by any court. Therefore he must find someone else, if he wants to recover his rights, who is of a free estate, to press his claim for him, someone who is of his lineage.)

Adam's legal and tenurial dilemma is a far more realistic presentation of the problems and complexities of landholding than is found in most literary repre-

[21] In seeking to determine the legal status of an individual, the burden of proof lay on the one whose status was in question. The burden was thrown one way or the other by seisin. The man who was under the power of a lord must remain so until he had shown his right to liberty. "If the burden of proof lay on the person whose status was in question, he had to produce free kinsman" (Pollock and Maitland, *History of English Law*, 1.426). See also Jean Scammell, "The Formation of the English Social Structure: Freedom, Knights, and Gentry, 1066–1300," *Speculum* 3 (1993): 591–618. From 1161 to 1177, freedom meant access to public courts. Following Henry's attempt in 1166 to ascertain the number of knights in his land, the barons had to decide whether to confirm their tenants as knights (607), which meant whether they would allow them to become free by keeping their land. Bracton confirms that novel disseisin was designed to withstand seignorial attempts to recover land that was held by those who had formerly acted as knights. In order to eject a man, a lord had first to prove villeinage – that is, free status is dependent on landholding. Bracton mentions some people who are of so high a status that they can not be reduced to *servitutem* without writ and judgment, which makes it clear that even people of a high status can be reduced to servitude.

sentations of knights. A major advantage of the rule of God over the rule of a secular king involves the application of justice. Whereas a vassal reduced to servitude through his own default would have no recourse in a feudal court, God's justice offers the possibility of perfect recovery, a principle that Grosseteste illustrates through the allegory of the four daughters of God (Mercy, Peace, Truth and Righteousness) who debate the fate of mankind.[22] There was a King who had a serf who, because of a grave misdeed against his lord, was judged and condemned to be turned over to his enemies who put him in prison in great distress. The King's four daughters disagree on the fate of the prisoner, Truth and Righteousness arguing for a strict application of the law while Mercy and Peace plead for mildness. The dispute is ultimately resolved by the intervention of the King's son, who offers to pay the debt of the prisoner so as to satisfy the requirements of his daughters. Divine law is a perfection of feudal law; God is shown to be a much kinder and more merciful lord than any king. The analogy between God's kingdom and secular political kingship serves to emphasize the liberating power of submission to God.

Comparing the state of fallen man to the status of a serf without legal recourse allows Grosseteste to emphasize man's complete dependence on God's grace to win salvation. Grosseteste's disinherited serf can in no way help himself by his own efforts. Grosseteste's explanation of the attribute of Counselor as applied to Christ contrasts the finality of the disenfranchisement of secular governments to God's infinite mercy. Grosseteste hypothesizes advising a once-powerful man who had been stripped of his possessions and exiled from his country simply to return and recover his rights with the help of his friends.

> A quoi va tu si mendis?
> Returnez en ton pais.
> Va par tut tes amis querre
> Si defendez vostre terre.
> Icel conseil bon feust
> Si achevis le peust
> Mes verrai conseil nest comie
> Puis ki nad ne naie. (892–99)

("What are you doing so disgraced? Go back to your own country. Go to all your friends and ask help to defend your land." That would be good advice if it were possible. But it is not true advice because he has no help.)

The patent impossibility of such a reversal of fortune in feudal society dramatizes the mercy of God who rehabilitates his disobedient vassal and restores him

[22] This allegory, which originated in Jewish tradition in the *Middrash Rabbah*, can be found in the Middle Ages in the writings of St. Bernard, Hugh of St. Victor, and the "Vie de Tobie" by Guillaume le Clerc. See Sajavaara's discussion, *Middle English Translations*, 61–89.

to his full rights, an unbelievably generous act in comparison with actual feudal practice. The analogy between fallen man and the political exile serves to emphasize the gratitude that man owes God, which Grosseteste repeatedly stresses:

> Com homme trovad esgarez
> De paradis engetez
> Ne jammes ne feust relevez
> Par soi ne par sa puissance. (903–6)

(He found man so confounded, expelled from Paradise; he would never have managed to raise himself again by his own power.)

> Nest celuy bon conseiller
> Kissi nus rechata chier.
> E ki nus ad fete la voie
> Que venir poums a la joie. (1191–94)

(Is not that a good counselor who bought us back so dearly? And who opened the way for us by which we could come to joy?)

Next Grosseteste likens fallen man to a disinherited serf and Christ to a noble kinsman who offers to help him win back his inheritance. Grosseteste uses direct discourse to increase the realism of the analogy he is drawing. Christ says to man:

> Jo te voi si esgarez
> Et de tun pais eissilez.
> E si veez apertement
> Ke par toi nas recovrement.
> Kar jo sui de ton lignage
> Si puis clamer ton heritage.
> E sui de franche natiun
> Si ert oie ma reison.
> Pur toi prenderei la bataille
> Saverez bone de famaille
> Kar jo enfui la veintrai
> E ton droit derainerai. (926–37)

(I see you so dismayed, and exiled from your land. It is clearly seen that by yourself you will never get it back again. Because I am of your lineage, I can claim your heritage. And as I am of a free estate, my reason will be heard. For you I will undertake this battle and you will have again the inheritance of your family, because I will win the cause and restore your rights.)

Grosseteste explains the Redemption in terms of the theory of the devil's rights, not current in thirteenth-century England,[23] but a theory which nonetheless allows Grosseteste to pursue his comparison of God's justice to secular justice. The passage is rife with legal references. The devil repeatedly describes his claim to mankind as a legal contract signed in the king's court: "le covenant est conferme / e en la grant cort cyrografez" (1018–19; "the covenant is confirmed and signed in the great court"); "Mes bien tendra le covenant / Ken sa cur fu fet avant" (1023–24; "He will certainly keep the covenant that was made before in his court"). Grosseteste's Christ is a brilliant lawyer whose expertise in debating the legality of the devil's right to hold man prisoner and the price of his release dazzles the devil and forces him to admit defeat:

> Mes donques te vient teu poeir
> Teu vertuz e teu saveir.
> Ka moi osiez enprendre
> Desputer e reison rendre
> Tut ai perdu en pleidant. (1037–41)

(Where do your power, your knowledge, and your skill come from, you who dare to challenge me, dispute me, and show me the law? I have lost everything in this plea.)

Hereditary right is the most important concept that Grosseteste employs to express the significance of salvation. Salvation itself consists of replacing the disgraced genealogy of Adam with that of Christ, a new genealogizing of man:

> Mes icele engendrure
> Feut a nus e pesme e dure
> Ke feust la grace jhesu crist
> Ke nus engendra en esperit
> Par adam fume dampnez
> E par jhesu resuscitez.
> Il est adroit nostre pere
> Qui nus engendra en cien manere. (1359–66)

(But that engendering was to us unfortunate and hard so that Jesus Christ did us grace, who engendered us in the spirit. We were damned by Adam and restored by Jesus. He is rightly our father who engendered us in such a manner.)

[23] Since Anselm, the theology of the Crucifixion emphasized not the pact between God and Satan but the redemptive value of Christ's suffering, thus the suffering, human Christ so popular in later medieval representation of the Crucifixion; see Southern, *Robert Grosseteste*, 220, and *Middle English Translations*, ed. Sajavaara, 41.

The significance of the sacrament of rebirth through baptism is that we are given a new heredity, literally a new engendering:

> Mes les creanz et le baptizez
> Serrunt mis en sauvetez.
> Apertement nus ad mustre
> Qil nus covient etre rene.
> E pus rene serrum
> E lamour dieu vineroins
> Cest leawe del esperit
> Qui nus engendra jhesu crist.
> E pus kil nus ad engendre
> Nostre pere est en verite. (1423–32)

(But the believers and the baptized will be saved. God has clearly shown us the need to be reborn. And after we are reborn will come the love of God, which is the water of the spirit through which Jesus engendered us. And since he engendered us, he is our true father.)

Adam's sin consists in having lost his inheritance not only for himself, but for all his lineage, while Jesus, like a good father, will restore it again. The recovery of eternal life through the Crucifixion and Resurrection is compared to the loss and recovery of a family inheritance:

> Adam de parais engete
> E trestut sun ligne.
> Mes jhesu crist nostre pere
> Nos heritez nus rent arere. (1449–52)

(Adam was thrown out of Paradise, and all his lineage. But Jesus Christ our father restored our heritage to us again.)

Not only are the values of Christianity and those of patriarchal, feudal society not contradictory in Grosseteste's poem, they are identical, and it is only by reference to secular values and practices that the implications of God's justice can be understood. Far from viewing lineage, heredity, landholding and lordship as contrary to the values of Christianity, they are the very basis of the organization of Paradise and the promised rewards of the faithful. Likewise there is no incompatibility between material prosperity and Christian virtue. While the proud and the rebellious are condemned, there is no reason why God's faithful should not have what any nobleman would wish for: castles, lands and power:

> Home peut avoir grant manantie
> Grant seignurie e grant hautesce
> Chasteaus e bois de grant largesce.

E si pout home bien deu servir
E son voleir acomplir
Pus qil vist en charite
En dreiture en loyaute
Kar dampnedeu nad rien tant sicher
Cume fin amur de quor entier. (976–84)

(Man can have great power, great lordship and great estate, castles and wide lands. And thus man can serve God well and accomplish his will as long as he lives in charity, righteousness, and loyalty, because great God holds nothing so dear as the good love of the whole heart.)

God in Grosseteste's poem represents not the renunciation of noble aspirations but the only certain avenue by which they can be attained. Although the *Chasteau d'Amour,* like the *Myrour,* urges its audience to reject the world in exchange for the rewards of heaven, it does not reject secular goals; rather, they can usefully serve as a model for desiring God. In this work, secular and religious ideals resolve themselves into mirror images in which heavenly society fulfills and perfects the goals of secular life.[24]

The allegory of the Castle of Love is easily the most striking in the poem. As in the case of the allegory of the four daughters of God, the motif of the castle of the body has a long history.[25] But Grosseteste's version of this allegory

[24] Man suld forsake resonably
All the welthes of this warld euermore and ay
For to haue the ioye of heuen only a day.
How mekil more then suld man ay forsake synne
While he lyued in erth that blis for to wynne?
The godenes of God, the fairnes, the wysdam, the my3t,
The ioye, the solace, the confort, that ay is in his si3t,
Passes all mannes vnderstanding, and wit. (1236–43)

[25] The body as a castle or edifice, the dwelling of the soul, has a tradition that dates as far back as Philo Judaeus (*Middle English Translations*, ed. Sajavaara, 92). The most often cited medieval examples of this allegory are from the writings of Anselm, St. Bernard, Hugh of St. Victor, and Serlon de Savigny. Bernard used the motif in Sermon 2, *On the Assumption of the Virgin*; he was interpreting Luke 10:38 ("Intravit [Jesus] in quoddam castellum"). Bernard interprets the castle as the womb of the Virgin Mother, or "castellum" (see Barbara E. Kurtz, "The Castle Motif and the Medieval Allegory of Love: Diego de San Pedro's *Carcel de Amor*," *Fifteenth Century Studies* 11 [1985]: 37–49). In England, according to Southern (226), it was first popularized by Archbishop Ralph d'Escures of Canterbury (1114–22) in a sermon which was translated into English in the early twelfth century. Thereafter it appears in numerous sermons. C. L. Powell, "The Castle of the Body, " *Studies in Philology* 16 (1919):197–205, notes that an important difference between the metaphor as used by Grosseteste and in *Sawles Warde,* which Powell considers to be derived from Grosseteste (though given the uncertainty about the date of Grosseteste's poem, borrowing could have gone in the other direction): in *Sawles Warde*, the castle is differentiated from its chief guardian and so is both inanimate and sexless.

is unusual enough to be considered original with him.[26] Grosseteste describes Christ's incarnation as his entry into and occupation of an extremely modern and highly fortified castle which represents the womb of the Virgin Mary. The features of the castle and their meaning are elaborated in great detail. The castle is located in a marchland situated on a strong rock (the heart of Mary) and surrounded by deep ditches. The central structure is protected by four towers (the four cardinal virtues), seven barbicans (the seven virtues), and three baileys (virginity, chastity, and marriage). It is painted in three colors: green below (signifying faith), blue in the middle (hope), and the pinnacle above red (love). The inside is white, and in the highest tower a fountain issues forth in four streams (the waters of grace capable of extinguishing every harm) that flow over gravel to fill the ditches. At the center there is a throne, reached by twelve stairs, whiter than day and more beautiful than any which ever belonged to a king or emperor.

The castle is both an impervious fortress and a place of great pleasure and delight. It is described as a castle "that no one can ever harm," "without fear of any attack" (594), a place "where no one who seeks refuge will ever come to harm." The number of fortified outworks highlight the military function of the castle, a structure of aggression and dominance. It is synonymous with lordship:

Onqes si bele chaere
Ne out Roi ne emperere
E donc vi ad ci beau chastel
Onke mes ve fu nul tel. (656–59)

(No king or emperor ever had such a beautiful throne, and never has there been such a beautiful castle).

Since the body of Mary is the castle of love, and her womb the throne of the king of heaven, the metaphor compares the value of a woman's body to that of a

[26] In Sajavaara's opinion, Grosseteste's allegory is connected to others only by vague similarities and no other allegories bearing the symbols of Grosseteste's have been found; therefore the "castle of love" must be considered Grosseteste's invention (*Middle English Translations*, 94). Southern (*Robert Grosseteste*, 226) and G. R. Owst, *Literature and Pulpit in Medieval England* (New York: Barnes and Noble, 1961), 77, agree that Grosseteste worked out the allegory with much greater elaboration than his sources. As Caroline Walker Bynum has shown, Mary's role in the Incarnation, that is, of providing Christ's flesh, was frequently represented by portraying Mary as a container for Christ. She quotes Gertrude of Hafta's vision of the pregnant Virgin in which she saw "the immaculate womb of the glorious virgin, as transparent as the purest crystal, through which her internal organs, penetrated and filled with divinity, shone brightly .... Indeed, one saw the little blossoming boy, the only son of the highest Father, nurse avidly in delight at the heart of His virgin mother" (*Fragmentation and Redemption: Essays on Gender and the Human Body in Medieval Religion* [New York: Zone Books, 1991], 198).

castle, which is both a military fortress and the seat of a lineage. The field of reference on which the entire allegory draws is the symbolic equivalence between the value of a castle and that of woman in feudal, patriarchal society. On one hand, possessing a beautiful "castle" is an attribute of lofty status, a symbol of dominance and power, and no earthly woman (or castle) offers the same ability to exalt and ennoble as Mary. It is also, however, a place of pleasure and delight, the castle of "amur," "solas," "socurs," full of "joye et deliz." The castle offers many comforts described in language that is evocative of courtly romance and open to sexual meanings. The castle is described in terms of an ideal woman who is the source of plenitude and fulfillment:

Sest li chasteaus de delit
De solaz e de respit.
Et desperance e damur
Et de solaz e de socour.
Cest le cors de la pucele. (666–70)

(It is the castle of pleasure, of solace and refuge, of hope and love, of solace and comfort. It is the body of the maiden.)

Symbolically, Mary represents the qualities of mercy and compassion in Christian love. She is both the second Eve and a defense against man's three enemies: the world, the devil and the flesh. Yet representing the womb of Mary as a castle, at once impervious to assault and the source of all pleasure and delight, assumes an analogy between the rewards of Christian salvation and the most fundamental values of feudal, secular society: marriage, lineage, inheritance, and estate. The representation of Mary draws on the tradition, popular in the twelfth century, of Mary as the Bride of Christ.[27] As the Bride of Christ, Mary, like an earthly wife, submits to her husband, to whom she is a source of service, pleasure and love. Not only is Mary the Bride of Christ, she represents the ideal lover for mortal man as well:

Cest la signefiance
Qe od tendrur en esperance
Servi tut tens son seignor
De grant delit e per amour. (697–700)

(This is the meaning, that with tenderness and hope she always served her lord with great pleasure and for love.)

[27] See Penny Schine Gold, *The Lady and the Virgin* (Chicago: Univ. of Chicago Press, 1985), for a discussion of the figure of Mary as Bride of Christ and Queen of Heaven, popularized in the twelfth century by St. Bernard's commentaries on the *Song of Songs*, and especially her discussion of the implications of the singularity of Mary (71–75).

The exalted prestige and status that God's kingdom promises are not limited to the next world. The putative lineage established by the ennobling desire for the inheritance of God's kingdom, the desire for God as father and Mary as spouse, of which the literary text is the vehicle, functions as a sort of self-recreation, evidence of spiritual nobility and thus of social superiority in the secular world. The following appeal by sinful man to Mary, expressed in the first person, is in the tradition, popular in the twelfth century, of addressing Mary in the mode of the love lyrics addressed to an unattainable woman:

> Duce dame, aie, aie.
> Reine dame ovrez ovrez
> Un poi reposer me lesser.
> De la grace que garit
> Les povres en esperit.
> Dehors un chastel sui asis
> De trois de mes enemis. (800–806)

(Sweet lady, help, help. My lady queen, open, open. Let me repose a little, out of the grace which heals the poor in spirit. I am besieged outside your castle by three of my enemies.)

In order to understand the significance of these lines addressed to Mary, it is useful to turn to the opening lines of the *Cursor Mundi*, a poem which drew on Grosseteste's poem and which is also a manual of religious instruction with the same didactic program as the *Myrour*.[28] The *Cursor Mundi* begins with a famous catalogue of "iestes and romaunce," the purpose of which is to point out that popular literature classifies the people who listen to it. The *Cursor* poet defines literature primarily as a means of self-definition. What begins as a catalogue of literary genres ends as a catalogue of *gens,* as the long list of the subject matter of "romaunce and iestis" defines not only the value and status of literary works but also of the people who listen to them:

> To rede & here mony are prest
> Of þinges þat hem likeþ best
> Þe wise mon wol of wisdome here
> Þe fool him draweþ to foly nere. (25–28)[29]

[28] Sajavaara reexamined the lines in the *Cursor Mundi* borrowed from Grosseteste's poem which had already been noted by other scholars (9375–9516; 9517–9764; 9765–9816; 9817–10122) and added the following: 9513–16; 16949–17100; 18661–18750; see "The Use of Robert Grosseteste's *Château d'Amour* as a Source of the *Cursor Mundi*," *Neuphilologische Mitteilungen* 68 (1968): 184–93.

[29] Citations are from Cambridge, Trinity College MS. R 3.8, in *Cursor Mundi*, ed. Richard Morris, EETS, o.s., 57 (1874; reprint: London: Oxford Univ. Press, 1961).

Since people read and hear the things that they like best, literature is a sort of self-description, a means of classifying socially and morally both poet and audience. The literary text inscribes its audience:

> Of good pire com gode perus
> Werse tre wers fruyt berus
> Þat I saye þus of þis tre
> Bitokeneþ mon boþe þe and me. (37–40)

Likewise courtly love is here defined not as an experience or an emotion, but as a kind of self-affirmation. Loving "paramouris" is a means to social advancement in secular society:

> For now is holden nought in shouris
> But he con loue paramouris. (51–52)

In competition with the "dame" of secular love poetry, the poet offers the Virgin Mary, also defined as a "lemmon" and a "paramoure":[30]

> Þerfore blesse we þat paramoure
> Þat in oure nede doþ vs socoure. (69–70)

Whereas the pretext of the love lyric is the poet's desire for comfort, aid, and fulfillment from an unattainable woman, in fact the subject of the poem is not the absent woman, but the exalted nature of the poet's own desire.[31] In other words, his desire is inseparable from the text itself. Mary is a literary text, or more specifically the "matere" from which one can craft a literary text in competition with other literary texts, which serves as a means of self-advancement:

[30] Owst (*Literature and Pulpit*, 17–25) believes that the love lyric may have originated in the homiletic tradition and from there passed into secular literature, although later the praise of Mary was fostered, especially by the Franciscans, to compete with secular love lyrics.

[31] This point has been made by R. Howard Bloch in his discussion of Thibaut de Champagne's "Aussi comne unicorne sui," in his *Medieval Misogyny and the Invention of Western Romantic Love* (Chicago: Univ. of Chicago Press, 1991), 149: "The lyric seems to have very little to do with women at all. On the contrary, it bears more upon the poet's relation to himself than upon his relation with others." In this discussion, Bloch notes the similarity of the lyrics to Mary and the tradition of "love from afar," both of which stress the necessary absence of the object of desire. "In the seemingly contrasting love lyric and the song to the virgin, Thibaut underscores the coterminous paradox of courtliness and virginity: to love, one must love perfection, or a virgin; to love a virgin is to love an abstraction; in loving an abstraction, one loves what is by definition unembodied; and, finally, by giving expression to the love object, one destroys it. Whether one desires the unattainable lady or the Holy Virgin, the object of desire is always absent in order for desire to fix upon it" (153).

Of suchon shulde ȝe matere take
Ȝe crafty þat con rymes make
Of hir to make boþe geest and songe. (85–87)

Because Mary is a pure abstraction, the textual representation of a concept of perfection that is by definition unattainable, she represents the best of all lovers, or, more exactly, she represents the best of all literary texts, since the text's ability to encode an ideal channels status and prestige from the text to its audience. The desire for perfection exalts and defines the poet, and through him the reader:

Materes fynde we may in dede
Rymes of hir to make & rede
Who so wol of hir fairnes spelle
Fynde he may ynouȝe to telle
Of hir goodnesse of hir trouþhede. (93–97)

Mary's perfection constitutes her textual superiority just as the inferiority of the secular lyric is defined by the inferiority of its object of desire. On the other hand, dedication to Mary, by the very nature of the abstract perfection which she symbolizes, is necessarily a means of self-exaltation:

Who þat loueþ trewely þis lemmon
He shal haue loue þat neuer is woon
For in þis lif she faileþ neuer
And in þat oþer lasteþ euer. (81–84)

The *Cursor* poet self-consciously invokes a comparison between religious and secular literature which reveals them to be mirror images of each other competing to offer the reader a means of self-affirmation. Both forms of literature respond to the conflict between the individual's desire to emerge and a hierarchical social structure that represses and contains:

In hir worshepe bigynne wolde I
A werke þat shulde be lastyngely
For to do men knowe hir kyn
Þat muche worshepe dud vs wynn. (111–14)

Praising Mary is thus self-praise, one more means by which Mary "wynns vs worshepe." One way of understanding the enormous popularity of works of popular doctrinal instruction is to realize that they represented more than exegetical models for understanding God's justice and hopeful promises of eternal felicity.[32] They represented a means to self-determination in this world. The Monk of Sawley's invocation of the romance genre as a response to Grosseteste's poem brings into focus the increasingly complex and problematic nature of the relationship between the individual's desire to emerge and the institutional authority of both Church and State to which later medieval man was increasingly subjected.[33] Two different literary constructions of the conflict between the aspirations of the individual and the submission and obedience required by political and religious institutions are possible, one which views authority as ultimately liberating and the other which sees authority as essentially a repressive force that must be resisted. Both respond to man's desire for reward and fulfillment within the terms that feudal society offers: land, status, marriage and lineage. Both show an awareness of literature as a means of imaginative self-determination, the only way of self-determination open to feudally restricted man. But they differ in how they construct the relationship between the individual and institutional authority. Homiletists such as the Monk of Sawley, whose chief aim was to teach the indispensable role of the Church in the salvation of the individual, saw in Grosseteste's "romance" tale of the personal triumph of the vassal/serf mankind a way of illustrating the role of the Church in liberating and empowering the individual. Many romances, however, show a very different role of institutions in the lives of the heroes. Insular romances in particular often

[32] It is well to keep in mind that homiletic literature was extremely popular, and that penitential manuals survive in many more manuscripts than the most popular of romances (Hopkins, *Sinful Knights*, 60). Competition between religious literature and romance took the form of claiming the superiority of one form of literature over another, not in laying spurious claim to romance status in order to increase popularity.

[33] During the later Middle Ages, both the emerging national states and the Church followed strategies of tying the individual directly to a centralized institutional authority, bypassing to some degree the traditional power located in the linear family. The Norman monarchs achieved this end by a highly centralized feudal administration, by making every vassal a subtenant of the king, by holding strict control of all property rights, by abolishing private warfare and thus the private settlement of legal disputes, by establishing the primacy of the king's court over the shire courts, and by directly intervening in disputes between lords and vassals; see Crane, *Insular Romance*, especially the introduction and chap. 1, for a discussion of these political strategies. The Fourth Lateran Council of 1215, which imposed regular yearly confession, interposed the mediation of the Church between the individual and God, placing the individual and his daily life directly under the control of the Church; see Bloch, *Etymologies*, 198–227, and especially 224–25, for his discussion of the parallels between the monarchic policy of establishing direct ties of allegiance between each individual and the royalty and the ecclesiastical regularization of penitential practice, and for the role of romance in inculcating these models. See also Georges Duby, *The Knight, The Lady, and the Priest*, 211–26, for his discussion of the role of literature in presenting the same models, and for his view that marriage is the perfect image of the hierarchical organization that allows both religious and political control of the individual. The Monk of Sawley showed acute perspicacity in understanding the close similarity between the position of the aspiring knight within the feudal hierarchy portrayed in tales of romance and that of the fourteenth-century Christian within the institutional structure of the Church.

portray a social landscape strangely free of political constraints, a world in which less than nobly born heroes move up the social hierarchy by their own efforts or amatory prowess and thus attain the rewards of aristocratic marriage, land, and children.[34] In addition, in romance, an inferior social position is often only an illusion, a temporary condition that can change at any moment when the real truth about the hero's birth is revealed. Heroes slide easily from servitude to power, as do Horn, Havelok, and Bevis. Romance heroes relate in a very egalitarian manner to kings who value them for their personal qualities and treat them as equals or even superiors, as King Athelstan does Guy. In addition, kings are not exalted by romance, in which they are frequently the villains whom the hero bravely defies, as do Havelok, Fouke, and Bevis. In other words, romance suggests the possibility of an individual reaching happiness by his own efforts rather than through the institutional channels of birth and feudal allegiance. Further, romance adumbrates a much more problematic relationship between individual and institutional power, often one of conflict. Diana Childress notes that a main difference between romance and hagiography is that romance frequently treats a noble hero who has lost his inheritance through no fault of his own and who recovers it thanks to his own virtues, while hagiography describes a hero who is allowed to prevail by surrendering his will to God, who acts on his behalf.[35] But even more striking than this difference is the similarity between saints' lives and romances in their construction of the relationship between the individual and institutional authority. Saints' lives tend to show an individual who, thanks to a direct and unmediated relationship with God, prevails against wrong. Moreover, saints' lives also tend to have a distinctly antiauthoritarian bias, often pitting the saint against a highly corrupt government. The two different literary responses thematize not different values, and not even different attitudes toward the proper goals of the individual life, but rather a different way of regarding the relationship between the individual and institutional authority which the penitential manuals see as a means to freedom and fulfillment and which romance and hagiography view as hostile to the aspirations of the individual. Points of convergence between literary genres directed at the same audience can be highly revealing of the concerns, values, and aesthetics that the literature encodes.

[34] Bloch (*Etymologies,* 194–95) makes the point that romances often feature heroes whose genealogy may be obscure but who marry heiresses, thus conveying the message that merit as well as birth elevates the hero to success. He refers to these as novels of social ascension.

[35] Diana T. Childress, "Between Romance and Legend: 'Secular Hagiography' in Middle English Literature," *Philological Quarterly* 57 (1978): 311–21.

Griselda's "olde coote" and Textual Variance

WENDY HARDING, *Université Paul Valéry (Montpellier III)*

With the publication of *The Riverside Chaucer* in 1987, F. N. Robinson's great contribution to Chaucer studies was again preserved for future generations of students and teachers.[1] In this revised form, the text edited by Robinson continues to be the preferred reference for critical studies of Chaucer's poetry. The claim made by George F. Reinecke in a 1984 essay, that the Robinson text "*is* Chaucer to millions in the twentieth century,"[2] holds just as true today. In general, the majority of us are happy to accept this situation and to offer new interpretations of Chaucer's poetry based on our readings of this standard text. In my own case, it was only after encountering a seemingly inexplicable difference of opinion in regard to a passage from the *Clerk's Tale* that I began to take notice of the variations in manuscript versions of the *Canterbury Tales* and the problems of undecidability that arise, not from the pleasurable ambiguity of poetry, but from the profusion of textual variants that the manuscripts offer.

The passage in question describes Griselda's return to her former home after she has been cast off by Walter. Having suspected that such an occasion might arise, Janicula goes to meet his daughter carrying the coat that belonged to her before she left his house. I quote the relevant stanza in full from *The Riverside Chaucer*:

> Agayns his doghter hastily goth he,
> For he by noyse of folk knew hire comynge,
> And with hire olde coote, as it myghte be
> He covered hire, ful sorwefully wepynge.
> But on hire body myghte he it nat brynge,
> For rude was the clooth, and moore of age
> By dayes fele than at hire mariage. (911–17)

[1] *The Riverside Chaucer*, ed. Larry D. Benson, 3d ed. (Boston: Houghton Mifflin, 1987), is the immediate descendant of *The Works of Geoffrey Chaucer*, ed. F. N. Robinson, 2d ed. (Boston, Mass: Houghton Mifflin, 1957).

[2] George F. Reinecke, "F. N. Robinson (1872–1967)," in *Editing Chaucer: The Great Tradition*, ed. Paul G. Ruggiers (Norman, Okla: Pilgrim Books, 1984), 251.

In my reading of this passage, Janicula's attempt to cover his daughter with her old coat is ineffectual. Rather like the magic girdle that reveals marital infidelity in Arthurian literature,[3] the coat seems unable to adhere to Griselda's body: "But on hire body myghte he it nat brynge." This strange incapacity demands explanation, and I have posited two different interpretations of the scene, one focusing on Griselda's characterization[4] and the other on the tale's development of the conventional metaphor comparing translation to clothing a text.[5] The passage demonstrates the impossibility of Griselda being returned to her former state,[6] of being reclaimed as Janicula's daughter.[7]

In my research into other scholars' interpretations of this passage, I discovered that it had been read in quite another way. Peggy Knapp argues that the passage disrupts an allegorical reading by introducing a realistic detail into the tale. Paraphrasing the passage rather than quoting it in full, she writes: "Worse still, the *olde coote* does not fit. The fabric is rude and the woman is older. Perhaps her fuller figure is the result of Griselda's child-bearing. She can never have back her only dowry, her maidenhood, as she says herself. The reader who accepts this gloomy tale of exploitation as a confident allegory has to be aggressive indeed in turning aside from its plain rhetorical effects presented in both the father's and the narrator's voices."[8] My initial reaction was to wonder how such a sophisticated reader could produce such a different reading of the text. Yet I discovered that other critics shared the same opinion. Christine Gilmartin reads Griselda's clothing as an indication of her status and argues that the heroine of the *Clerk's Tale* "cannot fit into her old clothes now, for she has been a wife and mother."[9] S. K. Heninger views the *olde coote* passage as a reference to mutability which illustrates the difference between Griselda's outward transforma-

[3] I make this comparison in "The Dynamics of Law in the *Clerk's Tale*," *Chaucer Yearbook* 4 (1997): 45–59.

[4] Harding, "Dynamics of Law."

[5] "Griselda's Translation in the *Clerk's Tale*," paper delivered at the Fifth International Conference on the Theory and Practice of Translation in the Middle Ages, July 22–25, University of Göttingen, Germany.

[6] Kristine Hansen, "Griselda's Abrahamic Test: Covenants and Clothing in the Clerk's Tale," *Literature and Belief* 12 (1992): 53–70, also reads these lines as a testament to Griselda's new state of integrity. Hansen offers an allegorical reading of the coat, which "symbolizes the old man of sin she put off at her wedding to Walter. Having been regenerated by that rite, she is still in a state of grace, which the smock may betoken, and it is not possible to cover that with sin" (63).

[7] If the clothing of Griselda is taken as a metaphor for translation, this passage represents the impossibility of back translation. The new text is "faithful" to the new author, Chaucer, rather than to the Petrarchan original.

[8] Peggy Knapp, *Chaucer and the Social Contest* (London: Routledge, 1990), 135.

[9] Christine Gilmartin, "Array in the Clerk's Tale," *Chaucer Review* 13 (1979): 240.

tions and her inner constancy.[10] In my own reading, it was clearly the coat that had aged rather than Griselda, who seemed impervious to the mutations induced by time. Fortunately, Knapp's observation that the detail of the ill-fitting coat is not in Petrarch's version of the tale sent me to Severs's monumental study, *The Literary Relationships of Chaucer's Clerkes Tale*, and to a discovery that paradoxically both clarified and complexified the problem.

Severs compares the *Clerk's Tale* to its probable sources in both Petrarch's Latin version of the tale and to the French *Livre de Griseldis*. In describing Janicula's effort to reclothe his daughter in her *olde coote*, Severs claims that Chaucer follows the French source, which adds "another realistic touch as to the ragged, worn-out condition of the garments, and the difficulty and discomfort of donning them after so many years."[11] He shows how the French text includes this added touch of realism, in comparison to Petrarch's less developed treatment of the scene:

> Audito ergo non tam filie tacite redeuntis quam comitum strepitu, occurrit in limine et seminudam antiqua veste cohoperuit.[12]

> Et le bon homs son pere ... vint a l'encontre des gens a cheval sur son seul; et de la povre robette, que tousjours lui avoit gardee, la couvry a grant mesaise, car la femme estoit devenue grande et embarnie et la povre robe enrudiee et empiree.[13]

The corresponding Chaucerian passage quoted by Severs is taken from Manly's 1928 edition.[14] It is identical to the Robinson version, except that in line 915, the pronoun *she* appears instead of *he*: "But on hire body myghte *she* it nat bryng ...." Severs gives a highly realistic interpretation of these lines: "She might not 'brynge' it on her body, not only because it had grown old and rough, but also because she herself, having married at about the age of twelve, had grown taller and stouter during the thirteen years which had elapsed."[15] Yet the com-

[10] S. K. Heninger, "The Concept of Order in Chaucer's *Clerk's Tale*," *JEGP* 56 (1957): 390–91.

[11] J. Burke Severs, *The Literary Relationships of Chaucer's Clerkes Tale* (New Haven: Yale Univ. Press, 1942), 245.

[12] Severs, *Literary Relationships*, 280. "Hearing the uproar, not of his daughter, who returned in silence, but of the accompanying throng, he ran to meet her at the threshold, and covered her, half-naked as she was, with the old gown" (trans. R. D. French in *Chaucer: Sources and Backgrounds*, ed. Robert P. Miller [New York: Oxford Univ. Press, 1977], 149).

[13] Severs, *Literary Relationships*, 281. "And her good father ... went to meet the people on horseback at his threshold and had great difficulty in covering her with the poor garment that he had always kept for her because the woman had grown and had children and the poor robe had become more ragged and worn" (my translation).

[14] *The Canterbury Tales*, ed. J. M. Manly (New York: H. Holt, 1928).

[15] Severs, *Literary Relationships*, 246.

ment about Griselda's physical transformation seems to be derived from sources other than the lines Severs quotes from the *Clerk's Tale*. The idea that Griselda has grown seems to have come from the French *Livre de Griseldis*, and the speculation that Griselda married at the age of twelve may derive from the Wife of Bath's Prologue, from an assumption about the normal age of marriage in Chaucer's time, or from the age of Walter's daughter at the end of the tale. Puzzlingly, the lines quoted seem not at all to support Severs's claim that Chaucer is following the French text. The obvious referent for "moore of age" in line 916 is the cloth, not the woman. Moreover, in the *Livre de Griseldis* it is not *she* (Griselda) but *he* (Janicula) who fails to bring the coat onto her body.

Fortunately, Severs clarifies the problem and supports his claims in an appendix, "Textual Notes on the *Clerkes Tale*, in the Light of the Readings in the Sources."[16] Here, Severs notes that though Manly selects the variant *she* in line 915, the Robinson, Skeat,[17] and Manly and Rickert[18] editions choose *he*. The manuscript variants listed in Manly and Rickert also offer a variety of other possibilities, including "hem nat,"[19] but Severs argues that "the French seems rather to support the reading *he*,"[20] despite the fact that this is not the version quoted in his discussion of the passage. More important, Severs notes that Manly and Rickert choose the variant "and *she* moore of age" for line 916. Their choice is based on their own study of manuscript stemma. They claim, "The revised archetype seems without doubt to have had 'she,' although 'she' clogs the line."[21] Working from the assumption that Chaucer is following the French text here, Severs supports the inclusion of *she* in line 916. He further argues for an editorial revision to correct the uneven meter: "Possibly the line is clogged through an error in the position of *was* in the archetype; if so, we should read: '*For rude the clooth, and she was moore of age*.'"[22] It seems, then, that Severs's reading is not so much based on any one extant edition of the *Clerk's Tale*, nor on any single extant manuscript, but on his own reconstruction of what Chaucer wrote in translating the sources published in *The Literary Relationships of Chaucer's Clerkes Tale*.

[16] Severs, *Literary Relationships*, 358–60.

[17] *The Complete Works of Geoffrey Chaucer*, ed. W. W. Skeat, 6 vols (Oxford: Clarendon Press, 1894).

[18] *The Text of the Canterbury Tales*, ed. John M. Manly and Edith Rickert, 8 vols. (Chicago, 1940).

[19] *The Text of the Canterbury Tales*, 6.350.

[20] Severs, *Literary Relationships*, 360.

[21] *The Text of the Canterbury Tales*, quoted in Severs, *Literary Relationships*, 360. Robinson admits that "there is strong MS support for the reading 'and she more of age' ... although it clogs the meter." *The Riverside Chaucer* lists the manuscripts omitting the pronoun and observe that the other manuscripts show *she moore* for line 916, "perhaps correctly" ("Textual Notes," 1127). They also note that the same pattern of variance is found in line 1013, where almost the same manuscripts clog the meter by adding a pronoun to "clarify" the syntax.

[22] Severs, *Literary Relationships*, 360.

Indeed, Severs argues for editorial decisions to be based on these sources: "Where the manuscripts of the *Clerkes Tale* offer variant readings, Chaucer's sources ought to be consulted to help determine the true Chaucerian text; for, when the manuscripts divide indecisively, the English reading which is closest to the originals should be adopted by the editor of Chaucer's tale – unless, as occasionally, there is evidence of author's revision."[23] Unfortunately, the possibility that this line of reasoning is circular cannot be ruled out. In this particular case, we can see that Severs chooses from among the variants on the basis of his arbitrary determination that Chaucer is following the French text closely. If one accepts Skeat's and Robinson's editorial decision, which in the case of line 916 is based on metrics, one could just as easily argue that this passage represents not a scribal error but a brilliant innovation on Chaucer's part.[24] The variant "and *she* moore of age" could represent the *mysmetring* of a scribe attempting to clarify the text in line with a personal interpretation of the passage.[25] Alternatively, the variants could represent various stages of revision by the poet. The problem is that there are no clear indications for choosing one version over another. Manly and Rickert's methods for recovering the textual archetype have not received unanimous approval in the scholarly community.[26] At the same time, the argument for basing editorial decisions on Robinson's more eclectic method of refusing to put "unreasonable or unmetrical lines into text"[27] has its adherents. The manuscript evidence thus offers two widely different variants of this passage: one follows the French text in referring to the physical change Griselda has undergone, the other revises this scene significantly in referring to the unseemliness of the old garment that has become unfit for Griselda because it dates from the time before her marriage.

Given the strong arguments for both versions, one sensible solution is to accept variance as a feature of the text, adopting Bernard Cerquiglini's attitude to medieval texts: "Or l'écriture médiévale ne produit pas de variantes, elle est variance. La récriture incessante à laquelle est soumise la textualité médiévale, l'appropriation joyeuse dont elle est l'objet, nous invitent à faire une hypothèse forte: la variante n'est jamais ponctuelle."[28] In a manuscript culture, the rewrit-

[23] Severs, *Literary Relationships*, 359.

[24] I elaborate this argument in the two essays on the *Clerk's Tale* cited above.

[25] Chaucer expresses his concern for regular meter in the prayer at the end of another poem in rhyme royal, *Troilus and Criseyde*: "So prey I God that non myswrite the / Ne the mysmetre for defaute of tonge" (5.1795–96).

[26] See George Kane, "John M. Manly (1865–1940) and Edith Rickert (1871–1938)," in *Editing Chaucer: The Great Tradition*, ed. Ruggiers, 207–29.

[27] From Robinson's Harvard papers, quoted by Reinecke, "F. N. Robinson," 239.

[28] "But medieval writing doesn't produce variants, it is variance. The incessant rewriting to which medieval literature is subjected, the cheerful appropriation of which it is the object, invites us to make a strong hypothesis: the variant is never accidental" (my translation; Bernard Cerquiglini, *Eloge de la variante: Histoire critique de la philologie* [Paris: Seuil, 1989], 111).

ing of texts, whether by scribe or author, is a continuous process, as the Chaucerian corpus reveals so well. Unlike the printed text, which is normally taken to represent an author's final decision on a work, a manuscript is merely a stage in a series of exchanges among participants engaged in the task of producing meaning, be they author and scribe, author and reader, scribe and scribe, or scribe and reader. Cerquiglini's theory may seem like a convenient means of cutting the Gordian knot of textual variance, yet it is also a convincing account of the historical circumstances of manuscript production and the differences between literary production in manuscript and print cultures.[29]

My investigation of the problem of variance in lines 915–16 of the *Clerk's Tale* has been instructive in several ways. First, it illustrates that a divergence of opinion among critics is not always a result of their interpreting the same text differently; sometimes, contradictions originate from the manuscripts themselves or from different editorial decisions regarding the manuscripts. Second, the manuscript variants can offer evidence of the way meaning is transformed in the process of transmission. Lack of consensus about the relative authority of manuscripts makes certainty about the Chaucerian text impossible. It therefore seems wise to acknowledge variance and to adapt our approach to texts accordingly. The task of editors becomes not the elimination of variance but its interpretation as a record of the reception and revision of the text. The task of critics in turn becomes a process that requires the consultation of manuscript variants, just as we consult contemporary critical views, before coming to conclusions about meaning.

[29] See Cerquiglini, *Eloge*, 17–29.

REVIEWS

Blanch, Robert J., and Julian N. Wasserman. *From Pearl to Gawain: Forme to Fynisment.* Gainesville: University of Florida Press, 1995. Pp. 207.

Blanch and Wasserman's latest joint publication on the *Pearl*-poet is, in their own words, a "book with a premise to be extended and explored rather than a thesis to be proven" and "a collection of connected observations rather than an argument" (1). Developed from a Kalamazoo session on the *Gawain*-poet [sic], these essays also owe much to the several decades of study and publications on the part of Blanch and Wasserman, both separately and jointly. This particular volume thus combines the old and the new – sometimes happily, occasionally less effectively – in a kind of meditation on key motifs and themes in the *Pearl*-poet.

One of the more markedly newer aspects is the authors' treatment of the four poems of the Cotton Nero A.x manuscript as a body of poetry. Rather than allotting a chapter to each poem, as has been the predominant approach to the *Pearl*-poet's work, at least until very recently, this book studies shared features of the poems, often paying particular attention to their context in the Cotton Nero manuscript, manuscript features such as the order of the poems, the illustrations, and other details such as marginalia and capitals. In addition to this and other newer critical approaches, there are some details of the discussions in *From Pearl to Gawain* that point to older stances, such as using "Purity" as the title for the poem that opens with the Middle English word "clannesse" – the latter being the title preferred by most critics and editors (except Menner). The authors' insistence on "purity" is even odder given their use of Middle English words in their own title, "forme to fynisment" – notably not translated to Modern English's "beginning to end." It must be admitted that Blanch and Wasserman offer, in their first note, a justification for their preference for the title "Purity" as "a matter of unabashed sentimental attachment." A similar justification is notably missing for another detail of their critical discussion; namely, their citation of passages from *Patience* by "stanzas." In this instance, the authors present no argument for clinging to a verse division that has not been universally accepted and is rarely followed in modern scholarly editions.

However, these are quibbles that in themselves are not all that important and, while they do suggest connections with older and somewhat outmoded readings, they also point to this book's greatest strength: it is so steeped both in the authors' immense knowledge of *Pearl*-poet scholarship and in their enthusiastic appreciation of the poetry itself that engaging with this study is like revisiting some of the *Pearl*-poet's best readers over the last half of the twentieth century. At times, however, Blanch and Wasserman's approach can be frustrating, since it is harder to follow commentary that is organized neither by the text at hand nor by a sustained critical argument. If the reader's task is difficult, the reviewer's is more so, since in many respects the appropriate response would be as disjointed as the book's discussion. Nonetheless, there are certain threads that run throughout the volume that are worth mentioning and responding to briefly, threads that should give some sense of what the authors are telling us about the *Pearl*-poet.

Chapter 1, "As Good as Your Word: Language, Culture, and Building Blocks of History," begins with the claim that creation was for the Middle Ages a linguistic act and a metonymy. From this premise the authors proceed to discuss first authorized discourse, especially in *Purity* and *Patience*, and later conflicting systems of communication, primarily in *Sir Gawain*. For chapter 2, "As Good as a Handshake: Covenantal History and the Fate of *Monkynde*," Blanch and Wasserman turn to the language of contracts, contrasting divine covenant with human contracts and oaths. Chapter 3, "Pardon the Interruption: The Miracles of God and the Convenant of *Kynde*," comes at history from a different angle – focusing on its narrative, with particular emphasis on miracles, which the authors see as divine interruption of the "natural cycle" of history's unfolding (46). During the course of this chapter, we are treated to some insightful discussion of both "wonder" (a mark of the Arthurian court) and *kynde*.

Chapter 4, "Tools of the Trade: The Hand of God, The Hand of Man," contains some of the richest and most frustrating material in the entire volume. Working with the iconography of the hand of God in illustrations drawn from a wealth of disparate manuscripts (some of them very distant from the *Pearl*-poet in time and place), Blanch and Wasserman provide a loose though intriguing context for the use of hands in both the marginalia and illustrations of Cotton Nero A.x and also in the poet's text. The lack of an organizing idea is especially noticeable in this chapter and leads to some occasionally strained and even slightly silly efforts to pull everything together, usually by a visual or verbal pun (and not necessarily the *Pearl*-poet's puns). For example, we are told that, while the controlling hand of divine providence is working behind the scenes at Belshazzar's court, "its nature ... is deliberately kept at arm's length" (107).

While chapter 4 is the least successful in this volume, chapter 5 is for me by far the most valuable. Bearing the not-especially felicitous title "Quicker than the 'I': The Hand of the Poet and the Pronouns of Narrative," this chapter, which does incidentally have a sustaining argument of sorts, examines the personal pronouns in all four poems as a basis for discussing the position of the poet/narrator vis-à-vis his audience and his story. Featured in this discussion is a close reading of what Blanch and Wasserman call the "Exhortation to Purity" in *Cleanness* – the hundred-line passage of narratorial comment that comes between the last two of that poem's three major stories. In this passage Blanch and Wasserman trace the movement from third-person to second- in the narrator's references to his audience. Drawing our attention to the brief but significant switch at one point to the first-person plural (*Cleanness*, 1111–12), the authors claim that the poet is here letting the first-person plural mediate between *I* and *thou* and is thereby softening his stern preaching tone with "a brief sense of commonality" and "the possibility of salvation" (130). Blanch and Wasserman go on to argue that by the end of these hundred lines of interpolated comment, the poet has "reformulated" the relationship between reader and narrator and minimized the distance between them, so that we see through the narrator's eyes and from his perspective and are therefore no longer excluded from the community that joins in prayer at the poem's end, "þat *we* may serue in his syȝt" (1812; Blanch and Wasserman's italics).

Recognizing the strengths of so much of the fifth chapter is not to say that I agree with all of it. Indeed, in this final essay of the book, there is almost as much to dispute as to accept. For one, there is the authors' unquestioned conviction that the narrator of *Cleanness* and *Patience* has adopted the persona of a preacher, a conviction of long standing in *Pearl*-poet criticism, but one which I find overly simplistic and unduly limiting. Blanch and Wasserman connect this view of the narrator as preacher to their assertion that the perspective of the first-person narrator of *Patience* and *Purity* "is never in doubt" – for he "remains immutable" while his audience's position is ambiguous and changing (139). I am not convinced, and indeed many features of the narratorial voice, insertions of phrases like "I herde" or "I wene" that Blanch and Wasserman themselves note, would seem to shift the narrator's position vis-à-vis his subject. In addition, there is that notable exception to the narrator's unchanging position (again an exception acknowledged by Blanch and Wasserman), the one that comes at the end of *Patience*, when the narrator's voice merges with God's. Moreover, as Blanch and Wasserman suggest in passing, the authority of the narrator in *Patience* and *Cleanness* comes precisely from the two poem's sources, which being sacred scriptures are free from the uncertainty that characterizes much of *Pearl* and *Sir Gawain*. While Blanch and Wasserman speak of the poet's "appropriating" biblical texts, I think this fairly trendy term and concept somewhat suspect and not especially helpful. Instead, I believe some attention should be paid to the medium by which the *Pearl*-poet knows his sacred scriptures, often, whether implicitly or explicitly, through the liturgy – the most notable example being his statement in *Patience* that he heard the Beatitudes "on a halyday at hyȝe masse" (9).

But here I am only demonstrating how fully this final chapter engaged me and how rich is Blanch and Wasserman's contribution to what is, as the best of criticism should be, an ongoing conversation about a fascinating and rich body of poetry. The more good readers who join that conversation the better, and this book should do much to make that happen.

Sandra Pierson Prior
Columbia University

Cooper, Helen. *The Canterbury Tales*. 2d edition. Oxford Guides to Chaucer. Oxford: Oxford University Press, 1996. Pp. xiii, 439.

This is, in fact, the second revision of a book that came out only in 1989, a few new references having previously been added for the 1991 paperback. This edition adds a further smattering of references to the big books of very recent years: Marshall Leicester's *The Disenchanted Self*, Lee Patterson's *Chaucer and the Subject of History*, Susan Crane's *Gender and Romance in Chaucer's Canterbury Tales*, Carolyn Dinshaw's *Chaucer's Sexual Poetics*, and Elaine Tuttle Hansen's *Chaucer and the Fictions of Gender*. In view of the hectic, third-world pace of development in medieval studies and the commitment of this series to up-to-dateness, we can expect regular revisions for the foreseeable future. The references to recent criticism here, however, have mostly been patched into the lists of recommended reading. Few are given any sustained comment; fewer still have influenced the basic structure of this book. (A ten-page chapter on the *Wife of Bath's Tale*, for example, is changed only by the addition of a one-line reference to Crane.) The virtues and defects of Cooper's work remain those of the original edition.

Readers of the *Chaucer Yearbook* will know – either from the much-praised previous edition or from Cooper's earlier *The Structure of The Canterbury Tales* (Athens: Univ. of Georgia Press, 1983) – what those virtues are: this book is informed and scholarly over the huge range presented by the *Canterbury Tales* and its scholarship; lucid and jargon-free; concise in its presentation of issues and arguments; and generally perceptive. It offers the reader new to Chaucer a sensible digest of basic information and guidance to at least some of the major criticism, plus frequently amusing and/or resonant asides, such as the remark that the Franklin should properly be considered less as a type of gluttony than a "fourteenth-century health-food addict" (46). Her textual judgment is sound and her skepticism about excessive source-hunting is welcome. Given the book's authority and its systematic tale-by-tale, aspect-by-aspect format, it will no doubt continue to be among the first items an undergraduate with a term paper assignment should consult.

A book like this is, for the rest of us, a great bundle of top-ten lists: it begs to be differed with. Most will turn directly to a favorite tale, looking for nits to pick. Few will agree entirely with any one set of recommendations. On the Wife of Bath, for instance, I noted the absence of any reference to important recent essays by Peggy Knapp ("Alisoun Looms," in her *Chaucer and the Social Contest* [New York: Routledge, 1990], 114–28), Susan Schibanoff ("The New Reader and Female Textuality in Two Early Commentaries on Chaucer," *SAC* 10 (1988): 71–108), and Louise Fradenburg ("The Wife of Bath's Passing Fancy," *SAC* 8 (1986): 31–58). These choices are a matter, however, of personal priorities and apparently severe space restrictions. Many readers will note, however, more important omissions, like Seth Lerer's *Chaucer and His Readers* (Stanford: Stanford Univ. Press, 1993), from the chapter on the afterlife of the *Canterbury Tales* in the fifteenth- and sixteenth-centuries. Still, one can argue that Cooper's role here is just to be the gatekeeper to the maze and that students who follow her preliminary directions will eventually find the omitted people. Exhaustive bibliographies, apparently, are for other readers at other times.

While I admire this book, I want to say as forcefully as possible what bothers me about it because it has been much praised and because it has been and should be widely used. The ground plan, for example, is methodical to a serious fault. After a brief general introduction to the *Canterbury Tales* as a whole, we follow the Ellesmere/Riverside order tale-by-tale from the *General Prologue* to the Retraction, with a chapter left over for "Imitations of the *Canterbury Tales* 1400–1615." Coverage of each tale is subdivided into sections on date, text, genre, sources and analogues, structure, themes, the tale in context, and style. (There is, you will note, no section for teller.) The fact that Cooper herself acknowledges "the artificiality of some of these boundaries" (2) is nicely disarming, but hardly solves the problem. It remains neither practical nor theoretically valid to try to discuss "style" in separation from themes or sources – what *is* the Clerk's style if not a sustained variation on both Petrarch's and Boccaccio's? – or "structure" apart from genre. Fabliaux have structural codes just as they have conventionally appropriate registers. At best, these subdivisions fragment Cooper's interpretation of a given tale and scatter the bibliographical references over half a dozen different places; at worst, they encourage her to treat the style of a performance in isolation from its context and speaker. If the format was imposed on her by the Oxford University Press, the press should reconsider its options for future volumes in the series. Coherent essays, like those in Derek Pearsall's *The Canterbury Tales* (London: Unwin, 1985), will do nicely, thanks, with a single bibliography per chapter, subdivided as the author wishes. I cannot see that the present format suits the needs of anyone save, perhaps, a student of the lazier sort who has been asked to write on, say, "the structure of the *Physician's Tale.*"

As with the other volumes in this series, Cooper's brief commits her to being both semiencyclopedic and personal, to providing both a sampling of current approaches and her personal reading. The two ends are not entirely compatible: the survey, predictably, becomes a part of the reading that proceeds through what Cooper thinks does or does not work. "My own approach," she writes, "shares in the recent critical stress on Chaucer's literary and stylistic awareness ... rather than in readings that see the tales as dramatic speeches by their tellers or as allegories of orthodox Christian teaching" (2). Those feet you see disappearing over the side of the boat belong to Talbot Donaldson and D. W. Robertson. Two of the most influential approaches to Chaucer of the last forty years are being dismissed without argument or analysis. A new reader trying to find "the lines of battle" (2) in Chaucer criticism is given no sense of the importance of their methods, of how these were justified, or why they passed out of favor (assuming that they have). Indeed, it is difficult to tell from this introductory passage whether they are to be seen as invalid or simply unfashionable. In their place we are offered an implied consensus – "*the* recent critical stress" – which I happen to think does not exist. The center, here and throughout the book, is the "drama of style" approach primarily associated with C. David Benson. If Benson is seen as the center, then historicists like Lee Patterson and Paul Strohm, Marxist critics like Laurie Finke, or deconstructionists (to choose an oversimplifying label) like Marshall Leicester must be the periphery. There is good reason, however, not to declare a center since, in fact, there has probably never been *less* consensus in Chaucer studies than there is at present. A guide to the *Canterbury Tales* ought to reflect that fact, both because it is true and because it is one of the most exciting things about the subject.

In any case, the most obvious thing this book needs is a substantial chapter surveying the evolution of the criticism, preferably since Manly and Rickert, at least since Donaldson and Robertson. At present, the reader is offered little more orientation than a page of one-sentence summaries of a dozen major books (21–22). In order to make sense of the relations between the critics to which s/he is directed on any given tale, a student will need access to Alcuin Blamires's volume in The Critics Debate series (*The Canterbury Tales* [Atlantic Highlands, N.J.: Humanities Press, 1987). I doubt I would assign Cooper's book except in conjunction with something like Peter Beidler's excellent collection of critical approaches to the *Wife of Bath's Tale* (Geoffrey Chaucer, *The Wife of Bath*, ed. Peter J. Beidler [Boston: St. Martin's, 1996]), assuming my students were rich and dedicated enough to afford both books plus the Riverside.

Cooper is, of course, aware that "Chaucer is not the kind of author on whom it is possible to be definitive" (3), but her readings habitually move toward a normative interpretation rather than displaying, as Beidler does, the range of interpretations in play. (Some alternative readings make it into the recommended reading; others do not.) It is disturbing, to me at least, that Cooper can get through a long chapter on the *General Prologue* without ever discussing Chaucer-the-pilgrim, either in Donaldson's original formulation ("Chaucer the Pilgrim," in his *Speaking of Chaucer* [London: Athlone, 1970], 1–12) or in the influential revisions by Leicester ("The Art of Impersonation: A General Prologue to the *Canterbury Tales*," *PMLA* 95 [1980]: 213–24) or Barbara Nolan ("'A Poet Ther Was': Chaucer's Voices in the General Prologue to the *Canterbury Tales*," *PMLA* 101 [1986]: 154–69). Benson (*Chaucer's Drama of Style: Poetic Variety and Contrast in the "Canterbury Tales"* [Chapel Hill: Univ. of North Carolina Press, 1986], 27) at least argues against the concept, saying that "no single 'Chaucer' will explain" the variety of the portraits; Cooper simply omits it. Here, as with most of the tales, she acknowledges no dramatized narrator; stylistic qualities are habitually referred directly to the author or to the genre of a particular text.

It seems to me that this antidramatic approach causes Benson and Cooper more problems than it solves. Little is gained, for example, by reading the Knight out of the *Knight's Tale.* Much is lost, including an attention to narrative voice that would warn Cooper against saying that "there is little [in it that] one can relate to the Knight as teller, and what there is is either trivial or inappropriate" (82). This narrator displays, among other significant qualities, a fascination with combat and military pageantry, a famously clinical view of death, and a combination of perfunctory idealization with underlying cynicism toward women. While we should not novelize the Knight or confuse him with a real person, we should remember that Chaucer has gone to considerable lengths to assign this tale to a particular pilgrim in a particular narrative situation. The tale has, after all, an obvious relevance, which Cooper omits mentioning, to the Knight's son. We do not have to know the whole story to know that a story is implied. The portraits and performances of, say, the Wife, the Prioress, and the Pardoner work most effectively by drawing us into the process (and frustrations) of imagining a character to account for the performance, just as Chekhov's characters do. Indeed both the Pardoner's and Wife's performances are sustained, unavoidable challenges to do so. Playing that game does not prevent one from attending to stylistic, exegetical or other matters. Indeed it may help. Trying to work out the Pardoner's sexual nature is a useful warning against confident assignments of his emblematic significance.

Refusing the premise of pilgrim narrators, as Cooper keeps trying to do, creates particular problems with the unsuccessful tales. If you have read the Physician out of his tale, you have no one left to blame for its defects except Chaucer. If you have erased Chaucer-the-pilgrim, you have to invent a "ghost Chaucer" to account for failures of the *Tale of Melibee* (322). Otherwise, you have to conclude that Chaucer wrote them in a fit of stupidity which, apparently, lasted long enough for him to bracket the Physician's text with the brilliance of the Pardoner's or the *Tale of Melibee* with the *Tale of Sir Thopas.* I think we should be skeptical of any reading that depends on Chaucer being dumb. When Cooper complains that the Manciple's "tautologous harangue" of maternal advice "runs for forty-five lines, and is unparalleled in Chaucer's works" (388), I am inclined to reply that that is because the Manciple does not narrate any of Chaucer's other works. Why not attribute his verbosity, crudity of judgment, and habitual self-contradiction to himself? That is a lot safer than attributing them to his author.

Perhaps, in fact, the next move in Chaucer criticism should be toward a sophisticated rehabilitation of the dramatic approach, one that recognizes that indeterminacy and dialogism are fundamentally dramatic, not antidramatic. The multiplicity of a character – whether Hamlet, Trepliev, or Alisoun – is what makes it worth performing. And the performative nature of discourse is one of Chaucer's great subjects.

This book, indeed, regularly acknowledges the multiplicity of appropriate critical responses to Chaucer. Cooper can well argue that the student who follows her recommendations will find other voices and methods. Much, however, has been excluded (much of Donaldson) or marginalized (most political readings). The interpretations of individual tales construct implicitly normative readings that will seem to the new reader to represent the (actually nonexistent) consensus of present opinion. I would like to see a guide to the *Canterbury Tales* that enacted the polyphony of current criticism rather than merely referring to it. Too often this book closes down what it ought to open up.

Arthur Lindley
National University of Singapore

Arthurian Women: A Casebook. Edited by Thelma S. Fenster. Arthurian Characters and Themes, 3. New York: Garland Publishing, 1996. Pp. lxxvii, 344.

Norris J. Lacy, series editor, opens *Arthurian Women: A Casebook* with an explanation of the Arthurian Characters and Themes Series, detailing the general contents of each volume and the concept behind the series: to examine the major characters in Arthurian legend. He warns the reader that styles vary among the essays in this particular volume due to constraints imposed by some of the original publishers. Of the 19 essays collected, four were written specifically for this volume: Ann Marie Rasmussen's "'Ez ist ir g'artet von mir': Queen Isolde and Princess Isolde in Gottfried von Strassburg's *Tristan und Isolde*"; Regina Psaki's "'Le donne antiche e' cavalieri': Women in the Italian Arthurian Tradition"; Muriel Whitaker's "The Woman's Eye: Four Modern Arthurian Illustrators"; and Constance W. Hassett and James Richardson's "Looking at Elaine: Keats, Tennyson, and the Directions of the Poetic Gaze." Many of the previously published essays have been revised and updated for this collection, and a few are chapters pulled from recent books on some aspect of women in the Middle Ages or other books.

Next, Sharan Newman, author of a fictional trilogy about Guenevere, contributes a forward, noting the necessity of achieving a balance in gender studies of Arthurian legend, as historically male characters have received the majority of attention. Next, Fenster includes a page of acknowledgments. The front matter concludes with Fenster's 47-page introduction to the volume and a comprehensive, select bibliography focusing on works published after 1975.

Fenster opens her introduction, which she divides into four parts, with a brief history of studies of female Arthurian characters, going back to 1909 and Myrrha Lot-Borodine's *La Femme dans l'oeuvre de Chrétien de Troyes*. In this introduction, Fenster includes cross-references to essays included in the volume. In part 2, Fenster answers the question, "Who are the 'Arthurian Women'?" (xxi). She considers Guenevere, Iseult, and Morgan le Fay to be the three major women in Arthurian legend and discusses them at length. She gives brief treatment to Morgause, the Elaines, Enid, Igerne, and Laudine and Lunete, ending with a brief discussion of the "Fairy Women." Fenster notes that she excludes the Loathly Lady from this book but gives no rationale for that decision.

Fenster's focus in part 3 is not explicitly clear, but she seems to be elaborating the discussion of Fairy Women from the end of part 2. She mentions Bradley's *The Mists of Avalon* and the treatment of Arthurian women in other modern works. Briefly, she mentions Chrétien de Troyes's depiction of the fairy world, and ends this section with a detailed analysis of Marie de France's

"Lanval" and how the fairy world, where women rule, contrasts with Arthur's court, where men rule. This discussion is the only extended discussion in the volume of Marie's contribution to Arthurian legend, one of the few flaws in the collection. Marie deserves more attention as one of the only identifiable female creators of Arthurian legend in the Middle Ages.

In part 4, Fenster discusses relevant themes and critical approaches, and introduces the contents of the volume. She begins with a thematic grouping of the essays. Then she regroups the essays into the six sections she uses in the book, explains the focus of each section, and provides individual summaries of each essay. This general introduction ends abruptly. While such a detailed introduction may be appropriate to a casebook, part 4 could be streamlined for clarity without sacrificing any of the detail required by the series. The quality of Fenster's summaries varies. The reader would do well to read the opening explanation behind each section and skip the summaries.

The sections are arranged chronologically, beginning with authors and works from the Middle Ages and ending with authors and works from the twentieth century. In section 1, "Resisting Tales," the four essays "challenge the way modern criticism has read certain medieval Arthurian texts" (xliii), "resisting" the traditional assumption of interpretation through a masculine glass. This section aptly opens the collection, both chronologically and thematically, as Fenster's overall purpose here is to examine Arthurian legend through a feminine glass. Roberta Krueger, in "Love, Honor, and the Exchange of Women in *Yvain*: Some Remarks on the Female Reader," discusses women in Chrétien's original courtly audiences and how they received Chrétien's heroines. E. Jane Burns, in "Rewriting Men's Stories: Enide's Disruptive Mouths," a chapter from *Body Talk*, discusses Enid as a storyteller retelling the male narrator's story. Rasmussen's essay, treating a mother/daughter relationship, is more about manipulation than resistance. She does raise a relevant point at the outset: frequently a woman is seen as she relates to a man, usually a husband or son. Rarely are women viewed in relationship to other women. This point would be fodder for a more detailed treatment in Fenster's volume, especially in the context of relationships such as Iseult/Brangain and Laudine/Lunete. Maureen Fries, in "Female Heroes, Heroines, and Counter-Heroes: Images of Women in Arthurian Tradition," discusses images of women in medieval Arthurian legend as created exclusively by men.

Fenster has trouble clearly articulating her plan for section 2, "Story, Gender, and Culture," consisting of three essays. The articles here, according to Fenster's explanation, seem to relate more clearly to her previous section and the idea of resistance. Sheila Fisher's article, "Leaving Morgan Aside: Women, History, and Revisionism in *Sir Gawain and the Green Knight*," discusses how women are marginalized in a patriarchal, Christian culture. Geraldine Heng's article, "Enchanted Ground: The Feminine Subtext in Malory," posits a "subtext of feminine presence" (108). Finally, Psaki's article discusses women in the

Italian tradition, which she holds basically follows the French tradition. Psaki's article reflects concepts about women's roles already voiced in this volume by Fries, Fisher, and Heng. This article's main value is its exploration of the Italian tradition.

In section 3, "The Fairies' Tales," four essays elaborate the role of the fairy world – a feminine world apart from men – and fairies in general and of specific fairies, Nymue and Argante. Laurence Harf-Lancner, in "Fairy Godmothers and Fairy Lovers," translated from his *Les Fées au Moyen Age, Morgan et Mélusine: La Naissance des fées*, mentions Marie's fairies and provides detailed background on the medieval development of fairies from the Fates. Anne Berthelot's contribution, "From the Lake to the Fountain: Lancelot and the Fairy Lover," treats fairies in the *Prose Lancelot*. Sue Ellen Holbrook, in "Nymue, The Chief Lady of the Lake in Malory's *Le Morte Darthur*," examines Nymue from Malory's *Le Morte Darthur*, exploring her various names, Malory's sources for Nymue, and Nymue as a luminary figure in the context of the men around her. Judith H. Anderson concludes this section with "Arthur, Argante, and the Ideal Vision: An Exercise in Speculation and Parody," a discussion of Argante as a parody of the elf queen Arthur pursues and as a figure of broader parody as well in Spenser's *Faerie Queene*. While Fenster does not include an essay on Morgan le Fay in this section, she does include one in the last part. This section is the most clearly coherent and relevant section of the work.

Section 4, "Guenevere and Iseult in the Nineteenth Century," consists of two articles. Barbara Fass Leavy, in "Iseult of Brittany: A New Interpretation of Matthew Arnold's *Tristram and Iseult*," discusses Iseult of Brittany's fantasy life. Carole Silver, in "In Defense of Guenevere," discusses the human psyche, particularly in the context of matters of the heart and how Morris adapts his characters from Malory.

Three essays in section 5, "Another Look," discuss Arthurian women as viewed through the work of women artists, specifically the photographer Julia Margaret Cameron and numerous female book illustrators. The concept behind this section is a good one but its execution is disappointing. Joanne Lukitsh's essay, "Julia Margaret Cameron's Photographic Illustrations to Alfred Tennyson's *The Idylls of the King*," better suits "Resisting Tales," as Lukitsh examines Cameron's philosophy regarding photography, her feminist presentation of Arthurian legend, and the details behind the project. Whitaker's essay, "The Woman's Eye," is sloppily documented, poorly written and generally the weakest essay in the collection. She discusses the illustrators Eleanor Fortescue Brickdale, Jessie M. King, Dorothea Braby, and Annegret Hunter-Elsenbach, and includes four illustrations and one photograph. Hassett and Richardson, in "Looking at Elaine," discuss Keats and gaze theory, which is relevant in the context of the whole collection, but not clearly relevant in the context of this section. The section on the whole skirts the fascinating and important topic of women artists portraying Arthurian women.

The final section, "Revisionary Tales: Guenevere and Morgan in the Twentieth Century," suitably ends the collection. Elisabeth Brewer, in "The Figure of Guenevere in Modern Drama and Fiction," includes a solid history of treatments of Guenevere. Marilyn R. Farwell, in "Heterosexual Plots and Lesbian Subtexts: Toward a Theory of Lesbian Narrative Space in Marion Zimmer Bradley's *The Mists of Avalon*," discusses a relevant aspect of criticism of Arthurian women – lesbianism – based on Bradley's *The Mists of Avalon*, and Morgaine's relationships with other women, particularly with Raven. She includes an extended definition of "lesbian narrative space" yet avoids a radical lesbian interpretation. Her treatment of the subject is gentle and accessible. Raymond H. Thompson, in "The First and Last Love: Morgan le Fay and Arthur," examines how modern female writers treat Morgan sympathetically.

Two sections of the collection, "Story, Gender, and Culture" and "Another Look," could be omitted and those essays either redistributed or omitted. Of the three major female Arthurian women Fenster identifies at the outset, Guenevere gets the most comprehensive treatment. While the closing essay on Morgan le Fay is effective, it treats a very specific aspect of Morgan in a very specific context. Morgan deserves a broader treatment. Fenster includes no "Contributors" page. While some authors are readily recognizable, others are less well known and some background on them would be enjoyable.

On the whole, the work is well organized, with clear movement from medieval to modern. Fenster covers a variety of Arthurian women and a variety of topics, authors, works, and approaches as well. With the explosion of interest in Arthurian women this work offers a feast for teachers, scholars, and anyone else interested in examining Arthurian women. With the variety Fenster includes in the collection, one can pick and choose and certainly not leave the table hungry. This diversity renders *Arthurian Women: A Casebook* useful in any course on Arthurian legend, not just courses on Arthurian women.

Donna Prescott
Green Mountain College

King Arthur: A Casebook. Edited by Edward Donald Kennedy. Arthurian Characters and Themes, 1. New York: Garland Publishing, 1996. Pp. lvi, 311.

The timely introduction of a casebook series on Arthurian studies reflects both continued interest in the genre and a comparatively recent trend toward publications that anthologize the best work in a given field. In the series editor's Preface Norris J. Lacy draws attention to the daunting proliferation of scholarly material available to the Arthurian enthusiast, noting that the most recent edition of the annual *Bibliographical Bulletin of the International Arthurian Society* (ironically enough the word "international" is omitted in the reference) has over 700 items listed worldwide. The emergence of the outstanding series *Arthurian Literature* and the equally informative journal *Arthuriana* bears testament to the popularity of the subject and its perennial appeal.

The casebook on King Arthur represents the first in a series which will also include Lancelot and Guinevere, Tristan and Isolde, Gawain, Arthurian women and other leading figures and themes from the Arthurian world. Each casebook will follow a standard format, comprising an extended introductory survey with bibliography, succeeded by twenty or so critical essays. As such each book is designed to provide the reader with a comprehensive review of the topic concerned, combining hitherto unpublished work alongside selected "classics."

It is Kennedy himself who provides an Introduction to the subject of King Arthur in an excellent essay covering thirty-five pages, including footnotes. The narrative discusses the position of Arthur in history and early chronicles, moving to an analysis of the king's representation in medieval French and English romance, the era of Malory and Caxton, the literature of the sixteenth to eighteenth centuries, that of the nineteenth century, and finally that of the twentieth century. Of its sort the survey constitutes the most concise and informative summary I have encountered. As one might expect of Kennedy the footnotes provide a wealth of references for the scholar to pursue, while the text offers a clear and detailed exposition of the development of King Arthur as a cultural phenomenon and icon, an exposition accessible to the academic and lay reader alike. As an introduction for students intending to study medieval or modern Arthurian literature I can think of no better place from which to start. Kennedy's other contributions to the volume include a revision of his comparison between King Arthur and King Mark in Malory's *Morte Darthur*, first published in 1975.

Of the remaining fourteen essays, ten are straightforward reprints. Donald C. MacRae's "Appearances and Reality in *La Mort le Roi Artu*" first appeared in 1982, and provides a useful counterbalance to Frappier's interpretation of this romance as revealing the all-pervasive hand of Fate, MacRae stressing as he does Arthur's own inability to distinguish between what is and what merely seems. James P. Carley's "Polydore Vergil and John Leland on King Arthur: The Battle of the Books" was published two years later, Carley providing us with a characteristically elegant and scholarly insight into a sometimes heated debate from sixteenth-century England on the existence of our most famous king. As today, those who would embark upon such a quest would be advised to acquire either a very thick skin or a suit of plate armor. It is forty-five years since Merritt Hughes published "The Arthurs of the *Faerie Queene*," and while this essay may appear somewhat dated in comparison, Hughes's article still provides some useful reflections upon Spenser's work. Elliot L. Gilbert's "The Female King: Tennyson's Arthurian Apocalypse" concludes the straight reprints with a perceptive consideration of Arthur's reliance upon self to achieve the perfect society. The discussion of Tennyson's characterization of a king often perceived as weak and helpless is placed usefully in the context of contemporary moral and philosophical concerns.

It is with the remaining six previously published essays, however, that the casebook makes an especially valued contribution by providing translations into English of articles that might otherwise have proven less accessible. Particularly welcome is Kennedy's own translation of Karl Josef Höltgen's 1957 essay "King Arthur and Fortuna": given Arthur's frequent association with the Nine Worthies and the *ubi sunt* theme, and his appearance on Fortune's wheel in the *Mort Artu* and alliterative *Morte Arthure*, for example, it is especially good to have Höltgen's work available to a wider audience. Also included in translation are Elspeth Kennedy's "King Arthur in the Prose *Lancelot*" from 1984, an essay that not only displays the author's usual erudition but provides the general reader too with some useful comments upon the presentation of Arthur's character in terms of the aristocracy of the period. Fanni Bogdanow's "The Evolution of the Theme of the Fall of Arthur's Kingdom," from 1986, notes a transition from the Vulgate, where Lancelot is the center of our attention, to the post-Vulgate *Roman du Graal*, where Arthur is given more of a sympathetic role and hearing. Bogdanow draws a useful comparison between modern narrators of the Arthurian theme and their medieval counterparts, noting that of his own attempts at retelling Arthur's story John Steinbeck wrote that he had wanted to make of the king a more "understandable character." In contrast the earlier authors were more concerned with using the Arthurian legend as a panorama upon which to project their ideological preoccupations. The two remaining articles translated from French are probably the weakest in the collection. Barbara Sargent-Baur's "*Dux Bellorum/Rex Militum/Roi Fainéant*: The Transformation of Arthur in the Twelfth Century" (1984) represents a survey of Arthur as warrior and creator of knights in the works of Geoffrey of Monmouth, Wace and Chrétien. Necessarily within a dozen pages this makes for a somewhat limited undertaking. François Gallix's "T. H. White and the Legend of King Arthur: From Animal Fantasy to Political Morality" (1981) is a disappointingly flat essay, content for the most part to draw attention to passages from White's personal letters in order to make some straightforward comments about the author's portrayal of Arthur. The episodic nature of this latter article contrasts greatly with some of the more analytical scholarship available elsewhere within the volume, although this may say more about the state of criticism on White's work than the article itself.

Several commissioned articles make a welcome debut in the casebook. Marilyn Jackson Parins's "Looking for Arthur" provides a fine opening essay for the volume, tracing the earliest distinctions between the Arthurs of history and legend, the later fascination with mythology and Arthur as symbol, up to the twentieth century, where the king is often seen as a romantic *dux bellorum* holding back the barbarian hordes. William C. McDonald's "King Arthur and the Round Table in the *Erec* and *Iwein* of Hartmann von Aue" provides a useful reminder that Chrétien's Arthur was not the only literary version on the scene in the twelfth century. Unlike the Gallic monarch Hartmann's Arthur in *Erec* is seen as a dynamic leader who "replaces infirmity of purpose with regal resolution," while in *Iwein* he becomes so exemplary a ruler that "one has the impression of reading a saint's life." It is all the more disappointing therefore that we do not have a companion piece of a similar nature on the Arthur of Chrétien's romances. Debra N. Mancoff's "To Take Excalibur: King Arthur and the Construction of Victorian Manhood" builds upon some of the themes evident from her *The Arthurian Revival in Victorian Art* of 1990. This fine essay proves a useful brother-in-arms to Gilbert's article – drawing attention to both the centrality of marriage in Victorian life and stereotypical views of male behavior – through an examination of Tennyson's works and subsequent illustrations. Thus Daniel Maclise's "Arthur Obtains Excalibur," an illustration for Edward Moxon's 1857 edition of some of Tennyson's earlier works, is interpreted by Mancoff as showing a natural ambivalence on the part of the king to take up the burden of power and responsibility. A manly and awe-struck Arthur is portrayed as ready to grasp the sword and take the challenge while simultaneously recoiling in trepidation; meanwhile the Lady of the Lake is "churning below in the water," waiting for Arthur to seize his destiny. It has always appeared to this reader, however, that Maclise's depiction is closer to the female king of Gilbert's argument: rather than taking the challenge the king, hands clasped like a bashful maiden, does not even take the rudder. As a result he appears in danger of running over his patroness in a shallow pond, seemingly oblivious to the fate of the Lady, who holds Excalibur aloft in the manner of a pedestrian brandishing in vain a "STOP" sign. Last, but by no means least in the volume, is Raymond H. Thompson's "Conceptions of King Arthur in the Twentieth Century," a useful summary of literary interpretations of the genre since 1900, none of which make mention of stories featuring Arthur as captain of a runaway boat.

The casebook accordingly draws together some of the best criticism of its kind into one book, although inevitably it brings with it the advantages and disadvantages shared by all anthologies. For example it is impossible to please everyone with the choice of essays published. For my own part although I found it useful to have a translation into English of Karl Heinz Göller's "King Arthur in the Scottish Chronicles" from 1962, it would have been more useful, I feel, to have published instead Flora Alexander's response to Göller in the shape of her 1975 essay, "Late Medieval Scottish Attitudes to the Figure of Arthur: A Reassessment." Scholarly work undertaken since 1962 has rendered much of Göller's work outdated: a reader of this essay would not necessarily know, for example, that John of Fordun's chronicle was widely known through the efforts of his successor and continuator, Walter Bower. Or that the MS. C referred to by Göller as Fordun's work (in fact Cambridge, Corpus Christi College MS. 171) is now known to have been a copy of the *Scotichronicon* (a title now reserved for Bower's continuation as opposed to Fordun's original) used by Bower personally. Again, on a personal note, while the series editor's Preface to the casebook states that the central focus of the series will be on literature, but not at the expense of other media, I was disappointed not to find even a brief essay on the portrayal of Arthur in cinematic versions of the legend. Finally, on a general matter, I was surprised that while several articles had been translated in full, on the odd occasion a word in Greek was printed in the original with no concessions to those unable to read the language. And for a casebook that covers so well so wide a range of material, having the bibliography at the end of the book as opposed to the end of the introduction would probably assist most readers. It was especially frustrating reading the essay on Spenser to know that I had previously come across a footnote in an earlier article on the subject, but that I had no means of returning to the footnote in question other than by skimming through what I had already read: the inclusion of an index for each future edition of the casebooks would make cross-referencing a far easier undertaking.

Kennedy is to be congratulated for introducing scholars and students alike to such a fine collection of essays on this most popular of subjects. The volume itself is attractively presented and I, for one, look forward eagerly to many more casebooks in this series.

John Withrington
Lancaster University

Laskaya, Anne. *Chaucer's Approach to Gender in The Canterbury Tales*. Chaucer Studies, 23. Cambridge: D. S. Brewer, 1995. Pp. 224.

Conceived broadly, the topic of Chaucer's approach to gender has been with us for over a century. Despite, or because of, our fascination, major questions remain very much open, and there is plenty of room for Anne Laskaya's attempt at a new look. Her book provides a wealth of references to other scholarship – literary, philosophical, feminist, and historical. But her distinctive contribution is not what she thinks it is.

In the abstract which prefaces her work, Laskaya writes that her book "concludes that on the question of gender issues, the *Tales* are best studied as *male-authored* texts ... *revealing* much about late medieval masculinities" (n.p.; my emphasis). This is either too little or too much. The first half of her assertion means only that Chaucer and most of his creations were male. As for the second half, to establish anything new about late medieval gender roles would require much more attention to both history and literature beyond the *Canterbury Tales* than we find here. Laskaya's best work is not found in her broad generalizations about "masculinities," but in her treatment of Chaucer's "female" narrators.

For Laskaya, Chaucer challenges the dominant gender assumptions and discourses of the time, even though from a contemporary feminist viewpoint he does so imperfectly. This is admittedly a version of Chaucer as prescient rebel, but I think the argument stands up. For me, though, her most valuable insight is that when Chaucer assumes the *female* voice, his strong female speakers and tale-tellers treat women, or represent gender, better than do his male narrators.

In order to accept this, however, we have to let Laskaya stretch a few points. Whose *are* these distinctive "female" voices? For Laskaya, one forerunner is Dame Prudence in the *Tale of Melibee*: here "Chaucer's persona, Geoffrey, begins this exploration, ... oscillating back and forth between the feminine voice and the masculine"; while Chaucer's "most imaginative experimentation ... obviously occurs in the *Second Nun's Tale*, the *Wife of Bath's Tale*, and the *Prioress's Tale*" (166). Chaucer's experiment, then, takes place in just four tales. Two of the crucial four, the *Tale of Melibee* and the *Second Nun's Tale*, seem peripheral, undistinguished, arbitrarily included in the *Canterbury Tales* and foisted off on hapless or exiguous narrators. It is hard to see why the prose *Tale of Melibee* is particularly suited for any of the pilgrims, let alone the narrator. The Second Nun, that unworthy daughter of Eve, seems to degender herself, as well as being so disembodied that we barely glimpse her in the *General Prologue*. As for the *Prioress's Tale*, its significance remains unsettled for many contemporary readers because of discomfort at its violent attack on Jews. (Laskaya pushes the "anti-Semitism" off on the Prioress herself, while endorsing the tale's religious core.)

Thus the Wife of Bath and her tale remain; but even that formidable dame cannot single-handedly bear the weight of Laskaya's generalization about female narrators. Laskaya's thesis (or my version of it) depends on convincing the reader that we can find positive "female" voices in out-of-the-way places like Dame Prudence, the Second Nun, and (less improbably) the Prioress, and that these four tales show Chaucer's delineation of womanhood speaking for itself.

The first eight chapters of the book establish Laskaya as a knowledgeable interlocutor. She draws widely on recent scholarship – historical, feminist, and philosophical, as well as literary. (It is often a pleasure to read her citations.) She catalogues Chaucer's gender-representations extensively enough to convince us to trust her when she finds a distinctive "female" voice in Chaucer. At the same time, these chapters – the bulk of the book – omit crucial discussions and illustrate problems in method and execution.

Laskaya is not a close reader. Rather, she pastes in passages like quick slides in a presentation, as broad illustrations of the points she wants to make. Sometimes her reader may want to dispute or merely clarify the literal sense of a cited passage – does it really support her argument or not? – but the steady canter of a survey of gender in the entire *Canterbury Tales* hustles her along without stopping for questions.

This is not to say that detail is sacrificed to the contemporary gods of theory or ideology. The work is in no way doctrinaire or "strident." From epigraph to conclusion, Laskaya embraces openness in interpretation and multivalence in texts. Occasionally, she will carry a feminist reading farther than I would, but that is to be expected. Adult readers will know how to push back. If the writing lacks the crackle and energy of the best theory-oriented work, it is at least steadily clear and comprehensible. For a contemporary feminist work on gender studies, Laskaya's book is quite untheoretical. Many readers may feel that this is not altogether a bad thing.

Actually, she might have examined some of her working assumptions more closely. She takes the *Canterbury Tales* as an achieved artistic whole, maintaining rigorous distinctions between fictive levels. Thus, writing on Chaucer's representation of the female voice, Laskaya misses the chance to look at the *Shipman's Tale* as if it had been written for the Wife of Bath. For Laskaya, the contents of a tale reflect first on its teller, then on Geoffrey the narrative persona, and only then, and only perhaps, on Chaucer the author or his culture and history. I have no great problem with this principle as a starting point. But though it is controversial, it is never clearly stated and therefore never discussed, even when it yields strained results.

Laskaya writes, for example, that "Adam and Eve, the Parson *claims*, 'naked weren in Paradys, and nothyng ne hadden shame of hir nakednesse.' This *as-*

sumes that one feature of Paradise is sameness; ... in other words, awareness of difference is a feature of sinfulness; ... Eve is different; ergo, Eve is sinful" (136; my emphasis). It is hard to see how it is the Parson's "claim" that Adam and Eve were naked. He simply repeats the well known Biblical account. (And how does the Parson, or the Bible, "assume" that innocence requires sameness? It might require an unashamed attitude toward sexual difference.) Nor is it fair to imply that the Parson has a particularly antifeminist attitude if he echoes St. Paul on the primacy of the male (136), or to fault him for choosing "the language of a male-gendered Godhead [which] locates women as 'other,' and outside" (137). Misogynistic (mis)interpretations of the Bible have been so common that a critic needs to show that their use reflects on a given character rather than the author or his culture. We cannot assume without argument that Chaucer labels patristic misogyny as misogyny, imports it into the Parson's reading of Genesis, and distances the *Canterbury Tales* from the Parson's position.

Laskaya often takes critique for text and too often accepts as "demonstrated" or "discovered" some scrap of someone else's elaborate argument. She writes that "historians have *ascertained*" that the late fourteenth century was a time when "women's experiential realm had become sharply circumscribed" (32; my emphasis) – as if many historians would claim to have ascertained such a thing. In support of this assertion, she cites David Herlihy. But Herlihy writes only that women were "not so indispensable in high administration as they once were" (32n) – far short of an entire "experiential realm" becoming "sharply circumscribed."

And she bases too much of her argument on insufficiently examined late twentieth century literary-critical stereotypes. Such are the four medieval discourses of ideal masculinity which structure her book: the heroic or epic, the Christian, the discourse of "courtly love," and the "intellectual." These are posited without much support. Laskaya does not show that her list is exhaustive, comprehensive, or even valid, as in the case of "courtly love." She ignores voices that we hear, not only in Chaucer's England, but in his tales – the voices of the artisan, tradesman, householder, manager, nonaristocratic landowner, lawyer, or public entertainer – in short, of those from the emerging middle stratum on which Chaucer in fact lavishes so much of his attention.

She overlooks the *Nun's Priest's Tale* almost completely. The index lists only three references (there is in fact at least a fourth, to Chauntecleer's *mulier est hominis confusio*) as compared with seven, including one extended discussion, for *Melibee*. This is a serious gap. In the evasions and ironies marching side by side with its apparent openness, in its playfulness as well as its appeal to graver thought, in the vividness of its mimesis and its polished deployment of convention, the *Nun's Priest's Tale* is quintessentially Chaucerian. If we suppose that Chaucer thinks about his representation of gender, the *Nun's Priest's Tale* must be one of the more eye-catching pieces in his whole kaleidoscope.

Chaucer's careful preparation for the *Nun's Priest's Tale* is part of an explicit gender debate. The Host reacts to the *Tale of Melibee* by contrasting wise, patient Dame Prudence with his own wife, Goodelief. By disparaging his manhood, by threatening to take his knife and leave him with women's work, Goodelief goads him into beating his servant boys and brawling in the street with anyone who fails to bow to her in church. Harry's joke about the Monk's supposed sexual prowess – he would have been a "tredefowel aright" – foreshadows Chauntecleer. When the Knyght interrupts the Monk (I was about to say "cuts him off") for making his stories too depressing, the Host calls on the Nun's Priest to take his place. "Sir John" requites Harry's aspersions on his poverty with his praise of the poor widow at the opening of his tale. The tale itself answers perfectly to Harry's requirements and to the circumstances of the moment. His tale is of a sexually prepotent Cock and of the wise and understanding wife who nevertheless goads him into risky action, despite his misgivings, by disparaging his "manhood": "Have ye no mannes herte, and han a berd?" At the tale's end, Harry does not merely acknowledge its success, but exalts the Nun's Priest in place of Chauntecleer and the Monk as the preeminent treader of hens, exemplary for both human and avian physical attributes and sexual capacity.

In the *Nun's Priest's Tale*, the male narrator's version of a female voice seems sympathetic. Pertelote is concerned, affectionate, highly knowledgeable on learned topics (but in a pragmatic way based on experience), independent-minded, and fully sexual. At the same time, she can goad her husband, question his masculinity, and happen, by sheer chance, or "aventure," or "caas," to be wrong in her advice. She lets Chauntecleer claim his arguments are superior as long as he does what she wants. It is true that the Nun's Priest narrator compares her "colde" counsel to Eve's, but he asks the women in his audience not to take offense at his deployment of antifeminist topoi, "for I seyde it in my game."

The Nun's Priest episode is important in Chaucer's treatment of gender. Further, it provides counterexamples to some of Laskaya's arguments – even what I take to be her most valuable assertions. Contrary to Laskaya's generalization, Chaucer and his male narrator seem to enjoy a high degree of imaginative freedom in this portrayal of femininity. The widow in whose enclosed yard the action of the tale takes place is herself a striking exception to Laskaya's analysis. She is an admired role model, a virtuous, prudent, independent woman in a position of governance who does not have to be married or killed at the story's end. And (perhaps because of his role as both confessor and servitor to a highly feminine Prioress, as a very old suggestion has it) the narrator seems highly conscious of feminine sensibilities in his audience, despite the low proportion of women among the pilgrims.

Pertelote's contest with Chauntecleer points to another area where I think Laskaya's analysis needs amending. She seems to equate contests, competition, and game-playing with aggression, and to read all of these as masculine traits. For her, as for her modern authorities, the masculine world is a perpetual fight.

It is true that Chaucer's men find "felaweshipe" to be problematic and often savage competition to be their state of nature. Still, either as generalization about the *Canterbury Tales* or observation about "real life," Laskaya's picture is incomplete. First, it omits aggressive women – not just the evil mother-in-law in the *Man of Law's Tale* or the Wife of Bath, but Alison's stone-casting threat and sexually aggressive japery in the *Miller's Tale*, Symkyn's wife taking up her cudgel in the *Reeve's Tale*, Goodelief's or Pertelote's goading, or, for that matter, Pertelote's spirited defense of her intellectual position. Second, competition is not simple aggression: it is successfully *redirected* aggression, as we see in the *Knight's Tale*. By transmuting a lawless duel into a rule-bound tournament, Theseus converts earnest into game and wins praise as a lord who "wilneth no destruccion of blood." Competition may even become what game theory and modern salesmanship call a "win-win" situation. In Harry Bailly's tale-telling contest that frames the *Canterbury Tales*, all the competitors can expect a good time along the way and a good dinner at the end.

Interestingly, Laskaya points to Griselda as a successful administrator, but does not discuss other examples of married couples forming a social unit with complementary roles. In general, she does not discuss roles within marriage except for the issue of subordination. She touches on bonding between men, largely as a prelude to their aggressive competition; she does not discuss bonding between women at all, despite the fact that it clearly interests Chaucer (the Wife of Bath, her mother, and her gossip; Proserpyne and May). She wields a broad (and possibly anachronistic) brush when she discusses "effeminacy" in Chaucer's portraits of males like Absolon or Chaucer's first-person narrator; and she does not discuss the Pardoner's problematic sexuality except in a cursory manner. She describes neither the degrees of sexual predation nor the kinds of cooperation between the sexes. In short, Laskaya does not paint a very complete picture of what varying narrators, including Geoffrey, think a man or a woman is and ought to be.

The question remains whether Laskaya's omissions vitiate her argument. In the end, they do not. As Laskaya shows, the world of Chaucer's pilgrimage, and its discourses, *are* largely masculine. This world is marked by destructive competition between males; its discourses do display a set of male-centered attitudes toward women. As Laskaya further shows, Chaucer quite characteristically allows few assumptions (of any kind) to go entirely unquestioned, so even his male narrators are capable of questioning the status and treatment of women. Finally, and most interestingly, his female narrators go beyond (most of) his males in their depiction of female autonomy and their questioning of masculine control. In short, Laskaya's book convinces.

Stephan Khinoy
College of Staten Island, CUNY

Nolan, Barbara. *Chaucer and the Tradition of the Roman Antique.* Cambridge: Cambridge University Press, 1992. Pp. xv, 391.

In this intertextual study, Barbara Nolan reads Boccaccio's *Filostrato* and *Teseida* and Chaucer's *Troilus and Criseyde* and the *Knight's Tale* in the light of the three French *romans antiques.* She is concerned neither with assigning a generic category nor with the question of which of these *romans* Chaucer and Boccaccio actually read. Instead, she sees their poems as fitting into a continuum with the French *romans antiques*: "the phrase 'roman antique' ... emphasizes a formally significant conjunction in all seven poems between a medieval vernacular language and the language and matter of classical history, ... it helps to differentiate the verse-compositions considered in this study from other medieval translations of Latin originals by emphasizing the centrality of ancient historical matter and classically based moral wisdom in the evolution of the tradition" (7). Central to her argument is the premise that all of these texts subscribe in varying ways to a tradition of interpretation that was taught in the academic schools through the use of classical texts with commentaries. In the introduction, Nolan maintains that the commentary tradition and the schoolmen's use of it provide enough of a guide to reconstruct the intended moral meanings behind the poems she examines. In taking this position, she affiliates herself with the Augustinian hermeneutic favored by those scholars who uncover moral wisdom in medieval literature through a process of exegesis.

The first text Nolan examines is Benoît de Sainte-Maure's *Roman de Troie.* Since there is no English translation and little scholarship on the *Troie,* Nolan's detailed examination provides students and scholars alike with valuable insights and descriptions of this lengthy text (six volumes in Léopold Constans's edition). Although *Troie* is generally considered the latest of the three French *romans antiques*, Nolan explains that she begins with this poem because of its more complex and self-conscious exploration of the relationship between a vernacular author and his classical sources. Benoît defines himself as both a translator and as the composer of his poem. His respectful attitude toward the Latin classics is balanced by an appropriation of their authority for his own poem. Nolan sees Benoît as extremely influential in shaping a new literary tradition through his combining vernacular literary conventions and "the canonical texts of the liberal-arts curriculum." She points out that Benoît takes the commentary tradition, in which multiple glosses often present more than one interpretation on the same page, as a model for his use of multiple perspectives in the poem. At the same time his use of medieval school traditions provides a moral guide for readers as they interpret various episodes: "in his own *livre*, Benoît always subordinates his management of perspective and impersonation to academic ideas of *auctoritas* and ethical responsibility" (44).

Nolan elaborates this idea over the course of the next two chapters, which examine all three *romans antiques.* These poems often stage dramatized debates which Nolan sees as connected to the form of disputation called the *quaestio,* popular in the twelfth-century schools. The debates between characters often occur at court in a judicial proceeding called a *plait.* The *plait* was also important in the chanson de geste (the trial of Ganelon is a well known example), but there divine judgment is usually invoked as a way of deciding matters. In the *romans*, however, public debates are not always resolved and this is an important distinguishing factor between the chansons de geste and the *romans antiques*: "Instead of celebrating accepted values and affirming royal power, debates in the French *romans antiques* open up circumstantial moral questions and draw the audience into the process of judgment" (54). Thus Nolan argues that these *romans* encouraged their aristocratic French audience to an active process of reading which required them to evaluate their own social and ethical practices. Of particular interest to me is her reading of the trial of Daire le Roux in the *Roman de Thebes*. Daire is accused of betraying Eteocles the king in order to save his son. Caught between his roles as father and vassal, Daire faces a death sentence that Eteocles is eager to impose. However, Eteocles's mother Jocaste intervenes and proposes a solution that stresses courtliness and mercy rather than the rigid application of feudal law. As Nolan points out, women play a crucial mediating role in this romance, trying to shift the male characters from using violence as a means of solving problems. This is an indication of a growing female audience as well as a generic shift away from the male-dominated action portrayed in the chansons de geste.

Perhaps the largest question the *romans antiques* pose for their secular audience is how to evaluate the practice of *fin' amors*. The three poems present love as both alluring and dangerous, and it is the task of the audience to decide which forms of love are legitimate and which are not. Nolan sees the *Roman d'Eneas* as presenting the most complete examination of both sides of the love issue. Dido dies because she ignores her queenly duties for love of Eneas, while Lavinia manages to be both passionate and prudent so that her love results in a "sound, political marriage." Repeatedly these poems suggest that private actions always have public consequences, and the transposition of *fin' amors* from lyric to narrative invokes a consideration of the political and ethical consequences of pursuing love in the more public and historical sphere of the *roman antique.* While these conclusions on the moral choices posed for the audience are certainly justified, at times in these first three chapters I found Nolan's pursuit of ethical meanings a trifle heavy-handed. Though she acknowledges that the poems delight in spectacle and language-play, her discussion of these pleasures is curtailed by her focus on ultimate moral truths.

The stories of Troy and Thebes continued to fascinate medieval audiences, and by the time Boccaccio arrived at the court of King Robert there were a number of translations of the story of Troilus in circulation. In her fourth chapter

Nolan sets about showing how the *Filostrato* invites moral interpretation in much the same way as the *romans antiques*. She acknowledges that Boccaccio has obscured the moral truths in his poem: "the poet's manipulations of narrative perspective, his play with various rhetorical forms, and his delight in designing his poetic *storia* mask his intention in such a way that modern readers have often missed his point" (120). However, while Nolan acknowledges the complexity of Boccaccio's poetry in the *Filostrato*, she seems reluctant to engage that complexity, preferring instead to label it as an obligatory poetic covering for the essential moral truth behind the poetry: "his [poem] is rigorously moral and simple at its most abstract level" (123). But surely almost all texts can be reduced to a level of abstraction where the same is true. The crucial question is how to read the specific instances of amorality in the *Filostrato*. For example, why are both Pandaro and Criseida portrayed as such unabashed and successful opportunists? And what does the narrator mean when he suggests that his male readers can avoid Troiolo's fate by taking up with older women who are less likely to prove untrue? Nolan says of this passage that "the narrator advises young men to love wisely, choosing prudent, faithful women as the objects of their desire" (153), but is this really what Boccaccio means us to think? Should we trust this narrator's opinions when he depicts the poem as a love offering to his own lady Fiammetta? Nolan does not really address these questions except to say that the narrator "provides a dominant model for his readers which is more deeply challenging and morally open than the readerly models offered by the authors of the French *romans antiques*" (154). This point ultimately contradicts her earlier proposition that the poem itself is "rigorously moral." It seems clear to me that Nolan's failure to engage the amoral aspects of the *Filostrato* arises from her desire to reclaim Boccaccio from those critics who have read him as a subversive writer who challenges the moral stance of his predecessors.

Perhaps this is why her interpretation of the *Teseida* focuses narrowly on the poem as a kind of mirror for princes, with Teseo representing "the good prince." In her scheme, Teseo symbolically represents the twelve Aristotelian virtues described in Aegidus Romanus's *De regimine principum*, a text in circulation at King Robert of Naples's court. Because the symbolic scheme she has selected cannot allow for much character development, this leads to some inaccuracies in Nolan's assessment of Teseo, especially earlier in the poem. In Book 1, Nolan labels the Amazons as cruel and militant, while Teseo is deemed entirely virtuous. However, Boccaccio depicts their queen, Ipolita, as a valiant leader, full of concern for her troops and determined to defend their honor. This makes her something of a parallel figure to Teseo. As I mentioned above, at the end of her chapter on the *Filostrato* Nolan makes the interesting point that Boccaccio challenges his readers by not ordering the multiple perspectives he creates in the poem. I think the war between Teseo and Ipolita could be read very productively in this way, but Nolan chooses to limit her interpretation of the episode by making Teseo a representation of unquestionable virtue. This is partially due to her taking Boccaccio's glosses on the *Teseida* as providing an authoritative key to the entire poem. Indeed, this is what Boccaccio's glosses want us to believe, but should we accept the voice of the glossator in the *Teseida* as a straightforward presentation of Boccaccio's own opinions? Given Boccaccio's slyness when it comes to assuming other people's voices, I would hesitate to do this.

Fortunately Chaucer left behind no glosses for *Troilus and Criseyde* and the *Knight's Tale,* and Nolan delivers more complicated and open-ended readings of these poems. In contrast to her attention to the moral meanings encoded into the earlier *romans antiques* and Boccaccio, with Chaucer's works Nolan is more interested in discussing how he uses multiple perspectives to show the transience of all earthly things, not only *fin' amors.* Thus she notes that what distinguishes *Troilus and Criseyde* from the *Filostrato* and the *romans antiques* is Chaucer's all-encompassing compassion for his characters and the tragic history that enfolds them. The pagan world becomes interchangeable with the secular medieval world as Chaucer depicts his characters struggling with a "worldly mutability" that plagues all mortal life. This mutability is encoded in Chaucer's poetics, in the way he allows us to see into his characters and in the way he reminds us of Troy's ultimate doom. Though Troilus is the only character who is saved from this world, Nolan's emphasis on Chaucer's compassion allows her to treat both Pandarus and Criseyde with much generosity. She reads Pandarus as a kind of Epicurean poet figure who manipulates those around him in order to stave off (temporarily) the coming tragedy, and Criseyde becomes the representation of "the plight of indecisive, limited human beings, ... located as they must be in *medias res*" (234). Rather than bearing a specific ethical message about human conduct, *Troilus and Criseyde* thus expands upon the hermeneutics of the *roman antique* by presenting an image of the world that calls more for understanding than for judgment. Troilus's apotheosis and the Christian epilogue of the poem do not offer any secular, time-bound solutions to the problems raised in the main narrative; rather they present two very different visions of poetry: "Chaucer locates himself *between* the pagan *auctores* and Dante. As a poet he has chosen to participate both in the secular literary problem of describing worldly mutability *and* in the prayerful lyric joy that reaches towards the certain, final truth of Christian salvation" (246).

In contrast to her reading of the *Teseida*, Nolan sees no abstract moral scheme in the *Knight's Tale* except the truth of a changeable world full of sorrow and death. If Boccaccio's Teseo is the representation of a positive, Aristotelian universe in which perfect virtue and salvation are attainable, Chaucer's Theseus is by contrast a Stoic, who must contend with a world that is controlled by irrational and unpredictable forces: "Chaucer's Stoic virtues provide only a human, rational means of responding nobly to the constant ravages of passion, time, change, Fortune, and death" (252). In this chapter Nolan begins by aligning Theseus with the Stoic virtues, that is, those qualities and practices that seek to maintain the social and political order in the face of "almost insurmountable odds in the mortal world" (251). She then moves on to look at Chaucer's use of *aventure*, the forces of chance that crop up repeatedly during the tale. Much of this chapter traces out the relationship between the chance events that propel the narrative forward and the efforts of the characters in the poem, especially Theseus, to maintain order and harmony in the face of the unpredictable. Without the rational exegesis available to Boccaccio's readers, the readers and Theseus are left to do the best they can without ever understanding the causes of things. In fact, Nolan sees this lack of causality as the heart of Chaucer's depiction of the pagan world of Athens, though it also reflects the Knight's perspective on life as well. She perceives a more powerful, though partial, note of hope in Theseus's famous "First Mover" speech. Though perfect harmony cannot exist on Earth, Theseus gives us a glimpse of a different state of being: "Theseus' concluding glance at a providential order in the universe and everlasting bliss does hint, however wistfully and briefly, at the possibility of perfection beyond the horizon of the mortal world and beyond the limits of pagan art and its medieval translations" (281). She thus enlists herself in the ranks of those who see Theseus as a figure of positive, moral leadership (rather than, say, as a pragmatic politician) who confers dignity and a cautious optimism on the tale.

Nolan's individual readings often have real depth and nuance; she brings considerable erudition to her discussions of the seven texts, and she moves easily and impressively between classical poetry, philosophy, and medieval academic practices. However, the connections she establishes between the seven poems are sometimes tendentious. I do not find that her readings of the French *romans* or of Boccaccio contributed much to my understanding of how Chaucer used his sources, and thus it seems that her final two chapters could stand alone. The notion of an ethical poetic could be (and of course has been) extended to cover much of medieval literature, and hence does not provide enough of a sense of what is different about these seven texts. Finally, the first five chapters show one of the drawbacks to moral, exegetical reading: one comes to the text with the final interpretation already in hand, and whatever does not fit is disregarded or downplayed. This book has much to offer and is well worth reading, but it will not convert those who read medieval literature for what is in the poetry rather than behind it.

Disa Gambera
Carleton College

Weisl, Angela Jane. *Conquering the Reign of Femeny: Gender and Genre in Chaucer's Romance.* Chaucer Studies, 22. Cambridge: D. S. Brewer, 1995. Pp. 133.

Conquering the Reign of Femeny explores Chaucer's relation to the genre of romance and the gender issues he both inherited with the genre and modified through his endeavors. Weisl's study attempts to show that genre is as much a subject of explicit concern in Chaucer's writings as gender itself. The two are so intimately connected, mutually defining and delimiting, as to avoid clear separation. In this sense her study is much in line with Susan Crane's recent *Gender and Romance in Chaucer's Canterbury Tales* (Princeton: Princeton Univ. Press, 1994). Weisl begins her book with a short and paradigmatic vignette from Italo Calvino's *Invisible Cities* which works to posit the equivalence of women and romance. While romance has been traditionally understood as a highly gendered form, focusing on the concerns of its female characters and audience, the genre might be seen, in Weisl's analysis, to undergo challenges similar to those faced by its female protagonists, thus *acting out* the gender relations romance has traditionally taken as its subject, that is, those relations the genre has been understood to be *talking about*. For instance, "Because Criseyde has defied the genre's expectations by failing to remain faithful to Troilus, the poem cannot remain faithful to romance's narrative conventions. Thus, her actions create *Troilus and Criseyde*'s slippery, generically problematic ending" (3). Chaucer's exposure and/or critique of gender assumptions, conventions, and possibilities is tantamount to a statement on the genre as a whole. Therefore, according to Weisl, while Chaucer questions the role and position of women, as much recent feminist analysis has shown, he simultaneously tests the limits of romance, which ultimately appears coterminous with femininity itself.

Beginning with various definitions of romance – Eugène Vinaver's, Patricia Parker's, even Erich Auerbach's – Weisl adduces the various stylistic and structural devices that define the French romance invented by Chrétien de Troyes and Marie de France, transformed by the Middle English redactors and then inherited by Chaucer. Weisl's account of romance hinges on the "double confinement" of both gender and genre, a term by which she explains the mutually delimiting power of women and romance. Not only does romance confine women to certain roles, the limited possibilities for female characters in turn restrict the stories the genre can tell. "Thus, in their confinement, women in the medieval romance come to stand ironically for the genre itself" (3). Conscious that she is working with a genre characterized by a uniquely "vague set of generic criteria," Weisl attempts to formulate a definition that takes into account this slipperiness in content, form, and convention while sustaining a relation to romance's "feminized" status. Chaucer's romances, according to Weisl, are self-conscious forms that "tell us as much about narrative as they do about love" (4).

Like the genre of romance itself, Chaucer's romances are an "idiosyncratic" group that reveals a wide variety of influence and source: twelfth-century French, Boccaccian, and Middle English. Yet, even where they differ widely, Weisl writes, "Chaucer's romances are unified in their preoccupation with gender issues, particularly the roles of women" (12). Chaucer problematizes and explores the romance genre, according to Weisl, through his depictions of women, whose "feminizing" influence on men, society, and heroic action defines romance per se. Chaucer deconstructs the distinction between romance and epic (a formulation Weisl never makes explicit but which can be discerned in her commentary). If women are nothing but conquered territory in the epic chansons de geste, romance disguises these status markers as willing participants. Chaucer's romances instead challenge their epic sources, as in the *Knight's Tale*: "by giving Emelye a chance to speak her mind – and making her desires impossible within the genre's structure – Chaucer exposes and questions the conventions of gender and the romance narrative in which they are enclosed" (19). The *Squire's Tale* in some sense furthers this critique. When Canacee refuses to play the romance heroine (symbolically, by building the female bird a sanctuary from men as a response to their deception) the tale falls apart. "Without her willingness to serve as heroine, there is no story to tell" (19). Likewise, the *Tale of Sir Thopas*'s total lack of a heroine reduces the poem to mere jangle.

Weisl's books offers some interesting accounts of particular works and of the relation between women and the structure of romance generally. But lacking here is a developmental story (of Chaucer's work with romance) or even a narrative of authorial self-consciousness. One wonders if Chaucer is repeating what is structurally necessary to romance, as, for example, in the rather conservative closings of the *Wife of Bath's Tale* and the *Franklin's Tale*, which put women back in their place, or if he is doing something else entirely. Moreover, there is little discussion here of the difference between texts that can be classified as romances, such as *Troilus and Criseyde* and various of the *Canterbury Tales*. What difference do the individual pilgrim-narrators make? How is narrative voicing significant here?

In general terms, Weisl's book might be considered a feminist study insofar as it takes women's position in the romance as its main focus. However, this is as far as such a consideration goes. The kind of theoretical and ideological engagement with the concept of gender and the cultural work of romance that we see in Crane's study, to name only one, remains markedly lacking here, as does any strong engagement with other feminist studies of Chaucer (Dinshaw, Hansen or Fradenburg). Weisl ultimately offers less of an argument than she explores a topic. The very closest she comes to an argument we see in the final sentences of her introduction, where she maintains that romance "allows itself to tell only certain kinds of stories. The romance itself is structurally bound by the very gender definitions it creates. Chaucer's romance stands out from its predecessors because it both employs its structures with profound understanding *and* at the same time, reveals its secrets" (20; Weisl's emphasis). The question of agency is as important to her discussion as it is to these sentences – who or what is acting here? Her "epilogue" (as opposed to a "conclusion") restates the findings of her individual chapters, showing how Chaucer's romances – for all their problematizing and questioning of the conventional assumptions of the genre – end with a return to those conventions, a return that interestingly accounts for critical dissatisfaction with them. Chaucer, it would seem, ultimately does not follow through with the kind of gender-generic critique he began. Or, perhaps, these formulaic and dissatisfying endings are part of the critique itself? Again, the argument remains unclear, as does any sense of development in the canon of Chaucer's works. One of the questions we might ask at this point concerns Chaucer's continued and prolonged deployment of the genre of romance. Why should he keep returning to romance if he remains ultimately bound by its terms and conventions in the end (not to mention why he should feel himself so bound when Chaucer is an innovator everywhere else)? Is this problem with unsatisfactory ends as clear to Chaucer as it is to Weisl? For me, there seems to be some missing end to Weisl's book, a final step in the line of her (implicit) argument that needs to be taken.

A final word about practical matters. While my general comments on the book as a whole suggest that perhaps an overview or revision of the book's largest concerns would have made it stronger, a revision at its most narrow – a careful proofreading of its bibliography – was absolutely necessary. Not only does one find various typographical inconsistencies from one entry to the next, each page of the bibliography is full of inaccuracies (mistakes that are often repeated in the notes). There are both misspellings of various names – William Kibler, Kathryn Hume, Arlyn Diamond, Paul Olson, and Chauncey Wood – and miscitations – Jane Gallop's book is *Thinking Through the Body* (not Reading); Laura Hibbard Loomis's essay is "Chaucer and the Breton Lais of the Auchinleck Manuscript," and it appeared in *Studies in Philology* (not *Speculum*). Derek Pearsall's essay, "The Squire as Story-teller," *University of Toronto Quarterly* 34 (1964): 82–92, while mentioned in the text, does not appear at all in the bibliography, and thus readers lack this information entirely. These are only the mistakes most easy to correct here; there are other misspellings, miscitations and obviously incorrect dates, for I am sure we have not gotten to a *PMLA* volume number 948 for the year 19483.

Elizabeth Scala
University of Texas – Austin